Football Inc.

HOW SOCCER FANS
ARE LOSING
THE GAME

Craig McGill

First published in Great Britain by Vision Paperbacks, a division of Satin Publications Ltd.

Vision Paperbacks
101 Southwark Street
London SE1 0JH
UK
e-mail: info@visionpaperbacks.co.uk
website: www.visionpaperbacks.com

Publisher: Sheena Dewan
Cover design © 2001 Nickolai Globe
Typeset by FiSH Books, London
Printed and bound in the UK by Biddles Ltd.

ISBN: 1-901250-52-0

Contents

Contents

Acknowledgements

Writing a book is a lot like a game of football. Very often one person gets all the glory but there are a lot of folk behind them doing a lot of work but not receiving as much credit.

In an effort to correct that, let me first thank everyone who took the time to speak to me or comment with regards to the book. Most of these people are mentioned in the chapters, so there's no need for repetition here. To those who spoke to me anonymously and can't receive full credit for what they said, thanks also.

At Vision, thanks go to the full editorial team, Sheena Dewan, Ellen O'Donoghue and Stella Wood for coffee, patience, inspiration and paycheques. All credit for this book ultimately lies with them, while the faults are my own.

Aside from Vision, thanks also go to Rob Bruce and Tennents Lager for allowing me to see a game from the VIP perspective, *Time* magazine and Neil McCarthy for letting me sample the joys of a French World Cup, as well as Stirling Council's Corrie McChord and the European Region of Parliaments for helping me to see Euro 2000.

Off the pitch, thanks to my mum and stepdad, Ann and Brian, for the obvious line of getting me here and keeping me in one piece, while other thanks go to my dad Jamie and Aunt Sally for taking me to my first game of football and putting up with me, even as I moaned about how cold it was.

Thanks also go to Eddie Burns, David Henderson, Greg Morton, John Cole and Robbie Lochrie for moments of football advice and explaining concepts like how unusual it is for a red-headed footballer to be from Venezuela. For encouragement, help and comments I'd also like to thank Phill Kennedy, Ewan Dryborough, Iain Hepburn, Daniel Gilbert, Peter Burns, Angela Fullerton, Stephen Colligan, Bill MacDonald and Neil and Ewan McIntosh. Some thanks for encouragement and inspiration from days gone by has to go to Pat Connolly.

Thanks to Karen Watson for 24-hour support and comfort, as well as being the first girl to ever explain offside better than a bloke.

Thanks also to Marty McMullen for summing up in one phrase what football can be at its best – it's that phrase that starts the book.

Finally, thanks to every good footballer there's been for the entertainment and passion and thanks to every good football fan for the cheers, the jeers and the banter. This book is for all of you more than anyone else, so without further ado, let us kick off.

Craig McGill
Scotland
March 2001

Introduction

'O jogo bonito' – the beautiful game, as football is called in Brazil. There is no other game in the world that inspires quite as much passion. The Americans may give their baseball and basketball tournaments titles like World Series and World Championships, but football (soccer) is the truly global game. Whereas American football is concerned with statistics, real football is concerned with romance, passion and adventure. Everyone has a goal, a moment, a team – normally 1970 Brazil – that they speak about in exalted tones. It is a game that can inspire pub quizzes (Q: Name the only British grounds to fly the swastika. A: White Hart Lane and Ibrox, when Germany played England and Scotland in friendlies in 1935 and 1936 respectively). It is a game that men can find more important than sex (according to a Teletext survey they'll even put reading about football ahead of sex). It can inspire hilarity (Prince Philip asking Arsenal trialists if the club was called Dreamcast FC because of the logo on their shirts). The point is: football inspires. For many the quote by Bill Shankly about football being more important than life or death is true. The game may have a large number of women fans, but they are, on the whole, more sensible than the grown men, who will cut back on almost anything to ensure they have enough money for a season ticket for their club.

Real fans will stand for hours in the rain to get a glimpse of a new manager or player. No one does that for the new signings at Microsoft, ICI or other international companies. The only similar comparison is royalty, and in some places footballers are even more revered. What makes football different from royalty, though, is that there is no elitism, as everyone has the potential to be a footballer, while you can only be true royalty by birth.

Football was set up as the people's game and has endured despite royal bans in the past, poor attendances, ill-thought-out laws, changing society and war. In an age when every activity can cost a fortune, football remains a simple game, and can still be a cheap game. All that is needed are two items – normally clothing or bricks – to act as goalposts and a round object to act as a ball. In the old days, empty cans would be used, while Brazilians would hone their ball control playing with tangerines. Football has more spin-offs than any Hollywood product. Computer games sell in the millions, and strips are big earners for companies like Adidas and Nike. There have even been games about football that involved hands and fingers more than legs, such as Subbuteo. Football is everywhere. It is a game that is becoming more and more popular, even in America, Australia and the Far East, where children under the age of 12 are playing organised football more than any other sport. It is also very popular in high school and college athletic programmes in America and is starting to be considered as seriously as their other sports. In Europe, South America and Africa it is a different matter. Football is the predominant sport, has been for decades and looks set to continue that way.

But if this is the case, why is there the need for this book? If football is growing and is the people's game, then surely everything is fine? Many countries have argued that football started with them. For years England claimed it started there, while South Americans, Asians, Scots and Spaniards have all tried to take the credit at one point or another. It doesn't really matter who invented it because if you speak to any football fan, regardless of team or nationality, you'll discover that they think it's their game, and if you ask them about the team they support, it's their team. Even in the days before shareholding, fans felt as though they owned the club, not chairmen and directors. Fans feel the game – and whatever team they support – is theirs, and the thought of their club being taken away from them is beyond comprehension for many.

But the fans do not have a say in how the game is run. They are the consumer who is ignored. 'Thanks for your money, now be on your way' seems to be the attitude of many in the higher echelons of the game. Fans are being shown the red card by the game's administrators and those who control it. They may say fans matter, but fans don't; only their money does.

Just over 30 years ago British football was at what many regard as its peak. England won the World Cup in 1966 and Celtic became the first British team to win the European Cup in 1967. Manchester United won it the following year. The conditions for fans were acceptable, not plush by any standards, but functional.

The only thing the game now shares from that time is 22 men on the pitch. Beyond that it has changed beyond recognition. Back then many players played part-time. Even if they were full-time, their wages were not the exorbitant sums they are today. Most of the players were local. And while foreign players and female football have been good things for the game, back then they were rarities.

Now, stadiums have become massive monster complexes, prices have risen much faster than inflation, football is shown at every time during the week if the fan can afford to pay for the satellite and digital television coverage, decisions about where to host the World Cup are decided more by politics than football and hooligans, racists, politicians and businessmen have all hijacked the game to suit their own ends. All of these things have affected the average football fan, but no one asked the fan, no one thought an 8.05 pm kick-off on a Monday night might be a problem for fans, no one asked what fans thought of having to buy three new strips a year, no one asked fans if they would mind missing out on the World Cup because it was in a faraway land that wanted to host it for the money, not the passion.

It may sound harsh to say that the fans are being shown the red card by those in command. If anything, it is an understatement, because the way fans are treated is an insult. But that can be changed. If fans realise what the game is like now and where it may be going, perhaps there is still time to save the sport that has inspired so many.

This book aims to show the state of things today, while looking at key moments from the past as well. It then moves on and looks at what's coming. It's a shot across the bows for those trying to take control of the game but it's also a warning for the real fans that they can't take it for granted that their game will survive. It may seem daunting for the fan with an average income to take on the might of companies like BSkyB and institutions like FIFA, but it can be done; it has to be done. In the coming years, football's biggest and most important moments may take place off the pitch instead of on it and if fans do not get involved and demand more of a say about the game, then it may change beyond recognition and the beautiful game will become an ugly, distorted version of all that it can and should be.

Game on.

Part One

Dramatis Personae

One

Fans

As the chants go, there's only one Kevin Keegan, one David Beckham, one Tony Adams, one Ronaldo, one Robert Pires. However, there's more than one of the people most important to the game – the fans. Never mind the 22 players on the pitch, the man in black, the managers or the chairmen, at the heart of it there is only one group of people who matter when it comes to football; without the fans none of the others would exist. Consider this: every week over 650,000 people in the UK go to or watch a game of football; across Europe that number is over 10 million. If these were medieval times, and they all stood together, they would form an army no one would stand a chance against. Unfortunately fans don't see themselves as an army – more often than not they act like serfs paying tribute to the gods and lords on the pitch, and that's the way those who run the game like it. It has been the only constant in the game over the last 25 years.

In the mid-seventies conditions at football stadiums were so bad that if you had been able to take a pet dog to the game, you would probably have been charged with cruelty to animals. People urinating in stands, jostling, shoving, hash being passed about. Pretty much anything you can imagine has happened in the terracing. Women were not welcome at a match – on Saturdays men went to the game, while the wife did the shopping. Besides, few women had the desire to stand in vomit for 90 minutes and pay for the so-called privilege. While all of the above might sound disgusting, for some it will bring back nostalgic memories of the 'old days', when things were allegedly better. It was all part of the macho culture that permeated football. You put up with it, and if you complained, then you were a 'wimp' or a 'poof' and that was all there was to it. John Sanderson has been a Leeds fan for more than 20 years and he remembers the way things were in the 1970s and 1980s, when many of today's fans were either just starting to go to football or were not interested in it:

'It was nothing like today. Even taking out the hooligans and the troublemakers, it was still a lot rougher. If you were going to an away game you'd try and get on a busy train so you didn't have to pay any fare, you'd have a few drinks and because of them you'd end up doing the toilet in a block of flats or down a lane if you couldn't find a pub.

'The game would be chaos and you'd constantly be on the move, being shoved about or looking for your mates, avoiding whatever was on the ground and then trying to stay upright if the place was packed and your team scored a goal as you didn't want to land on the ground as everything was down there. Trying to get home would also be an adventure too and you'd normally lose someone on the way.

'It sounds daft but when I'm sitting in some of these new all-seaters and there's no real smells, no real singing, and at times it seems as if I'm just at home watching it on telly, I miss those old days.

'I don't know if I could put up with being up to my ankles in urine again week in, week out, but I think it would be nice to try the old days again.'

Compare that to what the fan gets now. Seats that mean you can't get about to meet your mates, officials about the ground acting like little dictators, no drinking, no fun. A good example of this is when Newcastle played their first derby at Sunderland FC's magnificent Stadium of Light ground in 1997. Alan Shearer accidentally kicked a ball into the area where the visiting fans were. As he went to get the ball a fan tried to pat him on the back but got stuck and fell between the hoardings and the seats. Moments later the fan was led away by stewards, much to the disgust of all around, including Shearer, who looked quite irate at the over-the-top antics of the steward. In days gone by nothing would have been thought of a fan trying to touch a player. Now it's grounds for being thrown out of the stadium.

Changed days indeed, but one thing the seventies have in common with now is the sheer number of fans. The decline in attendance began at the end of the seventies, and did not stop for a decade, but the recovery means that now attendance levels are as high as they were 25 years ago. The last report on the game by Deloitte & Touche showed that over 25 million people watched Premiership and Football League matches in 1998/99 – higher than at any time in over two decades. In Division Two more than 4 million people went through the turnstiles – a figure not seen since 1976/77, while Division Three had over 2 million fans turn up for the first time since 1979/80. Both divisions saw their average attendance grow by 19 per cent. In the Premiership the stadiums were packed on a regular basis, with stadium occupancy figures of 91 per cent. In Division One the figure was 66 per cent, while in Divisions Two and Three the stadiums were 53 per cent and 36 per cent occupied.

Between the game of the seventies and the game now, football managed to survive, despite 10 years of poor attendance, but how and why? Everyone in football has a theory for this. Ex-referee Peter Willis thinks football is the best form of entertainment there is, because it is all about the opinions of referees, players, managers and fans, while football business writer Stefan Szymanski thinks it appeals because it is theatre of the highest order. Others argue that the mass appeal of football lies in its simplicity and cheapness to play. (However, to start being a fan does take a bit more money in terms of attending games, though many true fans now have no option but to stay at home and watch highlights on TV because they can't afford the prices dictated by the clubs.)

So why football? Why does it appear to be the number one sport in the world and not something like rugby, basketball or orienteering? A survey conducted by the author over the Internet (mailed to a number of e-mail lists hosted by companies like Topica.com and egroups.com, who were picked because of the large number of football e-mail lists that they have) saw fans give a number of reasons for their love of the game or their team. Most people who responded said that the appeal was that it was the game they had grown up with. It was the game played most at school, the game most people spoke about and it was something to do with your friends in the evening. Football was the main event for everyone to take part in – a form of peer pressure almost. A few turned to the game after trying other sports and not being either particularly interested in them or any good at them, while Americans said they liked it because it was different to their football and some felt it was more skilful. Others claimed that they enjoyed the passions of the game, the entertainment, the emotional rush. No one said they enjoyed sitting in a cold football ground miles away from their home on a soaking wet Monday night in December, which may come as a surprise to those who schedule the game on television for that time. The reasons that people like football, then, are quite simple, but it was far more complicated when people were asked why they supported the team that they did.

About half of those who replied to the question said that they supported the team they had grown up with, and even those who had moved away stayed loyal to their 'home' team. Others said that they supported their team because it was part of their culture and they had grown up alongside supporters of the team, so there was an indirect peer pressure influence. About a quarter of the people who replied said that they supported their team because of the way the team was said to play. In many cases this was because a team had a reputation for winning (Manchester United was the clear winner here), or because they were always an attacking team, though not necessarily one that always won. A few people said they supported a team because of one or two players in it, and that they were more fans of the player than the team, and would switch allegiances if the player did. Many who had moved away from their hometown teams said they supported their new local teams because that was the right thing to do, though many admitted always keeping an eye out for their old team's results. A small number – from cities where there are two dominant rival teams – claimed they supported smaller local teams because they disliked being associated with either of the larger sides. This was especially true for respondents from Glasgow, who said they were disgusted by the religious connotations and hazards that came with supporting the Old Firm of Celtic and Rangers and they would instead either support a local junior team or a team in a lower league like Clydebank or Partick Thistle. Growing up with a team is a factor that leads to the strong ties that many have with their club, and it has been viewed as an important bonding scenario early on in life between friends or father and son. Most children are taken to their first game by either their father or another male relative, though the advent of all-seater stadiums has seen more mothers and children at games.

But who are the fans of today? They are certainly not the same people who went to the game in the seventies. Vice-Chairman of the Football Supporters' Association, Dave Boyle, has noticed the change in fans. While stopping short of the view that football has abandoned the people who supported it during the dark days of the eighties, he does note that the old fans are certainly not the new fans and wonders if the latter will stick around to become long-term fans.

'We're concerned about lower-income fans being priced out of the game – the people who kept coming during the 1980s who kept the game afloat to become what it is today.

'There is a fear that football has become so fashionable that people wonder whether the "new" fans will still be turning up if football suffers a bust after the boom – in those circumstances the people who can't get into the ground who once did will be crucial – if they've not already left the game behind as the game did likewise.

'However, every fan at the game now is seen as merely a consumer, with a ceaseless thirst for all things football related.

'The rampant commercialism assumes that people's appetite for TV football and news is unlimited and that just isn't the case. They've worked on the theory of price inelasticity, whereby fans are so duped and blinded by loyalty that they'll put up with any increase in prices. That isn't the case – especially for the TV fan.

'FIFA have never looked after fans' interests. They seem to alternate between utter cynical commercialism and a general stewardship of the game that, however misguided, by aligning themselves against the major clubs, brings them temporarily onto the terrain of being fan-friendly, even though they would never see it as that, nor would they want to be there by choice.

'The FSA's view is that the match-going fan has definitely suffered – with matches rearranged, away fans are unable to get home after a weekday match. The problem with stay-at-home fans is particularly problematic in the lower leagues, where you can see the difference in attendance figures.'

Surveys by the Sir Norman Chester Centre for Football Research show the clearest picture of the modern UK football fan. Most fans are white and male. A lot of them have children. One survey by the Centre showed that 6 out of 10 fans with school-age children watch matches with their children, and half of all fans aged 41–50 do the same. It has also been shown that non-season ticket holders are twice as likely as season ticket holders to live 50 miles or more from their club's home ground, with half of all season ticket holders having been born in, or near, the town or city of their home club. Season ticket holders are also more likely to see their club as 'much more important than the national team', and are less likely to watch England play live. Season ticket holders are also deep pocketed, especially in the UK, where the best of the season tickets at clubs like Chelsea can cost around £1,000, while the average is around the £500 mark. Interestingly enough, in Europe the average ticket is cheaper, with this being put down to the different types of stadiums where seating is not as rigid as those in the UK, better usage of stadiums for other events than football games, councils owning the stadiums, with clubs paying a rent lower than the running costs and more money coming in from TV deals.

In Europe many clubs have frozen their ticket prices for a number of years, but more of their money comes from the individually negotiated TV deals that they are allowed to make. For years this has been used to excuse the higher prices in the UK – more money was needed to keep the top players. But this is a false argument as European clubs also pay more money to their players, so UK fans are being ripped off.

Regarding away games, it was found that regular away match attendees are much more likely to be fans who previously stood at matches. Ninety-five per cent of fans who attend all their club's away matches are season ticket holders. What is surprising is that fans who live furthest from their club's home ground are the strongest away match attendees, but less surprising is the fact that regular away match attendees object most to TV schedules affecting the time and day of match kick-offs.

More than 90 per cent of those who attend the large games in Britain are what a census would define as white UK citizens. Some grounds in the UK have no Asian season ticket holders, though grounds like Wimbledon and Leicester do have rising Asian support and most clubs do have some Asian fans. The apparent decline of racism in the game – as well as an increase in ethnic communities in Britain – has led to more and more members of ethnic minorities coming to games, not as afraid as they used to be that they might be attacked or insulted.

However, another group that goes to games and still fears persecution is the homosexual fans. Homosexuality is still a shameful area for football. Players can hug, kiss and squeeze each other's testicles on the pitch, but if two men started kissing in the stand, odds are there would be a scene that wouldn't occur if they were a man and a woman. Homosexual insults are thrown at players without a thought these days, having taken on the status of general insults; homosexuality is seen as a weakness. Very few chanters of the insults would feel at all uncomfortable singing homophobic songs. Indeed, while stewards at grounds across the country have thrown people out for making racist and bigoted comments, no one has ever been ejected from a ground for shouting homophobic abuse. Some fans, though, wonder why it has to be an issue at all. Mark Dalton is a gay Manchester United fan. He makes no secret of it, but in his own words:

'I don't keep washing the home strips I buy until they are pink and then wear them, though I know some gay fans do feel the need to let the world know that they are homosexual. I don't see the point.'

He feels that football and homosexuality are two things that will probably remain separate:

'Football is an aggressive game and a lot of heterosexual supporters seem to have a problem linking aggression with homosexuals.

'There's also the whole question of "being a poof" for the majority of fans being a decent insult to throw at others. I'm thick-skinned and comfortable enough with my sexuality so that it is not a problem but I know others hate that being chanted out.

'I used to shout it the odd time too as "poof" has now gone past, in my opinion, being a homosexual insult, it's now just a term for wimps of any sexual orientation, but then someone said I should change "poof" to "nigger" and ask myself if I would shout it out, though I suppose the counter-argument is that many blacks, even if it is in America, still call themselves and others "nigga" so perhaps – by an extension of that logic – only real homosexuals should be able to shout out "poof"?

'Being serious though, does it really matter who or what they sleep with as long as it is legal? I don't follow a club because I think a player is cute... or gay, I follow my team because it is the team I was brought up with. Sex shouldn't come into it. Everyone goes to a game to support a team, but apart from that everyone there will be quite different.

'Also why are clubs now allowing the set-up of gay-only supporter clubs? The division does nothing positive as anyone afraid to come out is hardly going to go to a gay supporters' meeting. It shouldn't be about sex, but if it has to come into it then people should just relax and accept each other for what they are, have a few jokes about it and that's it.'

Mark Watson of gay rights group Stonewall has called for the FA to launch a campaign to kick out homophobia in the way that they did against racism. Some people have called for players to come out of the closet and be open about their sexuality, saying that if they all come out, it will force fans to confront their prejudice, just as clubs signing black players forced fans to confront their racist attitudes, but this looks like being one area where the players will – for the next few years at least – keep quiet.

As noted at the start of this chapter, traditionally a woman shopped while the football was on. Or did she? And if that is the case, where did the one in seven women who are now Premiership fans come from? A factsheet compiled by Tessa Hayward for the Sir Norman Chester Centre for Football Research shows things not to be so clear-cut. According to the factsheet women were admitted free to games up until the mid-1880s but this was scrapped after a game in Preston, where it is said that almost 2,000 women and children turned up. Match reports of the era also show that women were found in the more upper-class parts of the grounds. The first half of the 20th century saw women becoming more independent, partially due to suffrage and their involvement in the war effort, and this allowed women to become more involved in sports, including football. Conditions at grounds also improved, making the facilities more attractive and appealing to women. Brentford FC was one club that seemed to gain a considerable amount of female support between the wars, leading to the club being referred to as a 'ladies' team', according to the factsheet.

The social changes of the 1960s and 1970s saw more and more women going to games as the new atmosphere of equality and more radical feminism swept the country, but by the mid-seventies things started to reverse as hooliganism took over. However, women never truly went away, and it is claimed that during the eighties at some games as many as 15 per cent of the audience were female. Indeed nine female fans were killed in the Hillsborough tragedy. The early nineties revolution in football seems to have brought more women into the game than ever before – as fans and as players – and this has led to them being taken more seriously than they have been in a long time. A 1995 FA Carling Premier League Fan Survey backed the finding of earlier surveys, and showed that female fans are highly committed to their clubs, as 7 out of 10 female fans interviewed were season ticket holders, while three-quarters of women fans had attended at least one away match. The big difference was that very few had played the game, while the overwhelming majority of men had. The Sir Norman Chester factsheet concluded:

Although female fans have always been, and still are, in a minority, it does seem as if more women are now attracted to football. With the recent growth in women's football and the increasing numbers of female administrators, officials, journalists and so on, women are now starting to find their voice within the industry. There are still many areas which need to be addressed and improved in terms of provision for female spectators, but football clubs and the industry itself are starting this process, and are realising the commercial potential of female support. Perhaps only now are women beginning to be more widely accepted as 'knowledgeable' fans who have an important place in the game.

A separate survey showed that Derby, Leicester and Nottingham Forest were the best at attracting female fans, while Celtic and Newcastle were the worst. Arsenal fan Maria Alridge says that being a woman who likes football is something that causes great frustration to her because of others' attitudes to her liking the game, and that in her opinion women being regarded as knowledgeable about football is some way off.

'It really gets annoying when you are at your work or whatever and you are talking about football or you join in a conversation about football. Some blokes go along with it, but you look at their eyes and you see that they are totally dismissing what you say purely because you're not a bloke.

'There's just this mental block that some folk have that you are female therefore you know nothing about the game and you only watch it because you fancy someone, which is not only annoying but insulting too.

'Female journalists and so on are dismissed by male fans because of it and I think it all boils down to the adolescent macho mentality that some have when it comes to football.

'It's as bad at the games because if you have a season ticket, which I don't but I've heard of this happening, you'll get accused of having stolen your seat from a real fan, in other words, a bloke.

'You might even get guys making passes at you or others complain that they cannot enjoy the game because they are next to a woman and it is ridiculous. Women have every right to enjoy football as much as men but for some reason men seem to have a problem with that.

'It's not something that should be an issue but it is and probably always will be because the odds are we will never get mixed teams at high up levels though I don't see why there cannot be female referees and lineswomen.

'Women going to the game is not a problem. The mentality of some men is though.'

Regardless of what gender fans sleep with or what sex and skin colour they are, they all have something in common other than the teams they support: they are being ripped off. They have shown that they have a voracious appetite for anything connected with their club, and clubs have exploited this without mercy. The dedicated fan can now buy mobile phone covers, bed covers, posters, official magazines and even television channels all featuring their club. The real die-hard can even apply for a mortgage, credit card or insurance through their club, though it is doubtful that being a fan for 20 years is enough to stop the debt agencies if they fall behind with their payments. At every opportunity money has been taken from fans in any way possible, from the sale of scarves and match programmes, to satellite television coverage, testimonials for already well-paid players and shares in the club – no financial stone has been left unturned. Whether it be club products with a sponsor's name on it, the television package or the season ticket, it is the fan who pays.

In some cases fans have paid with more than money. There are numerous examples of tragedies – Hillsborough being the one that led to some of the most monumental changes in football. Hillsborough was a tragedy brought about by a variety of factors, and it is looked at later in the book, but the resulting report by Lord Justice Peter Taylor transformed the game. As esteemed football writer David Conn has noted, the author, a man who did not have much contact with the sport, could not believe the conditions fans had to put up with. The report listed torrid, rubbish-strewn conditions, squalor and terrible smells, and among its suggestions called for seating and improved conditions. However, no matter how often one looks at the report – and it is something that every fan should read – there is no part that states 'Clubs shall build all-seater stadiums, get grants for this and then hike up prices above the cost of inflation to the fan'. Yet that is exactly what has happened. At the start of the 1990s it was perfectly possible to go to a football game with £10 and have enough money for either a seat in the stand (another football irony) or to stand in the terracing, as well as a pint or a pie, and even then go home with change. A tenner would even be enough for a parent to take their child to a match. Not now. At some grounds in Britain £10 would now only let you see the equivalent of 30 minutes of the game, as the average price is now £20–£30 for 90 minutes, and that is for what would be dubbed the cheap seats. Taylor never wanted the fans to be priced out of the game. The report states that it should be possible for clubs to offer tickets at prices comparable to those previously charged for standing in the terraces. Somewhere along the lines, that part of the report has been forgotten. Chairman of the Football Supporters' Association, Malcolm Clarke, has a strong opinion on the matter:

'The cost of going to watch a live game means that many traditional fans are being forced out of the market and we're particularly concerned that a lot of young people are, and people on relatively low incomes can't get access to it, so that's sort of our major concern. We certainly support the calls that there should be a wider range of ticket prices and that some of them at the bottom end should be lowered and ticket prices should not be increased more than the rate of inflation. I think over the last 10 years ticket prices have risen six times the price of inflation. £4 for terrace and £6 for a seat is not unreasonable. That would be about £10/£11 now but that won't get you into anything above third division in England. You certainly won't get into many of the premier grounds for anything even approaching £10.

'Without a doubt there are some clubs and chairmen where they just expect fans to turn up and give the money because they know they've got a captive market and regardless of how annoyed a fan might get, they cannot go and get what they need from anywhere else. Fans who don't get to the game normally retain an interest and watch from home.

'I know some Man Utd fans who cannot afford to take their kids to the games or can't get enough season tickets or certain game tickets together to go. What they do instead is go to the reserve games because that's all they can get to and they never see the first team and that's awfully sad in many ways, especially in terms of building the future and the next generation of fans.

'Football runs the risk of not properly building up a new fan base and being in trouble if the bubble ever bursts.

'It could be argued that going to watch the second team shows they are more loyal than many others, but it's a sad sign that those who we might call the true hardcore fans can't get to see the first team games.'

(As an aside, going to the second team games and youth team games can make fans money. When Leeds United fan Carl Darren spotted midfielder Stephen McPhail playing alongside Harry Kewell and Jonathan Woodgate for the youth team in 1996, he decided he was an outstanding prospect and put a £40 bet at 25–1 that McPhail would play for his country before he was 23. He did, winning Darren £1,000.)

What makes the matter of pricing for games even more scandalous is that some teams in the English and Scottish leagues are charging away fans more than the home fans at certain games, despite the fact that they are all in the same ground, watching the same game. This practice has been condemned but clubs are trying to get round it by saying that they are not charging away fans more, but are actually rewarding their home fans by charging them less. Fans have also been told they are being charged more for getting a better view.

Most fans feel that the Taylor Report was responsible for bringing in all-seater stadiums, and some will say that it is one of the reasons pricing has gone up. For some, as Clarke noted above, that means that they can no longer go to a game. The truth of the Taylor report, and the summation of it, is this: fans were being ripped off and neglected by those who ran the clubs and those who ran the game. Taylor called for changes that went a lot deeper than putting in plastic seating. He wanted the game overhauled and reformed – his report even went, in part, against the government view of that time. It was a brave report and a good starting point for saving the game. That Taylor's wishes were not implemented while those in power, like vultures, picked what suited them from it, is one of football's tragedies. It is morally repugnant that some cowards, who continue to profit from the game, hide behind the report and slur the work of a man who tried to make things better for the average fan, which is more than they have ever done. Even now, almost a decade after the Taylor Report, all-seater stadiums are a contentious issue. Another side to the all-seater debate is that a tragedy such as Hillsborough was not caused because there were no seats; it was caused by overcrowding and poor safety provision.

Since all-seater stadiums were introduced, some fans have campaigned for small sections of terracing to be reintroduced. There have been letters to politicians, campaigns on the Internet, and at one point New Labour said it might look at the issue, but after the 1997 election this matter faded away and if any work was done on it, it was kept quiet. Dave Boyle thinks the seating issue is one that raises many points:

'It's definitely the case that the Taylor Report wasn't fully implemented and there were sections ignored – protecting ticket prices the oft-cited case.

'However, it's also true that the Hillsborough tragedy was "framed" by the terrace versus seats choice. Has it been better? In some cases, the move to seats prompted the building of new stands and/or grounds with much better facilities that had been needed for years.

'On the other hand, there's the obvious fact that as capacity is reduced, prices had to rise to continue to meet existing income targets.

'There's also the whole atmosphere debate, which links in with issues about the "type" of fan that has accompanied the all-seater stadium, which is also linked closely to the issue of ticket prices. On balance, I can definitely see the benefits, but as a supporter of a lower league club, I still stand most of the time and prefer it.

'I also think that modern technology makes the safety argument much weaker – witness the Westphalen stadium in Dortmund with its huge terraces that are converted to seats for UEFA/FIFA-sanctioned matches. We should also be clear that it shouldn't ultimately be seen as a seats versus terraces issue – it's about allowing both to co-exist. Nobody's denying that many people like seats, but we'd like the modern ground to allow fans a proper choice. The polarisation is unhelpful and a solution that recognised the different preferences of fans could impact on different policy issues.'

Clubs also fare poorly when it comes to dealing with their public. Queues for tickets are nothing new, but in this high-tech day and age fans can now also spend hours on voicemail queues trying to get a pertinent piece of information from a human being at their club. Public relations spokespeople normally deal with the press and little else, although Newcastle United has recently appointed a liaison officer to work between the fans and the club.

It is a far cry from American teams like the Chicago Bulls basketball team, where four members of staff are employed solely for meeting and greeting the season ticket holders and every single phone call or letter from a fan – more than 400 per day – is met with an individual reply. There is nothing comparable at any football team in the Western world, if anywhere.

But why did fans let things get into this state in the UK? There are a few reasons, including the fact that back in the seventies there was still a 'doffing the cap' mentality that reflected the class divisions in Britain, where the lower class looked up to the higher class, which would have been the mindset of many fans. It is also the case that most football fans are not really great students of the politics of the game. In the aforementioned questionnaire, a number of fans admitted they were only interested in their team, nothing else, and for some that included off-pitch activities as well. They could put up with a lot for a win. Some weren't even interested in their national teams.

This has been a problem for people trying to get fans to look beyond their own team, to campaign for their conditions and rights. Some magazines have managed it; others have not, with thousands of pounds being lost in the process. One magazine that tried and failed was *Fitba*, which was edited by Scottish journalist Stuart Darroch. It was launched as a Scottish-specialist magazine, giving it a niche market and potential audience of 5 million, though they would have no doubt settled for a chunk of the 130,000 people who attend Scottish games on a weekly basis. It failed. Its aim of going past the two main teams in Scotland – the Old Firm – was its strength but also its weakness. According to Darroch:

'The thinking behind *Fitba* was to fill a gap in the marketplace for the average Scottish football supporter. For too long, we believed, all the attention had been on the Old Firm, whether that be from newspapers, magazines, radio or television. Obviously, Rangers and Celtic can claim the majority of supporters in Scottish football, but we believed if we could attract fans from every other club in Scotland then that would enable us to meet our circulation target. While the national press may dedicate only one or two paragraphs to the fortunes of Clydebank, we believed we could give these subjects and teams more space and coverage.'

And while there may once have been a time when magazines like *Fitba* could have succeeded, in modern times fans in many European markets care for little more than their own team and show no interest in anything else.

Some fans do get involved to change things but again, this is only to change things at a club level, with the latest stunt being fans running for election to government to gain national attention to their plight as well as to show up those whom they believed were letting the team down – normally owners who they felt were not putting in enough investment. Fans allow things to happen to them because they feel there is little they can do. Campaigning, letter writing and going to meetings can be very tedious, and the complete antithesis of what football should be.

So why then, any sensible person would ask, do fans not just say 'I've had it with your prices and/or your rotten football, I'm away?' For the pure and simple reason that they cannot. They are addicts, and doubly so, for not only are they drawn to football, but also to one particular team. A true Manchester United fan will never support Arsenal or Manchester City. It's got to be United. Versace customers may buy Gucci, but no Inter Milan fan will wear the AC strip. This fact – which is unique to sport in all the consumer economic markets – is what gives football fans their greatest strength. However, it is also their greatest weakness, as clubs know fans will do all they can to keep coming to the game, to buy the season ticket, to get the latest strip, to see the game on Sky. There is also another reason football fans do not desert the game: the romance. Dave Boyle sums it up:

'A crucial part of being a fan – especially those in lower leagues or who are outside the top 10 clubs in the big leagues, which make up the majority of clubs in football – is the possibility that one day, just maybe, we could make it into the top division or win the cup.

'I know that ultimately, it isn't going to happen as things stand – reason tells you all the time that there is a hierarchy and your team is at the bottom of the pile. You see the evidence every Saturday. Part of what keeps you coming back though is the hope, the dream – and that dream's harder to keep going when a key part of the romantic attachment to a team is also extinguished.

'Like Arthur Miller's salesman, a football fan's gotta dream.'

Some fans are starting to fight back. Later on in the book we will look at the supporters' associations that are cropping up across the UK and the rest of Europe, while some other fans are using the

Internet to lodge complaints about how the game is run or how their team is portrayed.

The most common forums are online e-mail groups for fans to swap opinions, or Web site fanzines, but there have been some unique protests. Celtic fan Stuart Cotterell felt that the club was always portrayed in a poor light by the *Daily Record* and that the newspaper was giving preferential treatment to their mortal enemies Rangers, so he registered the Internet domain names www.dailyranger.com and www.dailyranger.co.uk; accessing these sites took you to the official *Daily Record* Web site.

But for most fans the dream of winning tournaments and leagues is rapidly becoming a nightmare – financially and otherwise. This book will show what is happening to the fan, how events are beyond their control and what is happening to their game. Football fans may have to dream, but if they don't wake up soon, the dream will become a nightmare of Dante-esque proportions.

Two

Players

Who would be a footballer in this day and age – the chance to earn millions playing a game you love, perhaps even for a team you love, and at the end of the day there might even be a supermodel or pop star who wants to sleep with you. A hard life indeed. Or it is according to the players who moan about wanting more money, although some players now earn in four days what the average person earns in a year. In the UK this is certainly the case, with players on the upper scale earning £50,000 a week, while the national average wage is between £20,000 and £25,000 depending on the part of the country in which you live. But are players actually overpaid? There is no point in going back to the days when the likes of Sir Stanley Matthews received £20 a game, because the game was different then and the standard of living was different. It is better to look at the present, and though it is fair to say that the mega-money of now may stem from the fact that for decades players were underpaid, it is now going outrageously over the top.

A recent survey of UK soccer stars revealed that England's top footballers earn, on average, more than £400,000 per year, with the basic salary for Premiership players aged over 20 being almost £32,000 a month. The survey also showed that about 100 Premiership players earn over £1 million per year. Broken down, the figures make interesting reading. A youngster aged 17–18 will earn £19,000, while the average 19–20-year-old will get £45,000. Each year the average wage rises phenomenally, with 21–22-year-olds earning £126,000, 23–24-year-olds getting £364,000, until it peaks at 27–28-year-olds earning £572,000 a year. After that it drops, but by 'only' £100,000 a year. However, the British players are technically hard done by when compared to their European counterparts. In 2000, the top footballers' weekly pay before bonuses was:

Gabriel Batistuta	–	£95,000
Alessandro Del Piero	–	£72,500
Steve McManaman	–	£68,250
Patrick Kluivert	–	£60,500
Nicolas Anelka	–	£58,500
Christian Vieri	–	£58,500
Ronaldo	–	£52,500
Krassimir Balakov	–	£50,000
Steffen Effenberg	–	£50,000
Roy Keane	–	£50,000
Juan Veron	–	£50,000

However, looking at what other sporting figures earn shows that footballers are not the richest of people by any means. In Formula One Michael Schumacher brings in £25 million a year from Ferrari, plus endorsements, while boxer Lennox Lewis has an estimated purse of £5 million per fight – a figure that the top golfers can also easily make – and a Wimbledon champion receives just under £500,000 before sponsorship deals. On this scale Roy Keane comes in at around £4 million if Manchester United do well and he receives associated perks and bonuses.

In another entertainment industry supermodels Cindy Crawford, Claudia Schiffer and Elle MacPherson are all estimated to be worth more than £20 million, with Kate Moss and Naomi Campbell not far behind. However, compare this to the worlds of politics and big business. Top chairmen can routinely leave jobs and get five-, six- or seven-figure golden handshakes, as well as performance bonuses of similar amounts. Does this make it all right that footballers are paid so much? In truth, no. Footballers may say they are only getting paid the going rate when compared to other entertainment industries, but football is a special case. No one in their right mind would volunteer to be the CEO of a multinational for nothing, but offer a free starting place in the Manchester United, AC Milan or Barcelona line-up and people would fight for the honour. This is why there was so much disdain over the Roy Keane saga in 1999, when his pay was increased to around £50,000 a week. It looked as though the days of players wanting to play for Manchester United because it was Manchester United, the pinnacle of a player's career, were finally over. In truth they had been over for years, but the myth, started in Sir Matt Busby's days, was shattered, as other players in the team began to work out what they could be worth when their contracts run out in 2001 and 2002.

Not all players are obsessed with money. In truth, very few probably are, but they see what others are getting and they think they should be on similar sums because they are as good as, if not better than, them. Gary Neville was quite honest when he told reporters after a European game that he thought his value to Manchester United was about one-fifth of Roy Keane's. Republic of Ireland striker Tommy Coyne has said on numerous occasions that while what he does is work, he knows it does not compare to people who have to work in coal pits or do heavy industrial jobs, while worrying about mortgages and having to get children presents for birthdays and Christmas. In Coyne's mind that is real pressure, not playing football. Coyne, like others in his age group, is grounded in reality. They know they are talented, but they also know they are lucky. The same cannot be said for many of the upcoming young players, who are removed from everyday life at an early age. As the figures above show, between the ages of 17 and 20, a player could earn well over £25,000 per year, which is the average annual UK salary. There are people in their thirties and forties who do not earn that sort of money, and work a damn sight harder than footballers, while for the young pups their pay is only going to rise and rise.

However, things may be set to change, for no other reason than that clubs are running out of money. According to the most recent report into the game (published in 2000) by accountants Deloitte & Touche, the wages to turnover ratio for all 92 clubs was 65 per cent, compared to 52 per cent in 1994/95. In the Premier League it is an average of 58 per cent; 80 per cent in Divisions One and Two and 95 per cent in Division Three.

Eighty per cent of clubs now have a wage bill in excess of two-thirds of their income, compared to 60 per cent in the 1995/96 season, and only four clubs have wages to turnover ratios of 50 per cent or less.

These figures are high. In very few industries is there a comparable wage to turnover ratio because the higher the wages the less money there is to actually invest in a company or look after the customers. There is also the risk, as any wise accountant will tell you, that your income will drop unexpectedly, which still leaves you with a high wage bill but less – perhaps not even enough – to pay the wages.

Premiership players' wages were estimated at £241 million for 1998/99 – showing an increase of 266 per cent since 1993/94. The report stated that wage bills in the lower divisions are far too high for long-term financial strength and survival. Gerry Boon, head of the Deloitte & Touche football industry team, said:

'A gamble to break into the Premier League may cripple clubs with long-term commitments to expensive players if it fails to pay off. We are seeing polarisation within the leagues where top-paying clubs are able to out-pay the low payers four and a half times over.'

Glenn Hoddle has said that he fears professional football will collapse in England if wages continue to rise so dramatically:

'The game is becoming divorced from ordinary fans in so many ways.

'It has got out of control compared to other walks of life but it is being driven by money coming into the game. If the bubble bursts a lot of clubs will be left high and dry. There needs to be a controlled balance.'

But why are footballers paid more than the average person, many of whom work longer hours and do more dangerous jobs? Various economic theories are touted around, including a player's ability to transform a game with a single skilful touch. It is argued that in sport, other entertainment industries and business people can do an ordinary job at their level, but can also be capable of moments of brilliance, hence their higher value, which brings in improved returns for those involved. It has alternatively been argued that not everyone could go through the years of training that players do and have the talent to be developed or the self-control necessary to succeed at the top, so once they get there, the economic forces of supply and demand take over.

Most of these theories, while interesting, can be dismissed fairly easily: first, everyone is capable of moments of brilliance in their work and second, being signed as a young player does not involve any great sacrifice, as the money is always decent these days (as the figures above show).

The truth is that the money is there because of gate receipts, television and merchandising, all of which is paid for by the fan, the same fan who is sometimes snubbed by players after standing in the rain waiting for an autograph. But not all fans are just sitting back and taking it. For a while Reading fans had a club called PANTS, which stood for Players Are Not Trying Sufficiently. If the fans felt that the players were not trying their best they would wave underwear at them until their play improved.

However, there is a possibility that players may find their potential earnings increase diminished, as UEFA have suggested bringing in a limit on what players can be paid. They have proposed that clubs that want to play in UEFA events must have a UEFA licence, which would only be granted after a number of conditions are met – including proving that their finances are in good shape. Under this scenario, clubs may cut back on wages to players to show that they are financially solvent and capable of continuing in business.

Chief Executive of UEFA Gerhard Aigner has said:

'At UEFA we are examining the proposal to introduce a European licence for clubs with a control on balance sheets and, after that, limitation on the volume of salaries.'

The move came about after a survey showed some clubs to be living above their means, especially in Spain, where debts are forever delayed to the extent that clubs are sometimes more than £100 million in debt. Wage capping would have a number of interesting effects, and could make it harder for the less attractive leagues, like those in Scotland, to bring in top talent, as clubs in these leagues traditionally have to pay over the odds to attract that talent. It also leads to the question of whether players would strike if they felt they were losing out in terms of future potential earnings. If they went on strike over a limit on their wages, would the fans back them or would they be repulsed by the greed of the players? Would the players take the chance that the fans would not come back, especially if any strike action was long and protracted? It could even affect the European Championships and European cup tournaments. It is a scenario that many hope will not come to pass, but if UEFA made the move, it would be bold and – in the long term – probably for the best.

However, one reason constantly stated for the high wages is that footballers are rare commodities and they also have a high risk of injury, so their career could be ended at any time through injury. This can be dismissed because anyone can be injured at work, and many jobs have higher risks than football.

Players do face health risks, however, though these are rarely acknowledged. A report by the Professional Footballers' Association, called *Managing Injuries in Professional Football: The Roles of the Club Doctor and Physiotherapist*, showed that clubs can, and do, put injured players at risk by trying to get them back into the game quickly. Part of the pressure put on players came from telling them to play through the pain, to go through the pain barriers, as part of the macho ethos of football. The report pointed out that some clubs even tried to inconvenience unfit players in an attempt to hurry them back. For example, comparisons were made between fit players who would train until 1 or 2 pm while unfit players were kept back until 4 or 5 pm (though this could be partly explained by the fact that they are getting physiotherapy and other forms of treatment). The report also found that many football club doctors obtained their appointments through personal contacts of one kind or another, and that most physiotherapists did so via networking. The report added that there were very few full-time club doctors in England; even fewer were specialists in sports medicine and half of all club physiotherapists were not chartered and, as such, not qualified to work in the NHS. The report ends on an ominous note, stating:

'At the moment these processes constitute a catalogue of poor employment practices.'

Another survey showed that professional footballers often end their glittering careers suffering from osteoarthritis, which is a common form of arthritis caused by damage to the cartilage of joints. The research, printed in the *British Journal of Sports Medicine* and carried out by researchers from Coventry University, showed that almost half of nearly 300 players interviewed had been diagnosed with osteoarthritis after leaving the game, most commonly in the knee, and they were getting the condition in their forties – not their sixties as is the average. Players may also be suffering due to the type of ball used in the old days. Ex-Celtic and Scotland player Billy McPhail has campaigned for players to be given disability payments and claims he suffers dementia as a result of heading the old, thick leather football. There is also the possibility of damage from the drugs players now use to play through pain barriers, though it may be a few years before the long-term effects of these can be fully understood, as drug companies are continually developing more and more drugs that they claim can help players recover or improve their performance.

French superstar Emmanuel Petit has spoken about how he worries players may be forced to take drugs just to be able to play all the games that are taking place in the crowded schedule of today's football calendar. Petit has pointed out that even for fit athletes, playing games across continents in a matter of days, as well as training, can take its toll and players may feel the need to resort to desperate tactics to avoid being dropped.

Frank Leboeuf has also said that he fears the rate of games will lead to burnout amongst the younger players, as well as injuries not getting a proper chance to heal.

And while players at the top levels may be looked after in the event of an injury, if it occurs at the lower levels it can have a devastating effect on both the injured party and the person who caused the injury. In the mid-nineties Sunday League player Stephen Minnis broke an opponent's leg in a mistimed tackle. He was ordered to pay £20,000 in compensation because he was found to have been negligent in his tackle.

Not all injuries come from rushing back to training though. At the start of 2001, Leeds defender Rio Ferdinand injured himself watching television when he strained a tendon behind his knee through putting his feet up on a coffee table.

Injury aside, another worry many players have now is that they will be replaced – or frozen out of the game – by cheaper foreign imports. The UK Government almost tried to introduce a quota of foreign imports into the UK. Doing this, it was argued, would allow the UK players to blossom and develop. The Government said it was willing to bring in such a system but it would not be able to enforce anything because there were no regulatory rules for football. There was also the problem that trying to limit the number of EU footballers playing in the UK would be illegal under European law. The English FA, the Football League and the FA Premier League were all for the quota system. FIFA and UEFA issued comments stating that they were concerned about the number of foreign players in many national leagues, and that it might be affecting the performance – or may affect the future performance – of national teams.

However, the Government then backed down from starting anything, with an Education and Employment Committee report into work permits for overseas stars stating:

'Given that free movement of labour throughout the European Economic Area is viewed as one of the cardinal principles of the Treaty of Rome, we think it unlikely that sport would be given an exemption.'

An exemption to the Treaty of Rome would require the unanimous vote of all European countries and it was felt that the European powers would not make a special case for football. However, this has not yet been tested, though it may – and should – in coming years. Many countries, for example Spain, have made exceptions to national laws on the basis of football being a special case, and that could happen in the UK.

An area where players would love to see intervention – though it will never happen because of the difficulties of enforcing it – concerns the chants coming from the crowd. In the seventies, eighties and nineties footballers were subjected to horrible forms of abuse, including fans screaming that they had all slept with the players' wives, that the players were homosexual and downright ugly (and those are just the printable comments!). Normally the player just took it, or it inspired him to do a marvellous piece of football in front of the jeering fans in defiance, but in the 21st century the players won't put up with the abuse – they want cheers, not jeers.

One area where the jeering is particularly shameful is homosexuality. While gay fans may suffer some discomfort, players are subjected to far more. Only one player has ever admitted to being gay (see overleaf), though it is accepted that there are others. For years football players have been accused of being gay. The whole issue behind players' sexuality goes back to the image of football as a macho sport and homosexuality being viewed as a weakness or something unusual. Tabloid newspapers have run what they called 'ethical' outings by giving hints that players were gay, without actually outing them, but no player ever stepped up and discussed their sexuality.

Former Middlesbrough player Mikkel Beck has spoken of how claims of him being homosexual upset him and 'got to him'. He claimed one team-mate would not get undressed in the changing-room because he thought Beck was gay.

In the UK, the Labour government has made pleas for players to come forward and bring the issue out into the open. MP Tony Banks has mentioned the issue on more than one occasion, saying:

'Unless we can raise the issue, unless we can actually discuss it, then quite frankly people will pretend it doesn't exist.

'I have to admit that it would be a very, very brave footballer who admits he is gay and then goes out on the pitch.

'There is probably a significant number of gay footballers and many more gay spectators. If they have to submerge this sexuality in a macho display because that is what is expected of them, then, frankly, they don't feel – and I would agree – that they can give of their best either in terms of their athletic prowess or support.

'Homophobia is difficult to legislate for but it is something which must be confronted. A feeling is beginning to grow that sport is twisted if it isn't inclusive. Clearly it isn't if there is a great deal of homophobia in sport.'

Unfortunately, there is evidence that seems to suggest that coming out does not actually help get rid of homophobia. The University of Amsterdam, at the request of the Dutch government, commissioned a group of researchers to look into the experiences of gay men and lesbians in organised, non-professional sports in Holland. Their work showed that gay men and lesbians experienced little discrimination. However, the reason for this was because they kept their sexuality hidden. The report also found that when their sexuality was known, there was quite overt discrimination at times, especially for lesbians in football.

Only one player in the UK has ever had the courage to come out, and his story did not have a happy ending. The life of Justin Fashanu hardly serves as encouragement for others to come forward. Fashanu was one of the best players in Britain at the start of the 1980s. He was an extremely skilful player, playing for Norwich City while still a teenager, becoming one of their best centre forwards by the age of 19, and in 1980 becoming the first black player purchased for £1 million, by Nottingham Forest. He was also very bright; he could talk about sex with supermodels for the tabloids, while discussing the finer points of classical music in the broadsheets. He had it all. But as with many talented people he could never find a place where he felt comfortable, and when he came out of the closet he still found no peace, with sports writers, cartoonists and comedians all benefiting at his expense. At Nottingham Forest he was known for his involvement in the gay scene, and Forest manager Brian Clough, who was called a strict, old-fashioned kind of manager by those who admired him and a bully, if not worse, by his critics, did not take kindly to the rumours that were reaching him. His treatment of Fashanu was deplorable. He suspended and later sacked him, selling him to Notts County for just £150,000 in 1982.

Things might have picked up there for Fashanu, but a year later he suffered a long-term knee injury. He moved to America for a few years, found religion and returned home at the start of the 1990s to play for Third Division Torquay United. It was in 1990 that Fashanu came out publicly, telling the *Sun* that he had had sex with fellow players and a Member of Parliament. People praised him for coming forward, but it later transpired that he had lied in parts of the interview, for which he had been paid. He continued to wander up and down the country, never finding a place in which he felt he belonged, or that would let him belong. He moved back to America, to Maryland, where a friend gave him a coaching job. Those who knew him hoped that it would finally give him some long-term happiness. But it was then claimed that he had been charged with sexually molesting a 17-year-old boy. It later transpired that the relationship had been one of mutual consent, and that the boy was attempting to blackmail him. The authorities were only called in when Fashanu refused to pay any money. At the age of 37 he took his own life. His body was found hanging in an East London garage and he never had a chance to deny or fight the charges that had been brought against him.

I was passed some comments by a European player who played in the UK. While he is not gay, he had gay relationships when younger, and is now married. He said:

'Football is not a sport where homosexuality is really tolerated. I have heard comments from players in European teams saying they would not share a room with a gay player and they would also be uncomfortable in the same shower as them. It is sad.

'My wife knows what I did before I got married and while it would not bother me greatly to admit to what I did in the past – and it is no great secret – I am honest enough to know that it would cause a lot of problems for others as well as be the basis for a lot of juvenile sniggering.

'The Dutch are more tolerant of it because they have a more relaxed attitude about this sort of thing but even there football is still expected to be a macho thing.

'It's not something that would go away until a lot of top players admitted their sexuality, because if only one or two came out then they would be slaughtered by opposing crowd chants, but if most clubs had gay players then it would be different, especially if there was a threat of a fan being thrown out for making comments or a gay player who was a superb keeper or striker with 40 goals a season in him threatening to leave because of the comments.'

An example of the sort of treatment a gay player coming out could expect is provided by the experience of Graeme Le Saux. The claims that he is gay stem from nothing more than the fact that he comes across as an educated man, because of his hobbies of antique collecting and visiting art galleries. He also reads broadsheet newspapers, not the tabloids. It is because he has been perceived as not being a 'working-class hero' that he has found himself tagged as homosexual, something that speaks volumes for those who throw the accusation at him. He has endured seasons of abuse, which culminated most famously in an incident during a game with Liverpool in February 1999. It was claimed that Liverpool's Robbie Fowler had been making gestures to the crowd during the game, taunting Le Saux. When Le Saux prepared to take a free kick, Fowler turned his back and thrust out his backside. Le Saux complained to the referee and was booked for time wasting. He later physically attacked Fowler. Le Saux got only a one-match ban for the assault, though attacks of that nature usually bring a three-match ban. Fowler was given a two-match ban for bringing the game into disrepute. After the incident, more people spoke up and said that homophobia was no different to racism. Head of the Professional Footballers' Association, Gordon Taylor, said:

'When it gets to being involved in such gestures from other professionals it's something we want to get rid of, the same as we would if it was racist taunts.'

While some players object to suggestions that they are gay, being gay icons seems to be something that most players are not too worried about, and have the maturity to handle well. For example, there was no great outburst from Michael Owen when he was informed that gay men's magazine *Attitude* had voted him number one in their list of the 100 sexiest men in the world. In Brazil being voted a gay icon is nothing new, with many of the country's top stars posing for explicit full-frontal pictures for best-selling gay magazines like *G Magazine*. However, some players have been warned that very explicit shots could have a detrimental effect on their careers – not because they are appearing in gay magazines it is claimed, but because the explicit nature of the shots drags the game into disrepute. Some feel, though, that this is just an excuse, as South America is still having problems getting to grips with same-sex relationships. For example, when Daniel Passarella, captain of Argentina's 1978 World Cup-winning side, took over coaching the national team after the 1994 World Cup, he immediately banned long hair, earrings and homosexuals.

As well as the abuse a player could receive, sponsorship is another relevant issue. In the past, companies have been happy to use homosexuals and lesbians in their advertising to stir up some controversy but there have also been occasions when companies have pulled out of shows or productions involving gay people and depictions of gay life.

Sponsors seem quite happy to advertise at gay events, but when it comes to the larger events, which are more mainstream, it is not as clear cut. According to Mark Dalton, a gay Manchester United fan, a player coming out could lose out:

'He might be called brave by some groups but sponsors would probably avoid him like a bargepole. In the macho culture of football could you imagine the abuse a young kid would get if he was wearing the same boots as worn by a homosexual? At first people would always see those boots, or whatever the player was endorsing, as being a gay symbol.

'It doesn't help that the gay community does tend to iconise things as fashion and use them up in that context to the point of overkill very quickly, so if there was clothing endorsed by a gay footballer then everyone would wear it for a while and then it would get mainstream attention and folk would start taking the piss just as the more reactionary gay scene decided it no longer wanted anything to do with it.'

Groups like gay rights organisation Outrage think there may be some way to go yet. Spokesman David Allason thinks the working-class culture, which is at the root of the game, plays a part:

'I think a lot of players are still scared to come out. Football in many ways is still a homophobic game, largely because so many of the players quite frankly are not all that well educated. Look at players who have been branded a "poof" because they spoke properly and read the *Guardian*.

'Friends of mine who are into football have all said that they think it's not really in your best interests to come out to your fellow players and cite Fashanu and some of his experiences when he came out as a reason why.

'Also, being a gay fan and hearing thousands around you chanting that someone is a poof will affect you and you will feel the impact of it – obviously not as much as the player it is directed at, but you will feel it to some extent, just as black supporters are and were offended when racist abuse is flung at black players and this is part of the problem – Fashanu got it from both sides for being black and gay.

'I am quite sure that gay players coming out would help, just as happens in ordinary life that as more people – particularly younger gay people – come out it has a snowball effect that influences their friends, their fellow students who are gay to also come out if they see someone they know has come out and there has not been too much hassle about it.

'Also, people coming out has a knock-on effect in that heterosexuals who know the person start to question their preconceived notions and ideas of what being gay was all about, and that is passed on.

'If a gay player was really top notch and putting in the goals, keeping the club at the top of the league I think the fans would have enough self-interest to realise that if they attack him then they are attacking the team so they will back him even though they're not particularly less homophobic than before, and similarly on the other side it gives the opposition fans a stick to hurl at the opposing player who is gay, though they may have to avoid saying anything if they also have a gay player or gay players in their team.

'I think sexuality is becoming less and less of an issue and you could hope that one day it will not matter at all. Look at the situation in the UK with members of parliament for instance. There they are jumping out of the closet at a phenomenal rate and the same thing is happening in other walks of life, like television.

'It will take time – these things always do – but I think that gradually people will stop caring about sexuality and it will be on the same level as what colour you are or what your religion is.

'Leagues can make it more difficult for fans to barrack people by creating a climate whereby it is just not acceptable to indulge in bigoted chants from the terraces, in the same way as it is not acceptable to indulge in racist chants.'

Gay football is starting to come into its own. London-based Stonewall FC is a good example. This is a gay football club set up in the early 1990s, which was pilloried by the mainstream media when it launched. It was also cruelly ignored by the gay press, who were perhaps resentful that gay people would want to take part in something as mainstream as football. However, Stonewall FC has been a shining success, not only in terms of being an example of a successful gay football community but also in terms of footballing skills, with some of their players having had trials with Premiership and First Division clubs. In fact the Gay World Cup, also known as the International Gay and Lesbian Football Association (IGLFA) World Championships, is in many ways similar to the 'normal' World Cup, with the difference being that players and fans seem to have a better time at the gay event. In the professional World Cup, players are kept on strict diets and regimes until they are out of the event. At the Gay World Cup events, everyone parties from the opening games, though no quarter is given on the field. In one way the Gay World Cup is better, as it is an annual event, not every four years, giving British teams more chances to win a World Cup. They did so at the 1995 World Cup finals in Berlin, with captain Paul Baker being the first English football captain to receive a World Cup Winner's medal since Bobby Moore in 1966. According to David Allason:

'Events like the IGLFA World Championships can be a success if they get good media coverage and people can realise that a couple of gay teams playing is not that different from straight teams playing each other: after all, it's football that matters and not the identity of individual players.'

Londoners and the UK will get to judge for themselves, as the 2001 event is taking place in London. A spokesman for the event said:

'There's been a lot of demand for London. It's clearly a city with enormous football culture, wide gay and lesbian diversity and a fantastic footballing infrastructure. We want to put a grand party on for all of our old friends and to provide an everlasting and rewarding experience. We hope it will be one of the best yet.'

Just as gay football is succeeding, women's football is going the same way. The English-speaking countries – America and the UK – along with the Netherlands, are taking the lead in promoting the women's game, and there is now a women's World Cup. Reporting of the game is being heavily promoted on sites like goalnetwork.com, which dedicates special areas to it. A survey carried out by the Sir Norman Chester Centre for Football Research showed that football is still regarded as a man's game – mostly by men – though women's playing figures and attendances are up, as is the number of women coming into the game as administrators at a high level. However, the report also found that in comparison to continental Europe and America, the growth in the UK is slow. In Norway, there are more than 44,000 registered female players, which means there are actually more female than male players. Italy has had a semi-professional women's league since the early 1970s; matches there sometimes draw crowds of 20,000, and are regularly reported in Italy's sports newspapers. The most impressive figures for female participation are in America, where there are 3–4 million registered players.

In 1992 Jackie Woodhouse of the Sir Norman Chester Centre conducted a survey of players in the UK Women's National League. It provides facts and figures on who plays and where. Overwhelmingly, the female players were single (90.8 per cent) and had no children (93.0 per cent). This reflects the relative youth of the sample, but also says something about the difficulties involved in looking after a family while playing football.

Organised games for women date back at least to 18th-century Scotland, where an annual match between the married and single women would attract as many as 10,000 spectators. The modern game developed in the late 19th century, and the women's game achieved a measure of popularity, with teams in England, France and Canada. That first 'golden age' of women's football came to an end in 1921, when the English Football Association banned women's teams from their grounds, leaving them with few places to play. The rebirth of the women's game began in the 1950s, as football became a popular game for girls, even in England. Meanwhile, there was a massive youth soccer movement in the United States, as girls found they could take part in this skilful game. An unofficial European Championship was held in Germany in 1957. During the 1960s, eastern European communist countries encouraged women to participate in sports, including football. In 1969 the English FA lifted its ban on women's teams. By 1971, there was organised women's football in some 34 countries. By 1991, 65 countries had women's teams, and FIFA staged an official

Women's World Cup in China (at the time, FIFA was reluctant to use the term 'World Cup', but did so).

That first Women's World Cup was a tremendous success, with exciting games, a high level of play, capacity crowds and a worldwide television audience. In England, the English FA merged with the Women's FA so, ironically, the organisation that had dealt the crushing blow to the women's game in 1921 had come full circle, and was actively promoting women's football, even if half-heartedly at times. Another breakthrough came in March 1991, when the FA did away with their rule that banned mixed football in schools for the under-11s. A second Women's World Cup was held in Sweden in 1995. Less successful than the first in terms of attendance, the second event did feature exciting games and very skilful play. A major breakthrough for women's football came at the 1996 Olympics in Atlanta, where women's football was included as a full medal sport for the first time. Crowds were large; the level of play was, once again, high, and several of the games were very exciting. The final, between the US and China, drew a crowd of 80,000 enthusiastic fans, the largest crowd ever to attend a women-only sporting event. The trend has continued, with the latest Women's World Cup and the Olympic events attracting large audiences. FIFA has even allowed women players to be nominated as Footballers of the Century. The game is also picking up on the Internet with sites like www.womensfootball.uk.com giving fans regional details to get involved, and making sure women do not feel like second-class footballers, so the future looks bright.

For players overall the future looks positive, because the money is coming in, as the game is still on an upward curve. Players are going to be making more money for some time to come, and while fans might find this annoying, there is little they can do to avoid it. Going to the game contributes to a player's wages, but so does staying away from the game and watching it on TV. For a fan not to contribute to a player's wages they would have to have nothing to do with the club, which would be untenable for most. The main area where fans and players meet is in terms of money: it is the fans who pay the wages – directly and indirectly – and it is about time players started to recognise this because if a day comes when the fans stop paying, then we will see which footballers, if any, mean the oft-stated claim that they would play football for nothing. That day may never come – and players should hope it doesn't – but they should show more gratitude to where their wages come from if they are to retain the roots with the fans that have helped make the game so popular.

Three

Referees

Fans of different teams at a game will rarely agree on anything, but 9 times out of 10 the one thing that will unify them is their belief that the referee is rotten. Every other person on the pitch will have at least one person in the crowd sticking up for them, but the referee is on his own.

Every time a referee puts on his shirt, and accepts the wages of between £15 and £900 per match, he is risking being punched, pushed, spat on and having things thrown at him from the crowd. If the worst that happens to him is some cheek from a player, it's a good day. The latest figures suggest that in England alone there are more than 300 attacks on referees a year by players or fans in league and non-league fixtures. There are no European figures but it seems to be a problem mainly in England and Italy, though other countries – and continents – are not completely trouble-free.

Referees vary from country to country: in some they are professionals and in some they are little more than paid enthusiasts. What is consistent, though, is that they can never win. Fans, players and managers all moan about them worldwide. Recent years – as more technology has been brought in – have seen continual analysis of every decision a referee makes, from offsides and penalties to the running time of the game. He is expected to be omnipotent. And when modern technology backs the referee's decision, no one ever apologises to the poor man for criticising him.

If the referee's decisions resulted in nothing more than a few people grumbling and columnists filling some inches then it would not be a crucial matter, but referees are finding themselves more and more at risk, as fans get more passionate and the financial stakes get higher and higher. Referees have to make themselves above any form of reproach or accusations of being corrupt. One referee who found himself being accused of not being entirely neutral was Mike Reed, the referee at a Liverpool game, who celebrated a goal along with the team. The Birmingham referee was in charge during a game between Liverpool and Leeds United in the 1999/2000 season, which Liverpool won 3-1. Liverpool's Patrik Berger took a 25-yard shot that ended up in the net, but it was what happened next that surprised everyone. Reed looked as if he clenched his hand and raised it slightly as though he were a Liverpool fan celebrating the goal. He later claimed that he was celebrating the fact that he had allowed a situation that resulted in such a fine goal. Reed, who was in his last season on the Premier League list, said he was merely celebrating playing the advantage rule after another player had been fouled:

'Successful advantage doesn't happen very often,' he said. 'The referee loves to see the ball in the net when he's played an advantage. It proves he was right.'

Any outcry over Reed's behaviour was short-lived, as other referees spoke out in his defence and some said they had done similar things.

In Italy – where one referee was thrown out of football by UEFA for accepting gifts from AC Milan – the game found itself embarrassed when it was revealed that AS Roma had given gold Rolex watches worth more than 10 million lira to two match officials, and less valuable Rolexes to a number of other officials. Roma stated it had done nothing wrong as many clubs give presents – some more valuable than Rolexes – to referees and officials. It also questioned why it had taken a month for the revelation to come out, and then on the eve of a game against AC Milan. Nonetheless the Italian Football Federation ordered all referees to return Christmas gifts from clubs that could be regarded as excessive or inappropriate.

Italy considered bringing in foreign referees for the 2000/01 season after the outcry over Juventus's controversial victory over Parma in the previous season. Referee Massimo De Santis disallowed a last-minute goal for Parma against Juventus, and the win gave Juventus a two-point lead in the league over rivals Lazio. De Santis claimed there had been heavy pushing and shoving in the penalty area, but television replays could find no evidence to support his claims. Also, De Santis did not blow his whistle until after goalscorer Cannavaro headed the ball. The decision sparked death threats against the referee's family, street protests in Rome and an investigation into events before and after the game by Turin's public magistrate.

It was not the first time Juventus had been involved in controversy. They won the 1998 title in what Italian football fans now call 'The Season of Poison' because of a series of refereeing decisions in Juventus's favour. Juventus and Inter Milan were on equal points. In the closing weeks of the season Juventus won 1-0 at Empoli, with Empoli being denied an equaliser when the ball clearly crossed the line. Then a week later Juventus beat Inter 1-0, with Inter having a clear penalty turned down. Italian fans with even longer memories cite the 1982 season when Fiorentina were beaten to the title by Juventus on the final day thanks to what fans and journalists called dubious refereeing. Lazio striker Roberto Mancini found himself criticised when he hinted referees were more than incompetent:

'The last fair championship was won in 1991 by Sampdoria. Since then Juventus and AC Milan have shared the titles between them and have never fought each other for the championship.'

However, one Italian referee claimed there was no bias and that passionate Italians always forget that referees are just human. He told the author:

'These claims are always made. I have been involved at tournaments at all levels including the World Cup and it is nonsense. Others may have a bias. I never did. It is more common for a referee to get caught up in the excitement and atmosphere of a game and that can lead to delays in blowing a whistle but that is it.

'However, even amongst referees there have always been rumours that some have taken money or had threats made against them. We do not ask because the answer would be no whether or not they had taken something. There is no inner cabal dividing things up.

'It does get to you after a while though, as when people find out you are a referee you are setting yourself and your family up for constant harassment.'

In Britain, it's no different. In Scotland, during an Old Firm game that saw Celtic concede the league to Rangers, referee Hugh Dallas was pelted with coins and had his head split open. The windows of his home were broken after the result, and Glasgow saw high levels of violence. There were concerns about his neutrality after it was revealed a week later that he had been rejected for a senior post at Celtic. At the amateur level in the UK, one referee was assaulted by a player with a baseball bat. At another game, a sent-off player got in his car and chased the referee around the pitch in it. David Beckham was fined almost £4,000 by UEFA for showing 'clear dissent' towards referee Markus Merk during Manchester United's defeat at PSV Eindhoven in September 2000. The England midfielder was booked and showed his anger by spitting on the ground in the direction of the German official. However, the most famous incident to date involved Paolo Di Canio in September 1998, when the talented but temperamental then-Sheffield Wednesday player clashed with Arsenal's Martin Keown and was sent off in the 45th minute by referee Paul Alcock. Di Canio did not take too kindly to this, and pushed the referee in the chest, sending him tumbling to the ground. Although Di Canio claimed the referee had dived, Sheffield Wednesday suspended him after the match. The FA disciplinary commission later handed out an 11-match ban and a £10,000 fine, on top of the club's fine of two weeks' wages, around £50,000–£60,000.

In Romania drastic measures have been taken at times to ensure there is no question mark over the officials' honesty. A week before the 1998 Romanian Cup final, the Romanian Soccer Federation placed match officials at Snagov, 40 kilometres north of Bucharest, to keep them away from any possibility of bribery. This step was taken after allegations about corrupt referees, as Steaua Bucharest won their sixth successive title. And while some thought this was paranoia, Romanian football was shown to contain corruption when UEFA suspended two Romanian officials, the president of FC Ceahlaul Piatra Neamt,

Gheorghe Stefan and Florin Chivulete, a UEFA referee liaison officer for one year after it was revealed that they offered French referee Stephane Moulin and his fellow officials 'female company' prior to a cup match in July 2000.

Still in Romania, in 2000 referee Petronel Enache went on a short hunger strike and started giving his fee for games to players over what he called a lack of fair play in Romanian football, after he was passed over for promotion to covering games in a higher league.

In South America, referees are constantly being threatened off and on the pitch, but in 1995 it got to be too much for one referee. In a game involving Urubuetama and Ferroviario, player Semilde was being sent off when he gave the referee some cheek. Having had enough, the referee hit him with a savage right hook, flooring the player.

In Africa, referees have got used to the abuse. Referee Alousious Sesikwe let a player score from a free kick, even though he had not blown his whistle for the kick to be taken and then played 13 minutes' injury time, with the result being that he had to get a police escort away from the game as he was under assault from furious Angolan players, officials and fans.

So why be a referee? At the top level in England a referee will receive approximately £1,000 per match (in Scotland it is less than half that and on the European continent the figure is in between the two). This may sound like a nice sum for 90 minutes' work, but it takes a lot more time than that to complete the paperwork, stay fit, travel to the game and inspect the pitch, as well as the many other duties that a referee has to undertake. And few referees receive that much. Referees' Association spokesman Peter Willis was a referee at the top level in the sixties, which many believe was a golden time for English football. He thinks it is a totally different game now, though referees are still becoming referees for one main reason – they love the game:

'I got into football refereeing because the game has always been a part of my life. It's quite different now though. The pitch is different from what we had. The pitch leads to a faster game, the equipment, the tactics – everything is different from what we had, it's all a lot faster.

'But we did have physical players. We had the likes of Billy Bremner and Tommy Smith, there were about half a dozen players who were not known as being physical or hard men, they went in and tackled for the ball, but they were not classed as dirty or evil.

'We had problems then, we were questioned but it was more expressions of disappointment, the emotion was genuine. I think now it's totally different with refs as scapegoats and just as people are talking about electronic aids, using them and blaming refs is just others trying to excuse errors in their level of performance.

'There will always be someone unhappy with a referee's performance – a set of fans, both sets perhaps, players, managers, even chairmen. Referees are not perfect, everyone accepts that, but neither are players and more people should remember that.'

In England, becoming a referee is not an overnight process. There are weeks of studying, followed by exams. They then become Class Three referees and work up to Class One, but that is still very much at the lower end of the ladder. After referees get to Class One they officiate in the county leagues and act as linesmen in the league above the one in which they are refereeing. They then work up the local leagues, then the conference league and then the football league, meaning it can be at least six years before they would be in charge of a football league game. There are 33,000 registered referees. Seventy-four of them are on the national list for the premier and national leagues, and of that number 20 are on the Premier League list, with 10 on the international list. At the bottom of the ladder, referees are paid £15 for their time, with the rises coming sequentially as they get more experience and progress through the ranks.

When a referee makes the Premiership, the FIFA and UEFA lists, life does not get any easier; if anything, it gets tougher. Referees are assessed at every game. The FA has four referee coaches who are responsible for five Premiership referees each, and they will watch them on a match-to-match basis, speak to them before the game and also perhaps at half-time and full-time. In addition, they will discuss the game with them the following day. Referees carry out a self-assessment report where they mark themselves out of 10 and that self-assessment forms the basis of any discussions they have with their coach or FA officials. Referees also have to attend a number of weekend getaways for coaching, training and conferences, and this takes its toll. Of the 20 Premiership referees, seven have become self-employed in the last two years to give themselves more flexibility because they have not had the time to balance all their other commitments with football. Philip Don, FA Premier League Referee Officer and referee at the highest European and World Cup levels, agrees that people become referees for the love of the game, but that love can be quickly tarnished once they become a referee due to the level of commitment they have to give:

'Recruiting is one thing, but retaining referees is another.

'Some counties are appointing other referees to look after new referees as mentors, as retaining them can be a worry and then you have someone you can talk to after the game.

'However, we still have a lot of referees and there's a helluva lot of competition to get to the top, but once there, there's still pressure – mainly trying to juggle everything.

'Look at international referees. Each game there – and they could be called out for 10 or so games – is a three-day appointment. Now that is in addition to having a job, raising a family, travelling to Premiership games as well as the weekend meetings we have a number of times during the year.'

Technology

The main criticisms aimed at referees are for not calling fouls or penalties, especially in this age of multi-camera angles. Philip Don says that in the near future those situations will still be judged by linesmen and referees, but technology is going to be introduced – and soon – to the goalmouth. He also thinks that it's time referees had more praise for all the times the camera angles show that they got it right, instead of criticism for the rare occasions where they are wrong.

'Sky have, say, 15 cameras where the action can be analysed over and over. The referee has one view from one angle and he has to make the decision in a split second.

'I think the majority of replays justify the ref, but rarely do you see a camera looking at the game from the same angle as the referee. But we are not Luddites, we are looking at technology for the goal line, if the ball has crossed the line or not.

'We're not in the realm of looking at was it a penalty, free-kick or throw in, then you're transferring the opinion from the man on the pitch to the man in the stand and as we've seen in cricket, the third umpire doesn't always get it right.

'The game is about movement, fluidity, spontaneity and cameras would take away from that.

'We're not looking at using cameras for this, we're looking at something that will tell us if all of the ball has crossed the line or not and I think you'll see it in the Premier League before Christmas 2001.

'We'll trial it before it goes in. It will be something that delivers a signal to the referee. FIFA have said we cannot use cameras so you would need some form of electronic field around the goal with something on or in the ball so that when all of the ball has broken the field, a signal would be sent to the transmitter that the referee would have on his arm.

'Cameras would cause a time delay and you're having people look at those cameras and cameras could be obscured by players on the line.

'What it has to be though is 100 per cent foolproof and that's the difficulty so far, because if you have something at the centre of the ball, that's still not all of the ball over the line.'

Bias

Many people have put forward the argument that making referees full-time, professional officials would eliminate accusations of bias. Philip Don disagrees. He knows the FA already do what they can to stamp out favouritism, which is why referees are asked to state if they have any allegiances to teams. However, he does have a unique view as to why people complain that so few penalties are given against teams like Manchester United playing at home at Old Trafford. It's not, as the fans claim, because the ref is on the home team's side; there's a simpler reason:

'If referees have an association with a team then we keep them clear of those teams, but you also have to look at how teams play. When Manchester United are at Old Trafford they do the vast majority of the attacking and that means the other team is defending. When you are defending you are more likely to commit more fouls – it's the nature of the game – defending teams commit more fouls because they are under more pressure. Also, there will be less fouls or penalties given against the attacking team because they are attacking most of the time and not defending.

'We are looking at more professionalisation of referees. Perhaps not making them full-time referees but possibly looking at a situation where we pay them and remunerate them at a good enough level so that they don't have to think about working full-time.

'At the moment a referee gets £900 a game in the Premier League and then at the end of the season they will get an additional payment depending on the number of games that they've refereed, so you're looking at £1,200 a game over the season, but clearly that still doesn't compensate.

'One of the issues is giving them a full-time wage. If I was to take the present talent of referees – which is mainly from professional areas like accounting, teaching and so on, though there are some blue-collar workers – and look at their annual income, it's anything from £20,000 to £75,000, so where do you pitch the salary for a full-time referee? The guy who is on £20,000 will be happy with £40,000 but the guy at £75,000 won't be – he would want £85,000–£90,000.

'But there are various schemes I'm considering at the moment where we would employ referees on a part-time basis and give them the flexibility to work on their other careers at other times.

'If we had them Thursdays and Fridays that would be good, but how many companies will do that? But we do accept that we are putting far more pressure and demands on their time for when we want them so we somehow have to address that. It's something for the future.'

Indeed it is a matter for the future, but something that has shown no sign of changing is the way fans treat referees. While this book argues that fans should have a greater say in the game of football, refereeing is the one area fans have to stay out of, for obvious reasons. Referees, it can also be argued, are the purest fans in the game. They do not put on the black shirt to achieve fame, wealth or notoriety through controversial decisions. They are also not permitted the luxury of having a team to follow, as any allegiance would see them crucified in the media. They just get on with their job, and the reward is abuse and aggravation. Fans may complain that they are the hard luck story of football, in that they do not have a say in anything, but perhaps they should realise others make sacrifices too. This is unlikely though, because football is still just like the old cowboy films where it's easy to spot the bad guy – he's the man in black and he gets all the abuse.

Four

Managers

Players may be the front-line troops who get all the glory and some of the blame, but until recently there was one group that never got much credit and even now have the hardest job in football – the managers. If a team does well, it is normally the players who are praised – for scoring the goals, for defending well, for stopping the penalties. If they lose then a player might get some criticism for playing badly or missing an obvious shot at goal, but the manager will be the one who gets the abuse for playing them, or for paying too much for them. If a manager buys in too many players from abroad, regardless of how well they do, he is accused of abandoning local talent. If he buys local talent and the team doesn't do well, he is encouraged to cast his net wider. And all of the above can be thrown at him after his first game, so fickle and diverse are the opinions of fans.

Managers have a harder time than players. While players may moan about double training sessions, managers have to be in before players, plan for their upcoming games, look at the squad, check on injuries, train with the players, deal with any problems the players may have and go through tactics. And that's just for the first team. He also has to take an interest in the other squads at the clubs, see how they are coming on, if anyone is ready for the big time, look at videos of players recommended to him by scouts and after all that scrutinise his opposition.

As there's so much money in the game you would think that the managers must be as well rewarded as the players. Wrong. Granted none of them have part-time jobs in pubs but they are not in the same league as their players, who it could be argued owe their success and fortune to the tactical nous of their manager. Only six or seven managers earn more than £1 million, including Sir Alex Ferguson, George Graham, John Gregory and Arsène Wenger. That may sound like a lot, but more than 100 players in the same league are earning that money, with some earning two or three times that amount by the time bonuses are taken into account. Harry Redknapp has called for the managers' salaries to be brought into line with the players' earnings. However, there is some way to go before they are equal. One manager who tried to get his wages up there with the players was Ruud Gullit. While at Chelsea he negotiated for sums of around £2 million a year, with the club paying some of his tax. It didn't happen, but if his successor had known what was going to happen to him then he might have asked for a similar sum.

Gianluca Vialli proved that while a player has the luxury of going off form for a while, a manager does not have the same comfort zone. The Italian was the most successful manager that Chelsea had ever had, but that did not stop him being dismissed on 12 September 2000. A club statement read:

'The club feels that in a wider context, it is in our best interests to seek a change of direction.'

The club had a terrible start to the season, but only a handful of games had been played and everyone expected the squad – despite the stories of Vialli's poor dressing-room relationships with senior players like Gianfranco Zola and Frank Leboeuf – to recover. If these had been given as reasons for dismissal people could have understood, but the club's quote was baffling; after all, what other context can a football club have apart from football? The statement revealed more than it intended. The wider context of a football club in this day and age is to bring in money for its shareholders and owners. To do that the club must have expensive products like the planned executive facilities at Chelsea for corporate entertaining, which will cost £1 million a season. Those who want them will have to sign up for a minimum of 10 years. However, while the average loyal fan will pay to watch their team week in, week out, corporate sponsors will not spend £10 million on losers, so the team has to be winning and mounting a credible challenge, not losing all their games. It was against this backdrop that Vialli went. One Chelsea non-playing member of staff – who did not wish to be named – told me:

'If they were top the rest of the stuff wouldn't have mattered. The fans would have been happier – regardless of stories of people not getting on – and Bates would have been happier too. The results cost him [Vialli] his job but not because the fans were unhappy – which they were – but it was not the fans who sacked him.'

The players have also spoken out over comments that they had anything to do with Vialli's departure. Frank Leboeuf said:

'People are stupid to think I have the power to get a manager the sack. I'm not that important. Being booed by fans was quite hard to accept, when they were blaming me for what happened, but I could not get the manager the sack.'

Vialli's agent shed a little light on the situation after his client was removed. Athole Still said it had nothing to do with the club's results at the start of the season. He claimed Vialli had lost the confidence of some of the players and the spirit in the camp was not what he or Chelsea wanted.

He added: 'Gianluca accepts that he had lost the confidence of some of the players, and therefore completely accepts the club's prerogative in choosing to dismiss him. He is extremely disappointed with the situation, but he knows that something had to be done. There is no rancour involved.'

Vialli is not the only manager to be sacked quickly in the search for money. Italian Serie A giants Inter Milan sacked coach Marcello Lippi after the opening game of the 2000/01 season. In his first season in the job Lippi took the club to fourth in the league and he spent more than £40 million, including £13 million on the signing of the Republic of Ireland's Robbie Keane, during the close of the season to mount a strong attack in his second year. While the league defeat was not the worst thing that could happen to the club, getting put out of the Champions League in the qualifying round was, meaning the club would have to do extraordinarily well at home to recoup the money spent. But Lippi never got the chance, despite winning the Italian league, the Scudetto, three times in under 10 years with Juventus. One thing neither Lippi nor Vialli appeared to do is blame themselves. This is something that managers seem reluctant to do, with the exception of Kevin Keegan when he walked away from the England post, which we will return to below.

According to psychologist Martin Thompson there is a reason for this:

'Managers, to succeed, have to believe that they are in the right, that what they say is best. Football management and dealing with players is still a very machismo area. Attempts by a number of managers to treat players like human beings have failed miserably as most players act like squabbling children. If a player thinks he can exploit a manager he will. It goes beyond cockiness; it is the attitude and arrogance that comes with the pantheon these people play in.

'A manager may have moments of doubt, but they will be saved for private moments, either alone or with their wives and partners, who also have to be very strong to put up with the lifestyle and the stresses of the job.

'Therefore when it all goes wrong, it can be easier for a poor decision by a referee or linesman to be blamed or bad playing by their team or fouling by the other team than to accept that perhaps there was something wrong with the selection the manager made, and even if they do think that, they will rarely admit it in public as every manager is involved in a psychological battle with each other.

'Keegan was unique in that the nice-guy approach had always worked for him and by being so honest it also deflected a lot of the criticism that would have gone his way otherwise.'

While criticism is nothing new for managers, support from the powers above them is, and it is an old footballing cliché that if the chairman gives the manager a vote of confidence then the manager is living on borrowed time. But the old days of a manager having no protection are no longer with us. An organisation called the

League Managers' Association (LMA) was set up in the early 1990s as the official representative body for professional football managers. As well as that, the LMA members are signed up to the Manufacturing, Science and Finance trade union. The union gets involved in areas such as disciplinary matters, contractual problems and job security issues. The situation is similar in Scotland where the Scottish Professional Footballers' Association and Scottish Managers' and Coaches' Association are affiliated to the GMB union. However, in the rest of Europe there is little along these lines.

The LMA is split into non-executive and executive parts, with both parts reading like a who's who of management. The president is Kevin Keegan, while Brian Clough, Lawrie McMenemy and Bobby Robson are amongst the vice-presidents. On the executive side Howard Wilkinson is chairman, while Dave Bassett, Sir Alex Ferguson and David Pleat are all committee members.

Before the LMA there was the Football League Executive Staffs Association, which covered managers, secretaries, coaches and commercial managers. However, many people felt that managers needed their own forum through which they could express their views to legislators, decision-makers and others in positions of power. They could also put their years of experience back into the game, helping younger managers and passing their wisdom on. The money for the setting up of the LMA came from the Premier League and BSkyB in return for managers taking part in live television broadcasts for the latter. No money goes to the managers though. Any extra the LMA has is used for research into areas such as how the French and the Dutch develop young players. LMA members are the 92 managers in the English leagues plus anyone made redundant within one year. After a year's unemployment they move into the coaches' association. There are also some honorary members with lifetime membership because of their contribution to the game. Members are offered free legal advice to help them check their contracts.

The LMA advisers also try to ensure that every contract contains provisions for health, insurance and pension cover. Support is also given to managers who find they cannot deal with the stress of the job or off-pitch matters. There is even a benevolence fund for older members who have fallen on difficult times and whose pension provisions are not enough to allow them to maintain a decent standard of living.

One of the most significant early breakthroughs was the introduction into Premier League regulations of a code of conduct governing the appointment of managers and the termination of their contracts. The code, which was conceived in the early 1990s, relies on gentlemanly conduct and honour amongst the professionals, and is split into nine parts, as shown below:

1. A Manager shall strictly observe the terms of his contract with his Club and shall not (either by himself or through any third party) enter into negotiations with another Club relating to his employment without having first obtained the permission of his Club to do so.

2. A Manager shall not take any steps (including the making of statements to the media) to induce or which are intended to induce any Player or other employee employed by another Club to act in breach of the terms of his contract with that other Club.

3. A Manager shall comply with the Laws of the Game and the Rules of The Football Association, the Rules of The FA Premier League, the rules of any competition in which his Club participates and his Club Rules and he shall not encourage or invite any person (including Players and other employees of his Club) to act in breach of the same but shall take all possible steps to ensure that they comply with them.

4. A Manager shall use his best endeavours to ensure that there is in force at his Club a fair and effective disciplinary policy applicable to Players and other employees under his control and that it is applied consistently.

5. A Manager shall take all reasonable steps to ensure that Players and other employees under his control accept and observe the authority and decisions of match officials.

6. A Manager shall not make public and unfair criticism of any match official or any other Manager or any Player, Official or employee of his or another Club.

7. A Manager shall forthwith disclose to his Club the nature and extent of any direct or indirect interest he may have in any transaction or arrangement involving his Club and he shall account to his Club for any benefit which either directly or indirectly he derives therefrom.

8. A Manager shall conduct himself at all times in an ethical and professional manner and shall observe the highest standards of integrity and fair dealing.

9. A Manager shall take all possible steps to promote the reputation of the game of Association Football and to prevent it being brought into disrepute.

The LMA is also more forward-looking than many other organisations. A £200,000 deal with Cisco Systems saw all its members get laptop computers that allow them access to a secure corporate intranet, which could be the forerunner of a new way of dealing in the transfer market. While some detractors claimed this could lead to managers receiving illegal payments during transfer deals, the LMA said the intranet would only be used for above-board transactions.

While the LMA may be forward-looking in that regard, one idea that has taken time to be accepted is that of mandatory qualified coaching in Britain.

England is different to continental countries like Germany and Italy where potential managers have to work through what could be called an apprenticeship or sit tests before they can manage a club in the Bundesliga or Serie A, but this seems to be a European fad as the rest of the world makes no such stipulations.

In Germany, at least two years' experience in the lower league is a mandatory requirement. While there is sense to this in that a trained manager should be a better manager and a better manager should make the game more interesting, it was thought this would never happen in Britain. It was felt that the already europhobic tabloids and British public would scream with outrage if, for example, David Beckham was one day not allowed to coach because of a ruling from some eurocrat stuck behind a desk somewhere in Europe. It would also be a brave chairman who ignored a popular choice and went for a more technically competent, yet unknown, manager. However, the end of 2000 saw the FA in England ruling that future managers would have to have some form of professional licence. What remained to be worked out was whether or not they would need the licence for mainland Europe only or for the mainland and the UK, with some teams, managers and lawyers hoping to find a loophole.

Regardless of qualifications, there appears to be one managerial job that you cannot give away – the England post. How hard the life of a manager can be, especially in England, is summed up perfectly by the circus surrounding the search for a new England manager following the departure of Kevin Keegan in October 2000.

Keegan was brutally honest about why he had to go. 'I have not been quite good enough... I feel I have had more than a fair chance... There's no one to blame but myself. I am not the man to take it a stage further and I know that.'

While tabloid newspapers – for once blameless over the removal of an England manager – frothed with anticipation at the likes of Ferguson and Wenger being linked with the job, the candidates were more likely to be taking a frothy glass of painkillers after learning they were being considered. Managers enjoy the challenge and pressure of the job to a certain extent. They are dedicated professionals and enjoy prestigious occasions, but many looked at the pressure that would come with the England job – including from the press and the public – and said no thank you.

Within 36 hours of the post being open, three of the favourites had said just that. Of the new names nominated, Peter Taylor, who was a superb coach of the national under-21 team before being controversially dismissed, said he was quite happy staying at Leicester City. Peter Reid, who also worked with the under-21 set-up but left to concentrate on Sunderland, refused it with a light-hearted comment, saying:

'If I lose two games on the trot here I get a bit of stick locally. If I did that with England I wouldn't be able to go for a night out.'

The comment may seem light-hearted, but it reveals the pressure that goes with the position. Most managers get at least a few hours a day to themselves. The England coach is like a monarch. He is in that position 24 hours a day. Meanwhile, the fact that the FA was thought to be considering foreigners to lead the team showed (depending on your point of view) either a mature European outlook or panic that no one from the land of St George was up to taming the dragon that is the England job. Sir Alex Ferguson was ruled in for a while, but then as people remembered how patriotic the Scot was, he was ruled out. Thoughts then turned to Arsène Wenger, who has been linked with the job of coaching Japan when he leaves Arsenal. Wenger, however, was swift to rule himself out. That left French World Cup-winning coach Aimé Jacquet, who was also quick to dismiss any speculation with a brief statement saying:

'I have no intention of returning to the playing field in high-level soccer in England, or elsewhere. At the French Federation, I lead and I am pursuing passionate work with the coaches. That is fully sufficient.'

The post was eventually filled by Lazio's Swedish coach, Sven-Goran Eriksson. Reactions in Britain were split down the middle; some called it a brave move, while others said it was a disgrace that an Englishman was not in the job. Some put the latter comment down to misplaced nationalism, while others said it was nothing less than racist. Still others claimed it showed the standard of English management. The LMA said the FA had to find ways to get English coaches into the top jobs and LMA chief executive John Barnwell, while saying Eriksson would get co-operation from the LMA, wondered what encouragement there was for younger managers and coaches if the best jobs were going to people outside the English game.

Despite all this, if Eriksson wins the World Cup with England, there will be few people in England saying anything negative about him.

Most of this book sympathises with the everyday football fan and how they are losing their game. It is no shock revelation to call fans the game's gullible victims but after the fans, managers are next in line for that title. They know that the odds are against them and that in all likelihood they will be sacked from their jobs, yet they still queue up for most positions just as fans queue up for the game. In the end, both are used and abused, just in different ways.

Five

Chairmen

While players and even managers can be replaced, there is one person who has more security than most, and until recent years was fairly anonymous in the game – the chairman. In days gone by chairmen and directors were local businessmen who wanted to put some money back into the local club, quite often inheriting the running of the club from their father or the family business. If they weren't a fan living in or around the team's area, then they were perceived to be local boys who had left the area, done well for themselves and were now investing in something back home.

In the 1980s that began to change. Up and down the country new chairmen and board members started coming into clubs with large sums of money, promising great glories for the team. This was still before football became 'sexy' (which was around 1992) but people with capital sensed that things might be about to improve. The timing was fortuitous. The Hillsborough disaster saw funds poured into football to improve the stadiums, with little cost to the owners. Since then, many people have bought into clubs, looking for a business return, which is the wrong reason to invest in football.

But as the business side and off-pitch activities have become more prominent, chairmen and board members have found themselves in the spotlight more and more. Until recently, chairmen were rarely seen to be involved in club matters, except when a manager was looking to deflect attention from himself by blaming the chairman for not giving him enough money to run the team, buy new players or improve the star player's wages enough to keep him at the club. But as the game became more fashionable and the media looked for more and more angles from which to cover it, the chairmen and fellow directors came under greater scrutiny. The most infamous example of the latter was Newcastle United directors Freddy Shepherd and Douglas Hall, who were exposed by a Sunday newspaper, which showed them mocking Newcastle and the fans for buying over-priced merchandise. The pair resigned, but rejoined the board four months later much to the fury of fans, who were powerless to stop the move. Newcastle didn't worry about the reaction of the fans, a practice that continued after the scandal, as we shall see later.

But not all chairmen are bad and at least one football chairman says he is never worried about coming up against teams where the main concern seems to be running the game as a business. Wimbledon and Cardiff chairman Sam Hammam has always believed that football cannot be treated like a normal business and is not there to be profited from:

'When I hear a chairman saying football is a business I know that I'll beat that person. Football is not a business; it can never be a business. Football is a love affair; it's like a family.

'The mother raises the children and gives her time and attention because of love, because of a passion, because of something she wants to do.

'Of course, you have to make some business considerations – you have to know that you don't buy a mansion if you can't afford it. But when you're running a football club, it's a passion, it's a love affair, it's never a business.'

One chairman who has been attacked on a more regular basis than most is Martin Edwards of Manchester United. Now there is no denying that Edwards has done well for himself through his association with the club, but he seems destined to be remembered more for being involved in the attempt to sell the club to BSkyB than anything else. Club fan Jonathan Davidson thinks this is unfair:

'What a lot of people don't remember though is that he has often underwritten bank overdrafts of large sums. Most fans when looking at the history of the club probably won't remember him well, but it should not be as harsh as it is. Yes, he disagreed with people and yes, he made a lot of money, but he did also do a lot of good for the club.'

As football moves into the business age, directors and chairmen are no longer as invulnerable as they once believed themselves to be. Once a club becomes a plc, or some other form of shareholding, all it takes is a certain amount of votes to remove them. And if enough fans have enough votes or shares then they can potentially dictate who stays or who goes. Aston Villa chairman Doug Ellis found himself in that situation after a recent AGM vote.

Shareholders had accused him of destroying the team, citing a massive drop in the club's share price as proof. The Aston Villa Independent Supporters' Association had started things by saying he had too much power but not enough ambition and that it was time he stepped aside for a younger chief executive. Many shareholders agreed, but Ellis survived because he had the majority shareholding and also the casting vote in any decision involving the club.

Chairmen don't always sit back and take the abuse that they get from players and fans. West Ham striker Paolo Di Canio has found himself in potential legal trouble due to comments he made about the former Celtic chief executive Fergus McCann. These claims were made not only in his autobiography, but also in print and on television while he was at Celtic and after he left the club, and they incensed the former accountant. McCann made it clear that he would take legal action if Di Canio did not withdraw his comments.

He said: 'I am taking Paolo Di Canio to task over his recent false and damaging remarks. Legal papers will be served. It is important that individuals such as Di Canio are not allowed to get away with misleading the public and particularly the Celtic support. I also have a personal obligation to defend my reputation.

'On reflection I wish I had taken this action some years ago and exposed Di Canio for the disreputable way he abused the backing of Celtic Football Club by spreading false and damaging statements, when the club had acted professionally.'

The majority of people may look on chairmen with disdain, but there are those who are happy to help a club out in times of dire need. McCann saved Celtic by putting in £9 million of his own money to save it from bankruptcy.

In England Peter Johnson, who once had an interest in Everton, gave First Division Tranmere an interest-free loan. This, along with the money he put in, allowed the club to show a profit of £46,023 for the financial year 1998/99.

However, chairmen in Britain are tame compared to some of their continental counterparts. Spain provides some of the most controversial examples. There, the men who run the clubs are known as 'caudillos', which loosely translates as 'leaders'. They have a reputation for arrogance, doing what they want to get what they want. Atletico Madrid chairman Jesus Gil is one such man. In recent years he has found himself under investigation for fraud, including the disappearance of millions of dollars. Prosecutors have demanded that he be jailed for decades, banned from public office and pay massive fines. Gil is not the only one. Ex-president of Barcelona Josep Lluis Nunez and Real Madrid's Lorenzo Sanz were known for running their clubs like personal fiefdoms, buying and sacking on a whim and running up huge debts for the clubs. And while all caudillos are egocentric, very few can match Betis owner Manuel Ruiz de Lopera, who named the club's stadium the Ruiz de Lopera stadium.

This sort of hubris has seen the caudillos also overrule the managers on many occasions, buying players that they want – normally attackers – and not players that the teams need or the managers want. Then when things don't work out, it is the manager who gets the blame for it all, and who is often sacked.

Spanish fans cannot complain too much, however, because they can vote for the chairman they want. In this regard Spanish football is very different from English football. Under Spanish law football clubs were, up until recently, all non-profitable institutions, meaning fans and investors could not buy shares in them, though moves are now afoot for the clubs to be allowed to become semi-private institutions if the fans vote for it. Instead, fans became 'members' of the club, normally by being a season ticket holder. This, as well as getting the fan/member into the games, allowed them to vote in elections to decide posts such as club president. This system might seem quite attractive to football spectators who worry about clubs being controlled by one man, or his family, or the club being sold off to a television company, but there are disadvantages.

Like real-life politicians, many club presidents are elected on the strength of their promises, such as to sign a certain player (normally a striker, as Spaniards love attacking, passionate football) or to win a trophy. However, just like politicians, those running for club president may make promises that they cannot keep, the major difference being that they rarely have to worry about money. This is the flaw in the system.

The members are not accountable for the debts of the club, and all too often all a president/chairman does is delay debt repayments so that they are a problem for the next president, who then also puts them off. As debts are not a worry for the members, they normally vote for the president who promises the best players. Ultimately the onus is on banks to chase repayment of debts, rather than on clubs to pay what they owe.

In the short term this might seem fantastic, but most of the top Spanish football clubs owe tens of millions of pounds, with some going over the hundred million mark. This cannot go on forever, and experts predict that within 10 years Spanish football will face an unprecedented crisis as clubs move towards becoming private corporations. English journalist Thomas Peyton spent a year in Spain and was amazed at how the football system worked:

'It's all highly entertaining stuff and vastly different from the way the game has gone in the UK. In theory it's a good system because it stops the game being taken over by big business and the fans who turn up to the games have a say in how the club is run.

'But the changes in football, with more and more money being needed to sign players, has seen a ridiculous amount of spending as clubs all try to keep up.

'Banks are ultimately responsible for the debts but if any bank dared to call in the debt, which may result in clubs having to close or sell players, there would be outcries at the highest levels and any government which went along with it, or allowed it to happen, would not be popular and would lose the next elections without a shadow of a doubt. Spaniards love football above all else, but the whole thing is a house of cards as it could so easily fall down – and probably will one day.

'Occasionally, someone calls for common sense to intervene but they are accused of running scared or making excuses for defeat, but some day Spanish football is going to have to bite the bullet and probably sell off a lot of the expensive players so they can rebuild the game.

'The only other option is that the game becomes more similar to ours with the abolishment of the rule that says football clubs are non-profit institutions.'

A perfect example of how the Spanish system works took place in July 2000, when it was time for the members of Real Madrid to vote for their president. The two men running for the post were successful in the construction industry. It was a battle between the then president, Lorenzo Sanz, who had presided over the club since 1995 and whose term had seen Real win the Champions League twice, and the lesser-known Florentino Perez. Perez seemed to have no chance when he was announced as a runner, mainly because in Spanish football, the office-holder normally always wins again. However, when Perez announced he was going to sign Barcelona's Luis Figo if he became president, despite the £40 million buy-out clause in his contract, he was suddenly taken far more seriously. The battle quickly got very heated, with Sanz saying Perez's offer was a joke that would probably be followed by the signing of supermodels like Claudia Schiffer. Perez turned this against Sanz by persuading Figo to reveal that he had already been offered a £2 million advance and £5 million a year in wages to go to Real. Sanz then launched a campaign called Save Real Madrid, saying that the attempt to sign Figo was an insult to Real fans, as it was nothing more than an attempt to buy votes, and was pure fiction. Sanz also claimed to have a video where Figo, with his hair dyed in Barcelona colours, was insulting Real after Barcelona won the Primeria Liga in 1999. However, Sanz quickly forgot his stance on promising to sign certain players in the run-up to an election, and claimed that if he were re-elected he would sign Mallorca striker Diego Tristan. On election day 65 per cent of the 66,000 eligible to vote turned out.

The result was every bit as surprising as Perez's announcement that he would sign Figo, as Perez won, taking 30,320 of the votes. Only 13,302 went to Lorenzo Sanz, with the rest being spoiled or left blank. This made Perez the first outsider ever to win an election. He immediately made good his promise, and Figo signed a six-year contract at a cost of £37 million.

There was also election excitement at Barcelona. President Josep Lluis Nunez left after 22 years as president when Barcelona suffered a catastrophic season, winning nothing. He was succeeded by Joan Gaspart, who won 54.87 per cent of votes cast by club members. Gaspart, previously the vice-president but seen as a man with new ideas, promised the fans Marc Overmars if he became president, and he delivered, at a cost of £25 million to the club. The departure of Nunez was seen as a victory for the fans, notably the internationally famous campaign group The Blue Elephant. They claim that a number of reforms brought in under Nunez's regime saw an erosion of the fans' rights in the democratic running of the club. They cite the mysterious random selection of 3,000 out of the 100,000 members to form the assembly of delegates, and a reluctance to reveal who is on the assembly. The Blue Elephant fears club executives will try to transform the club into a purely commercial company that may one day be quoted on the Stock Exchange. They see the scheme put forward by Nunez and others, dubbed Barca-2000, as a nightmare vision of where the club could go. Barca-2000 was to be a Disneyland park surrounding the stadium, with all sorts of bars, cinemas, shops and other facilities totally irrelevant to football. As previously noted, Barcelona fans are football purists and the crass commercialisation of schemes like this has them howling in protest. It is early days under the new regime, but fans are hopeful that things will improve.

Italy is just as exciting as Spain, as a club president has managed to become ruler of the country, setting the stage for all of the powerful Italian club presidents to try to gain greater fame and power. Silvio Berlusconi is a man Italians either love or hate. He is the most dramatic example of the confluence of media, politics and football, and has provided football and political analysts with hundreds of hours of work spent trying to uncover how the man has stayed in his privileged position, what he has done and why. He has been dubbed

'Citizen Kane on steroids' by some sections of the media. The AC Milan president owns a number of television stations. His three national private networks, Canale 5, Rete 4 and Italia 1, control more than 90 per cent of the television advertising revenue in the country and half of the audience, putting him in a unique position with regard to football and television rights. This alone would make him an interesting character and powerful figure, but he has also moved into politics and in 1994 became prime minister, though he was removed in 1996. Nonetheless his party, Forza Italia, is still the main opposition in Italy. His prominence is aided by his television empire, and he is also secure in the knowledge that he will benefit from a good run by AC Milan. His control over television means that a number of Italians remain less than knowledgeable about the charges of political corruption, fraud and association with the Sicilian mafia of which he, or some of his associates, have been accused. His move into politics also means that he can accuse other television companies who investigate him of being politically motivated, effectively muzzling them.

While many say Berlusconi is the most powerful man in Italian football, there is one man whose name is hated by many – Juventus general manager Luciano Moggi. He has worked at Juventus, Roma, Torino and Napoli, helped his friend Luciano Nizzola to be elected president of the Italian FA in 1996 and is known as a shrewd operator in the transfer market. His son Alessandro is one of the leading players' agents in Italy, and between them they are alleged to have 250 players within their sphere of influence. Moggi is on friendly terms with a number of teams from Serie A to Serie C. His critics – who include a number of former managers – say he has influence with everyone important in the game, and that he has the ability to make or break a career. Roma president Franco Sensi once said:

'Why do the Rome teams find it difficult to win the title? Ask Moggi. It will be this way until Moggi isn't against us. It is not enough to invest millions to win.'

There is no perfect solution for fans dealing with chairmen, but it is the one position that adult fans who no longer have a chance of playing actually have a possibility of getting, if they are educated and lucky. Money also helps. There is no chance that Britain will emulate the foreign clubs in allowing fans to vote for their club's chairman, so for the foreseeable future the best chance fans will have to attack chairmen or influence the running of clubs is through the votes that come with owning shares. However, if their club is a listed business on the stock exchange, there is the danger that someone else will buy all the shares, allowing that person to appoint the chairman and board of directors that they want, so fans could end up with someone who is not best for the club. It's not just on the pitch that football's a game of risk.

Part Two

The 'Green' Game – Passing the buck

Six

The Grass is Greener

Football is no longer just about the 22 men on the pitch. The fans may think so, but to others there's more to it. For fans interested in the game, green is the colour of the pitch, but to businessmen green is the colour of money. Worldwide, football is a money-maker. At the moment the highest grossers are in UK football, with half the top 20 world domestic teams – as ranked by 1997/98 and 1998/99 turnover figures – coming from Britain.

The figures, from accountants Deloitte & Touche, rank clubs according to how they raise income and take into account gate receipts, transfer fees, income from corporate facilities and TV money. The two columns show the turnover for the 1998/99 and 1997/98 seasons respectively.

1.	Manchester United	£110.9m	£87.9m
2.	Bayern Munich	£83.5	£65.2m
3.	Real Madrid	£76.1m	£72.2m
4.	Chelsea	£59.1m	£47.5m
5.	Juventus	£58.5m	£55.3m
6.	Barcelona	£55.7m	£48.6m
7.	Milan	£54.1m	£48.6m
8.	Lazio	£50m	£41.1m
9.	Inter Milan	£49.1m	£48.2m

10.	Arsenal	£48.6m	£40.4m
11.	Liverpool	£45.3m	£45.5m
12.	Newcastle	£44.7m	£49.2m
13.	Parma	£44.4m	£33.4m
14.	Dortmund	£43.9m	£39.8m
15.	Tottenham	£42.6m	£31.2m
16.	Roma	£39.4m	£30.7m
17.	Leeds	£37m	£28.3m
18.	Rangers	£36.5m	£32.5m
19.	Aston Villa	£34.9m	£31.8m
20.	Celtic	£33.8m	£27.8m

In the UK only, the figures for 1998/99 are as follows:

1.	Manchester United	£110.9m
2.	Chelsea	£59.1m
3.	Arsenal	£48.6m
4.	Liverpool	£45.3m
5.	Newcastle	£44.7m
6.	Tottenham	£42.6m
7.	Leeds	£37m
8.	Rangers	£36.5m
9.	Aston Villa	£34.9m
10.	Celtic	£33.8m
11.	Middlesbrough	£28m
12.	West Ham	£26.5m
13.	Everton	£25.4m
14.	Sunderland	£24m
15.	Leicester	£23.8m
16.	Derby County	£22m
17.	Blackburn	£21.2m
18.	Sheffield Wednesday	£19.1m
19.	Coventry	£18.8m
20.	Nottingham Forest	£17m

The earlier chapter on fans showed that a lot of a club's revenue comes from them. However, this part of the book will show that a great deal of money also comes from elsewhere, including television, sponsorship and shares. It will examine the influence these have on the game, and what they mean for the fan. It is worth pausing, however, to examine just how much money comes into the game. The English league is the easiest to analyse due to the work carried out by Deloitte & Touche. For almost 10 years, the company's excellent football division unit, headed by Gerry Boon, has looked at the state of the game. The unit has worked with more clubs, leagues, governing bodies, stadiums, financiers and owners than any other advisers to date and their reports are taken seriously by all who care about the game as an indication of the state it is in. The majority of their analysis was based on the financial statements of clubs for the 1998/99 season, of which club accounts were available for 83 out of the 92 professional clubs that make up the Premiership and Football Leagues. Their analysis for the 1998/99 season, published in August 2000, showed that English football's income rose by 10 per cent to £951 million.

In 1998/99 the 20 Premier League clubs brought in £69 million, which was the same amount reported in operating losses by the 72 clubs in the first to third divisions of the Football League. Due to an increase of £55 million in transfer spending, Premier League clubs reported a reduced pre-tax profit of £13.6 million, while the Football League saw its losses grow by a further 45 per cent to £75 million. Turnover grew 15 per cent in the Premier League, dropped 13 per cent in Division One, grew 25 per cent in Division Two and 16 per cent in Division Three. This was an overall increase of 10 per cent in turnover across the leagues, but was set against a rise in the total bill for wages and salaries of 18 per cent, and a jump of £89 million in transfer spending. Seven out of every 10 Premier League clubs recorded operating profits in the 1998/99 season, contrasted with 9 out of every 10 Football League clubs making operating losses. Ever higher wage demands in the Football League place increasing pressure on clubs. And outside the Premiership only five Football League clubs – Sunderland, Bradford City, Gillingham, Walsall and Preston – reported making operating profits, while no club in Division Three reported an operating profit. Between the time of the report and the time of writing this chapter, the first two teams have climbed to the Premiership, while Preston is also doing well, emphasising how financial control and having money helps the team become a success.

In the 1998/99 season overall, English clubs spent an unprecedented total of £316.9 million on transfers, compared with £227.9 million the previous year. The flow of transfer money to overseas clubs has increased to £142.2 million from £70 million, and money spent by the Premier League on transfers from the lower divisions provided a net cash flow to the Football League of £27.5 million compared to £1.5 million for the 1997/98 season. Transfer amounts between English clubs are up 9 per cent from £160 million to £174.7 million, mainly due to large increases in spending by Premier League clubs. Smaller clubs like Oxford United, Crewe and York City joined a host of more illustrious Premier League clubs who made pre-tax profits of over £1 million. The highest pre-tax profit-makers were Manchester United with £22.4 million, Aston Villa with £20.2 million, Nottingham Forest with £8 million and Derby County, which brought in £6.7 million. For Oxford the news was especially welcome as the club had struggled for a while and there had been fears of it shutting down for ever.

The figures for the near future make encouraging reading. At the league level, in 2001/02, Deloitte & Touche Sport predict a Premier League turnover of £1.3 billion, up £630 million on 1998/99, and a Football League turnover of £500 million, up £219 million. Both leagues will have almost financially doubled in size, but the income gap at league level will then be a phenomenal £800 million per year. Gerry Boon said the figures show that the English game has learned how to use commercial opportunities:

'English football has come of age commercially, with another impressive year. Income is up £85 million. But football clubs continue to spend the increases on transfer fees in particular, and wages.

'With the recently agreed broadcasting rights deals set to bring £2.4 billion of revenue into the game over the next four years, the challenge for clubs will be to manage their money sensibly and ensure that some of it goes on strengthening business infrastructure rather than straight into the players' pockets. This would generate a stronger professional game in England.

'The average Premier League club is now five times as large as its Division One counterpart. Promotion to the Premiership brings clubs ever greater rewards and is still the "holy grail" for all football clubs.

'But too many clubs over-extending themselves in pursuit of one of the three coveted spots in the Premier League on offer each year cannot result in a healthy situation for football. This is the major problem in Division One, and at a number of other clubs.

'Profitability is the key indicator of a club's ability to invest in new players, in youth development, the stadium or other club infrastructure. To ensure survival in the long term a football club does not necessarily need to make profits, but it does need to avoid significant losses. Losses caused chasing success are fine in the short term, if the gamble succeeds, or the benefactor picks up the tab, and if having succeeded the rewards of elevated status are used to repair the club's financial position. If not, the risk can damage a club for a number of years. That can, and usually does, generate instability at all levels within a club.

'English professional clubs are limited companies and that brings responsibility to the directors. Those responsibilities are heavy ones, they go with the job. In the past some clubs have sat back, taken their fans for granted, acted weakly when faced with demands from players and their agents and have been cushioned by central "handouts".'

With regard to clubs and their finances, the report revealed that at the end of the 1998/99 season, £1.15 billion of finance was tied up in the 92 clubs, with four-fifths of that sum coming from shareholders, directors and related parties. The four divisions moved from being net cash depositors to borrowers, which occurred for the first time in 1997/98. Ten clubs accounted for £128 million of net bank borrowings; the three largest bank borrowers are Coventry, Bolton and Middlesbrough. There was an overall cash flow deficit in 1998/99 of £111 million – £44 million in the Premier League and £67 million in the Football League. The Premier League has 85 per cent of English football's £686 million net assets and 84 per cent (£426 million) of its £507 million capitalised value of purchased players. Promotion to the Premier League is currently estimated to result in an increase in revenue of about £12 million, the vast majority of which is directly attributable to an increase in TV revenue. This cash boost will increase in the future, to an estimated £25 million in 2002/03. According to Gerry Boon:

'Putting themselves in the Premier League "shop window" is attractive to every club and to the players. Aside from the significant TV money, promotion brings new revenue streams.

'Clubs become more attractive to fans, sponsors, broadcasters and corporate customers. Newly promoted clubs need to resist the urge to spend all of this expected bonanza and often before it has actually been received.

'Yo-yo clubs can, with the aid of TV parachute payments, survive in Division One, but if return is not swift, they may succumb to the effects of Division One inertia. It is a great financial challenge to remain outside the Premier League for more than two seasons.

'While the goodwill effect on attendances may allow short-term maintenance of Premier League costs, this is high risk and unless a quick return to the Premier League is achieved, the club may become structurally damaged for many years.'

The above figures show that the game should be buoyant. The clubs that are doing well are doing very well indeed and that should act as an incentive for the others. However, just as Faust had to give something away to get his end of the bargain with the Devil, so too do the clubs, and it may be their souls – the fans. Television might be enjoyable on a cold winter's night, but in the long term it could be responsible for destroying the fans' game because people might decide that they prefer to stay in and watch the game rather than actually attend it in person. Football is a spectator sport and while TV companies may continue to pay high sums for big audiences at home, most players would rather have that big crowd at the stadium cheering them on. Gods like to be worshipped, after all.

Many people say that football is no longer a sport, it is a business; but it is not. At the moment it is a mix of the amateur ethos that shows all that is good about the game plus the intrinsic selfishness of capitalism and big business.

However, economics lecturer and football business writer Stefan

Szymanski has taken the unique approach of looking at football as a normal business rather than regarding it as a sport that has business values attached to it. While his views may run contrary to those who are concerned about the soul of the game, it is good to know how professional financial analysts are looking at the game for one reason if no other: know thy enemy (this is not to imply that Szymanski is an evil man in any way. I found him to be extremely charming, informed and pleasant to speak to).

He is of the opinion that asking if football is a business is no longer a moot point:

'I don't think anyone questions the fact now that football is a business. They may not like the fact but they have to accept it. Some people may say it would be great if you could take the commercialism out of it but no one has any real suggestions as to how you might do that.

'Business was always in football, but how business has been in football has changed. It was just done in a very European and British way in that business was not an intrusive factor in the game.

'But when you think about the people who run football clubs, they were always very high status, very heavily involved in the local community and with serious business interests. However, the ethos was always that you could not treat football as a commercial enterprise, whereas you look at the United States where it has been commercial from the very beginning and no one questioned it at all, it was just accepted.'

According to Szymanski, the difference in culture between America and Europe is partially responsible:

'In America business is not seen as a dirty word so it was seen as acceptable for sports like football to be exploited commercially.

'With business and making money, one of the problems is the European attitude which is that there is a long tradition of thinking of business as something which is not quite respectable, it's not quite right to provide people with goods and services for money. The thinking is that you should do it because it is the right thing to do and in some sense it goes back to the old religious days with the church mentality.

'Meanwhile in the US the society started out without the

traditional suspicion of the business motive and business went on to be seen as a good thing and therefore for sports to be associated with it was no bad thing.

'Americans may moan about some of the people involved in the business side of it, but they do not – or rarely do – criticise the actual idea of business being involved.'

Another reason for the distrust of business in football, according to Szymanski, is that there is a general lack of understanding of how business works in our society. However, he does not feel that this is an area of great concern because:

'Business can be viewed like politics, in that people know as much as they need to know.'

Szymanski thinks that the involvement of business in sport can be exciting to watch because there are few areas as ruthless:

'Sport is an area in which the success or failure of an investment is more brutally exposed than any other business activity that you can name. For example, most businesses, if they make a bad decision, can conceal it one way or another, and things only come to light if a large number of mistakes are made and then they get really punished for it.

'However, in sport each bad decision is mercilessly exposed and pitilessly punished and I think that's a strength rather than a weakness. The business of football is a completely unforgiving environment where your failures are mercilessly exposed and that's why we enjoy it. It is great theatre. Also football is so competitive and open and I think that keeps and brings a certain amount of sanity to the process.'

While some have said that football and business are incompatible, Szymanski thinks that football has shown that in many ways it works as a normal business, and normal economic theory can apply.

'The one thing about football is that it is not easy; it is tough and most of the clubs are going to fail and if the objective is to win the league or a cup then most are going to fail regularly. Even something like avoiding relegation, a large number are going to fail.

'Ordinary economic policies can be very similar to the economic policies used in football. People keep going on about the amount of money coming into the game and ask if it is good the way it is spent. The answer to that can be looked at similarly to national economics when a country is doing well and the comparison can be made between rich people, rich football clubs and poor people, poor football clubs.'

If he is correct in his assumption, football could be in trouble – if it is treated purely as a business in the years to come.

'Are people getting rich and are people making money? Yes. But is it balanced? Are the poor seeing an equal share of the money? Is it sustainable in the long term? The answer is probably not. The poor are not gaining as much as the rich and they seldom do; so no, it is not sustainable in that there will be a recession of some sort in the future. You can be absolutely sure the economy will go into reverse at some point, there will be bankruptcies and failures, but in the longer term the economy will bounce back and there will be improvements. All of this is applicable to football.'

However, Szymanski feels that those worried about business being the death of football are missing the point. He says that even if the current business model used produces some kind of crisis in the future, the consequence would not be that no one would watch football any more. He feels the game is safe because it is ingrained in people's minds as the dominant sport in Europe, not to mention the world, and it is unimaginable that the majority would not watch football as their preferred sport. In other words, it has its own monopoly.

'I don't think there is any fundamental crisis looming over the horizon which is going to cause the whole deck of cards to come down. I've thought and thought about this and I know that others, like [football writer] David Conn, can come across as prophets of doom, but I don't see it the way they do. In one sense those like Conn are right in that there will be a financial crisis of some kind somewhere, but in a more profound sense they are wrong.'

As regards television – the main source of the money converting the game into a business – Szymanski does feel that viewing habits may change, but the current popularity of the game and the amount of money coming into it is, in his opinion, a testament to how popular and successful the game is.

'At the moment the game is growing in popularity, relentlessly in terms of its media profile and there's no end in sight. The fundamental economics of this are that football is a product aimed at people's leisure times and leisure is a product for which demand increases as people's incomes increase.

'So as long as you expect economic growth in a community you can expect demand for leisure to grow too. Leisure demand grows more than proportionately with income. For example, my income may go up by 10 per cent but my demand for football goes up by more than 10 per cent and that is a fundamental point that underpins the whole football scenario.

'The game is not like an Internet dot.com story. With football there is a real demand which underlies this product, and whatever happens to the various structures of football and whatever way it is organised it is going to be an incredibly successful business for the foreseeable future.

'Presumably there may be a slowdown at some stage in the game's future. You can't have accelerated growth forever, although if you look at a chart of things like TV rights, you have an exponential growth pattern where each deal is four or five times the value of the last one.

'You say to yourself that that cannot last forever. But then you look at the growth of something like the NFL in America, where since the sixties there have been exponential rises 30 or so years before it started to happen to football, and the rises continue, so it may be that the exponential rises could continue for another 20 or so years in football.

'I've been looking for reasons for it to all go wrong but I cannot see it; demand is unlimited more or less in this case.'

For the cynics who believe there is a bubble about to burst, Szymanski says look at America:

'Every night you can watch two or three different games and the demand has to be there. It has to be because broadcasters are not putting this on out of sheer kindness as people are paying and that's the way it could go here.

'At the very least there is the scope and scale to expand demand, to expand the market to where it is like the US, and no one in the US thinks the bubble is ready to burst. They think it is going from strength to strength.'

And even if the bubble does burst, Szymanski thinks the powers that be will just put on their thinking caps:

'In theory it is possible for the market to be saturated but this is a function of consumer income in that the more they earn, the more they have and the more they are willing to pay, and what the sports organisers will do is find more ways to charge people money.

'Look at luxury boxes. When football grounds were first built there were no luxury boxes; there was no demand for that. It was a new market invented later on and this will happen in the future.

'For example, there are all sorts of digital products coming out that can easily give me match updates if I want them. There will be a demand for many more products which will generate money for the football business.'

Generate money for the football business. Perhaps it is the case that fans have not lost a game after all. Maybe they never had anything to lose. Perhaps football has always been a business. Perhaps the greatest piece of business was carried out years ago when the fans were convinced to have no say in how things are done or how their money is spent, despite putting so much money into the club. In any trade, getting someone to give you money for nothing is indeed the best form of business you can do, but outside the business world it has another name: a con.

However, there is one flaw in Szymanski's argument, educated, informed and well reasoned as it is. No one ever stood in the rain for hours to get a glimpse of Microsoft's new hot shot board member, no one frames a share certificate for an oil company and gives it pride of place in their living room, no one buys a brick from a company's original headquarters when they move or steals bits of carpet as a souvenir.

Football fans stand in the rain to see new players, place share certificates for shares that will never be sold in pride of place, buy bricks and bits of turf when stadiums get upgraded. That is the game's strength. Rational people cannot understand why a person would pay a £15 service charge on top of the cash value of £10 worth of shares just for a piece of paper saying they own a small part of an institution, but to a football fan it is perfectly logical.

How can it ever be only a business when people do these things?

Football has outlived many economic policies and hopefully it will outlive the current phase of capitalism, but it will not be easy. Money is an awfully strong temptation and the clubs are being offered a lot more than 30 pieces of silver these days. The main tempters are the television companies.

Seven

Television

Football may be a game about a round ball, but for today's game the square box in the corner of the living room is almost as important.

Television coverage from companies like BSkyB has made watching the game from home entertaining and enjoyable, with multi-angles, player-cameras and so forth. In years to come it will be clear to football historians that it was the money from television that both transformed the game and made the players into the new rock and roll stars for a generation.

It all seemed so innocent decades ago, in 1938, when the English FA Cup final was first televised live by the BBC. Other countries were gradually getting involved in the televised football scene, though it was in the 1950s and 1960s that the blossoming of football on television began – or the cancer started to spread, depending on your point of view. Italian company RAI started regular Serie A transmissions in 1956 and two years later the first live worldwide coverage of the World Cup was broadcast.

In 1960 TV rights for the European Cup final between Real Madrid and Eintracht Frankfurt raised £8,000, and companies made hasty preparations to get footage of games out of Chile, where the World Cup was played in 1962. It was eventually decided – this was pre-satellite of course – that the quickest way of doing things was by flying video footage to Europe.

In 1965, the BBC paid £5,000 for the right to show regular highlights on *Match of the Day*, with the money being distributed equally between all the clubs in the league. By the 1966 World Cup television producers were having a field day, with action replay machines and videotape being used for the first time.

By 1970 a man had walked on the moon, and football also entered the space age, with the 1970 World Cup in Mexico beamed by satellite to Europe. In the same year, live league football started to be heavily developed in Spain.

After the introduction of satellite television, football continued to improve by tweaks instead of leaps, with more cameras and more flashy graphics though no major innovations. What did increase in massive leaps was the size of the audience and the number of businesses trying to take part in covering football. In 1990 167 countries around the globe bought Italia '90 television rights for an audience of just under 30 billion. This audience has grown over the years. When the total number of viewers for every game at USA '94 was tallied, the figure was more than 30 billion – which means either every person then on the planet watched five games or a lot of people watched a lot of football. The figure for France '98 was nearer 37 billion and the estimated figure for the 2002 event is 41 billion.

When football coverage started, it was claimed that it was intended for the fans that could not get tickets or get to a match, which was true at the time. In Britain and Europe, up until the 1990s, football and television were not as synonymous as they are now. The BBC and the ITV network showed only a handful of live games a year, and edited highlights at the weekend. A game was normally only shown on television for a special event such as a cup final or European away leg. Money for league coverage was divided between all the clubs in each league, but some clubs wanted more, bleating that the Taylor Report (published in 1990) costs for upgrading their stadiums were a heavy financial burden, players wanted more money, foreign players were expensive and how could they compete in Europe without the cash? Of course, they claimed, it was all being done for the fans, as they were the ultimate beneficiaries by getting better entertainment. So in 1990 Greg Dyke, then chairman of ITV Sport and now Director General of the BBC, invited a number of the top people at the leading English clubs to discuss the possibility of ITV gaining exclusive rights to televise matches involving their clubs. The obvious incentive for the clubs was more money.

It was eventually realised that one of the best ways for this to happen was to do away with tradition and start a new league – a premier league. The only problem was that to do this, clubs needed permission from the English FA, otherwise the whole thing would have been nothing more than a moot exercise – or at worst a long-drawn-out legal battle. Surprisingly, the FA allowed the breakaway to happen, and the clubs to start clawing back more money for themselves.

By 1992 the plan that would change the shape of UK football for ever came to a conclusion when BSkyB tabled a bid of more than £300 million, beating ITV's offer by £30–£40 million. Greg Dyke may have planned to kill off satellite television by what he did, holding meetings and talks to try to secure football rights on terrestrial television, but in effect he did the exact opposite and gave satellite TV the chance to move into the game and dominate it to the extent that it does today.

To be fair, it may be a little extreme to lay the blame with Dyke. Some, if not all, of the top clubs had wanted more money for a long time. It was just unfortunate that Dyke's idea, the satellite companies looking for a ratings-grabber and the greed of the clubs all coincided. As the first deal went through, few could imagine the dangers that lay ahead.

Fast forward to the summer of 1999. The £300+ million bid made by BSkyB for the first deal has been long forgotten and under the current £743 million four-year deal, which expires at the end of the 2000/01 season, the average Premier League club receives around £71.2 million a year. At the other end of the scale, the average Third Division team receives just £250,000. But for the Premiership clubs, the amount was about to rise massively as it was announced in June 2000 that the latest three-year deals, starting from the 2001/02 season, would bring in around £1.65 billion.

Some of the money was brought in by an auction system, which was used for terrestrial highlights. The BBC lost these rights to the ITV network and Greg Dyke was understandably not too happy. He told the media:

'The only conclusion one can draw is what mattered to the Premier League was to get the most amount of money – I'm afraid this is the world of football we live in today.'

While that might be a reasonable comment, it's a bit, if you pardon the pun, rich coming from the man who helped start the ball rolling in the first place.

However, Dyke and the BBC made a successful bid of £70 million for the terrestrial rights to screen the FA Cup as part of a £400 million joint three-year deal with BSkyB where FA Cup games will also be shown live on both networks, with all matches to be played on Saturdays or Sundays and both sides showing highlights of games shown on the other channel. There is also a further deal where the BBC will be able to show all competitive England matches live, while BSkyB has the rights to all competitive and friendly internationals. The complete breakdown of the deals makes fascinating reading, especially when the amount of options and games involved is considered. BSkyB paid £1.11 billion for 198 matches over three seasons: 66 live games a season played at 4 pm on Sunday and 8 pm on a Monday, with the right to also show a highlights programme on Sunday mornings. Each Premiership club must appear on BSkyB three times a season. The cost to BSkyB per game breaks down to £5.6 million a match and they also get first pick of what games to show, with the others fighting for the crumbs. This maintains BSkyB's dominance in a field that once saved them.

Sir Frank Barlow, chairman of BSkyB from 1991–95, has stated in interviews that the company was probably saved from severe financial problems at worst and ridicule at best by the live football rights that it picked up. He also feels that clubs are being bought up by television companies in order to exert their influence on a number of matters. It is his opinion that the FA and the Premier League are losing influence, with the clubs and TV companies increasingly dictating terms.

Amongst the other deals announced in June was pay per view, which was a new concept for the Premiership. It may yet not happen, after ntl, who were awarded the contract, pulled out as they embarked on a financial restructuring programme. The Premiership says discussions are continuing over the rights to show 40 live games per season on Sundays, with each team appearing at least once but no more than six–eight times. Saturday and Sunday highlights, as noted above, were awarded to ITV, who paid £20 million more than the BBC. The other contracts handed out involved clubs' in-house TV channels, which at the moment can only show old material. In future they will be allowed to show their own matches on a delayed transmission basis. While club channels are something that may not take off for another decade, or until digital TV is well established (Manchester United's channel being the obvious exception) the Internet is a different matter. Premier League clubs can show their own Saturday, Sunday and Monday games on their Internet sites after midnight on Monday. Keeping up with new technology, the Premiership also said that the rights to games for video on demand (where video can be sent through phone lines to televisions) will be awarded on an experimental basis. But there's more. £1.65 billion might seem like enough, but the Premiership has yet to put overseas TV and radio rights out to tender.

Almost 150 countries pay for the rights to show English Premiership matches, bringing in around £32 million a year, while UK radio rights – sold in three categories of national, local and London rights – bring in just under £10 million annually. Both of these figures are expected to rise considerably in the coming seasons.

More money came to English football through television at approximately the same time when pay TV operator Ondigital paid £315 million to acquire non-Premiership Football League and Worthington Cup rights. This was on top of money paid out for UEFA Champions League matches, the rights for which are shared with ITV. Their money bought them the right to show a minimum of 88 games per season from divisions one to three, in addition to extra pay-per-view matches and the Worthington Cup.

Strangely enough, while the Premiership and the English FA have realised how to make money from the league in Britain, they were a bit slower in the international market, and actually cost the game millions in lost revenue. The FA used to only allow one broadcaster at each international game, depriving companies from the countries of visiting teams of the chance to broadcast. They only saw the light at the last England–Germany World Cup qualifier in October 2000, where both BSkyB and a German TV station had a number of cameras.

The old saying that money brings its own worries is very true when it comes to television and football, according to Gerry Boon of accountants Deloitte & Touche:

'It is the involvement of the media and TV deals that are now driving football's funding. The shot in the arm from the new TV deals paradoxically presents many clubs with a predicament. Can the clubs hold on to the windfall or will it trickle through their fingers into the pockets of the players?

'It remains to be seen whether the new Football League television and Internet deals will radically alter Football League economics because it depends on how chairmen spend the money. It remains to be seen whether the money will go straight into players' pockets or into building a sound business infrastructure. The challenge for clubs will be to manage their money sensibly.

'In 1998/99 only 23 per cent of Football League clubs were profitable. Will the new deals relieve the pressure on them to sell their best players? Will they result in more Football League clubs being profitable? Or will the extra money be spent on the pursuit of Premier League or other glory?'

While £1.65 billion does seem like an incredible amount of money to be put into the game, it does not compare with Europe, where the top clubs do even better. A report by Deloitte & Touche found that in the last few years television deals negotiated by the big five European countries (England, France, Germany, Spain and Italy) were almost the same as each other. The difference appears when you consider that many European clubs are free to negotiate their own individual TV deals, and this brings them in massive sums compared to what is handed out in the UK.

Individual rights allow a club to sell its own matches at a price it finds agreeable. There is no need to compromise and, more importantly, there is no need to share the money. The ultimate form of individual rights is pay per view, where a company pays to show one game. In theory the money should be divided between the teams taking part, but there are also arguments that most of it should go to the home team as it is their ground and facilities that are being used.

Individual contracts and pay per view are excellent for the big teams that get even more money, but they are not so good for the little teams, as few people take an interest in them compared to the Manchester Uniteds, Lazios, Inter Milans and Barcelonas of the world.

A survey by company UFA Sports, published in the middle of 2000, concluded that pay TV is a growing element of sport viewing in Europe. It revealed that one in four football fans in Europe is a pay-TV subscriber, with half of all football fans in France receiving it. BSkyB is the leading provider of pay television in the UK, with a strength similar to that of Canal Plus in France, with almost a third of those with cable and satellite in the UK and France paying to watch football games. Spain is pay-television king though, with 70 per cent of all subscribers in Spain being football fans. The vast majority have already paid to watch some games and 78 per cent have already viewed a football game on pay TV. The report also claimed that one-quarter of Spanish television viewers who claimed they were football fans would watch more than five games a week if they could choose which games were shown.

In 1999 an attempt was made to allow UK football teams to negotiate their own television deals, instead of working collectively with all the other clubs as currently happens. The present system sees every club get some money, but under individual contracts that would not be guaranteed. The attempt to obtain individual contracts resulted in the Office of Fair Trading arguing that collective bargaining was restrictive. However, the Restrictive Practices Court claimed that the collective arrangements were in the public interest.

Those for the new contracts argued that more money for the big teams would allow them to compete more successfully at the highest levels, while those against said it would see some teams lose out on television funding as no one would be interested in watching them. The Restrictive Practices Court said it was not persuaded that there was sufficient demand for more televised football, which it felt would be the outcome of individual contracts.

This was a monumental decision – if it had gone the other way it would have opened the floodgates for individual games on pay per view, bringing in more money for a select few clubs, but losing others millions, while fans would have spent even more money to watch their teams on television. One thing that was not pointed out by the Restrictive Practices Court is that English football has done quite well for itself in European Championships over the last few years anyway, so perhaps it is not necessary for the clubs to break up the TV contract to try and get more money to improve their teams.

Pay per view is not only a threat at the domestic level. FIFA president Sepp Blatter has said that some matches in the 2002 World Cup may be shown only on pay television. Until now, FIFA have insisted that the tournament be shown on free-to-air terrestrial stations, as it was felt this was a good way to promote the game around the globe. However, there had been criticism from UEFA president Lennart Johansson that the World Cup was being undersold. Blatter has said that maybe only the opening match, the two semi-finals, the third-place play-off and the final will be on free channels. In addition, all teams in the finals will have their games transmitted on free television in their own countries.

Nonetheless, back in England it is only a matter of time before the challenge is made again, and it may be that football's dabbling with business will be what causes the split, because business rules and laws are not necessarily compatible with those of the football market.

At the moment football clubs that are not on the stock market can make their own, independent decisions. However, traded companies have a legal obligation to consider any offer that is to the benefit of their shareholders. What is beneficial for shareholders (normally more money) may not be so for the fans or the game in general, but that concern will be swept aside by stock market rules unless a new way of protecting the fans and the game is found.

If individual clubs are given permission to sell their television rights, it is not too far-fetched to imagine the day when individual players sell the rights to their moments of glory. This is already in its early stages. There is nothing at the moment to stop players claiming repeat fees for every time a goal or certain action is shown, but it has not yet been put into practice. According to lawyers, nothing could legally stand against it because actors, writers and others involved in the entertainment industries already receive repeat fees. For example, Ronaldo could charge a fee every time a certain spectacular goal is shown, with the payments coming in like musicians' royalties or actors' repeat fees. The matter has been discussed at football conferences and the FA has also talked about it. Sports lawyer John McIntyre thinks players owning the rights to their goals is inevitable:

'There's no doubt that players will argue that moves or goals are their own property. Just as a book is the author's intellectual property and creation, they will claim that goals are their creation. Copyright law is on their side in this one.

'The odds are that players will not claim for every goal that they score, but a player scoring from a spectacular overhead kick in the dying seconds of the World Cup to give his team the lead could earn a massive fortune from repeat rights.

'Agents will try and expand into this area because, even if the repeat fee is small, all those 10 per cents would soon add up.

'As soon as one player gets the rights to his own goals, watch the stampede.'

While all this money seems very nice for the players, shareholders and those who run the game, there's a group that sees very little of the money, mainly because in the long run it's their money – the fans. It is the fans that pay the television companies the money but they see no decrease in prices and it is arguable if the service continually improves.

Companies are there to make money. They are not altruistic, so whatever they pay out for TV rights, they will want back. Who will pay for that? Advertisers and fans. The same fans that cannot afford a ticket that costs at least £20 per person per game may be able to afford £30 for a season of football on their TV. As ticket prices go up, more and more fans will be forced to stay at home, and the television prices will also slowly rise, with more pay-per-view one-off events eating into the fans' pockets.

However, there has been a far more insidious side effect during the rise of football and television, and that is the literal coming together of the two. In England, many clubs are now partially owned by television companies and while the naïve may say this is just because of the shareholder market and the fact that football is a 'sexy' investment at the moment, the truth is more sinister. If a television company owns a football club then it obviously has a say in anything that affects that club, including future television bids, which are kept confidential from other TV companies – who do not own a share in the club. This would mean that all bets would literally be off, as the TV company on the board could see the bids coming in and then make a higher bid, with the eventual cost being passed on to the consumer. In America Rupert Murdoch's News Corporation owns the Los Angeles Dodgers baseball team, together with shares in the New York Knicks basketball and New York Rangers ice hockey teams, giving it a say on the boards and in relation to what happens with the television rights. Similarly, as of August 2000 BSkyB has an interest in Manchester United, Leeds United, Chelsea, Tottenham, Sunderland and Manchester City. Ntl is involved with four clubs – Newcastle United, Middlesbrough, Aston Villa and Leicester City – and Granada has interests in Arsenal, Liverpool and Manchester United's TV station.

Two of the largest UK deals took place in 2000. Arsenal announced a deal with Granada that had a number of benefits. In return for a 5 per cent stake in Arsenal, Granada invested a cash amount of £47 million to help pay for the Gunners' new 60,000-seater stadium. The two companies also set up a joint venture called AFC Broadband, a global portal to develop Arsenal's new media rights, which will include delayed coverage of the club's Premiership matches to computers, televisions, WAP phones and personal digital assistants like hand-held Palm Pilots and Handspring Visors. Vodafone and Manchester United also announced a multimillion-pound deal that in years to come will allow for games to be shown on hand-held Internet devices.

And while it may seem unlikely, given fans' paranoia over big businesses, could it be that in the far distant future a television company that owns a club might put off upgrading its stadium in an attempt to get more people to take up television options instead, as it would be more profitable?

While one can imagine boardroom meetings where companies try to block TV deals by their competitors, it may be that the British government and the football bodies have found a way around this. Unsurprisingly, it involves greed. The government has done incredibly well from selling things like frequencies for mobile phones through auction-style systems, and it may be that all future football television deals will be conducted in this way, with the top bid winning. This would do away with much of the secrecy and boardroom manoeuvring that goes on now and allow for a more open process. However, it would also mean a more greedy process, with higher and higher sums being put forward to win the rights, and at the end of the day, the fan will have to pay for this through raised TV prices. Television rights are not going to go away and will probably continue to increase over the coming years as the mobile and Internet platforms get powerful enough to actually broadcast games at the same quality as television. Again these costs will be met by advertisers and the fans, who will have no option but to stump up if they want to follow their teams. But this may result in a new version of the old days, when fans listened to their rivals' games on radio while watching their own team; we may end up with a generation of fans following another game on mobile phones or hand-helds while attending a game involving their own team.

The incredible thing that football never seems to have noticed is that it is in a better position than the television companies, as the television stations need football more than football needs them. If TV went away tomorrow, the game would continue, but the television companies would not get the viewing figures that football brings in without great effort and expense. Even then, they may not get them as regularly.

Fans complain about the night-time games and the early morning weekend games; they moan about BSkyB and the other companies changing match times. And while it may be the companies that set the schedules, the final say lies with the football authorities, who could quite easily stipulate at what times the televised games are shown. The television companies would moan, bicker and threaten, but they would have no choice but to capitulate because there is only one football league. Football is not like the cinema, where if a studio does not have a Tom Cruise for a film, it can try and get Harrison Ford, Mel Gibson or Bruce Willis. There is only one Manchester United, one Barcelona, one Inter Milan and one Celtic. Football fans will pay money to watch football from other countries but the leagues they will pay the most for are the home leagues in which their teams play. There is no doubt that some people in England would take up Scottish and European football if there was no Premiership to watch, and that the same would apply across the world in terms of domestic leagues, but people would not watch as often or in the same numbers as they do now.

Football saved BSkyB in terms of the viewing figures it brought in and BSkyB, as well as the other companies, is fully aware of how beneficial it is to them, hence the large amounts of cash they throw about, but those on the footballing side, especially in the Premiership and FA who deal with the bidding, are letting the fan down. They seem to think the fan is used to the status quo and should accept it, but many of these men have not had to make 200-mile journeys on a dark Tuesday or Wednesday night before having to get up early for work the next day, or suffer the disruption that this causes at home, or the financial difficulties. Football on TV may seem like a great thing for fans, but ironically it is the real fans that suffer most because of it, and as a result, the game suffers. Rupert Murdoch has always been a businessman, he has never hidden that fact. The football associations, however, are meant to be looking out for players and fans. Someone's not doing their job right – but it's not anyone who works at BSkyB.

Eight

Sponsorship and Shares

In the mid-nineties in English and European football the phrase SAS meant the combination of Alan Shearer and Chris Sutton, who were a devastating strike force at Blackburn Rovers. Recently, however, the impact of another SAS could prove to be even more dangerous to the game as a whole – sponsorship and shares.

It would be hard to hazard a guess as to which has had a worse influence on the game, under the guise of improving it. Fans are told that the money is a good thing as it allows conditions to be improved, better players to be brought in and keeps their club in contention for the big prizes. They are also told this when it comes to paying for the annual increase in season tickets and merchandising, so how much of this is true? It's hard to tell, especially when one considers that the point of any institution that has shares is to make a profit for its shareholders. It's not about winning games, keeping top players or weathering a bad performance run. It's purely and simply about money. In the world of business anything that makes a profit is good; everything else, no matter how much emotion is attached to it, is bad.

Sponsorship

Sponsorship is one way that businesses get involved in football – sponsoring events, players, the match balls and even the strips. With the exception of Barcelona, which has rejected any corporate logo on its shirts as it would ruin the aesthetics, club shirts carry a variety of logos, from multinationals to local double-glazing companies.

Even referees are being used to peddle wares. From 2001 Spanish referees are to be the first in Europe to wear advertising on their shirts. Referees in the First and Second Divisions will carry the name of broadcasting platform Quiero on the front of their shirts during league and cup matches.

Carlsberg has been involved in sponsorship for longer than most. As well as sponsoring teams like Liverpool, the company backed Italia '90, numerous European Championships including Euro 2000, a variety of European Cup Winners Cups, the Champions Clubs Cup, the Champions League, the UEFA Cup, the UEFA Super Cup (1998 and '99) and the Carlsberg Cup in Hong Kong. A company spokesman said that while their sponsorship was natural because both football and the company were global 'brands' (his word, not mine), he admitted that it was also about reinforcing Carlsberg's image as an international, premium beer.

Sponsorship is not a new phenomenon in the game. Its roots go back to the early days of the 20th century, when tea company founder Sir Thomas Lipton sponsored the Lipton World Football Trophy in Turin. While there had been some forms of sponsorship beforehand, this is the first recognised one involving two European teams. When the World Cup was proposed in the 1920s there was no trace of sponsorship. Jules Rimet's vision for the game – a football Olympics – precluded such vulgarity, even though it was beginning to happen in many countries across the globe. The one exception to the use of sponsorship in this opening World Cup involved Romania, where the King had given royal privileges to the team. However, there was a price to be paid for this in that he had quite a say in the team selection. That would not be the last time this happened.

As the World Cup grew in popularity, companies realised they could get exposure through sponsorship. Adidas gave shoes and boots to the West German team of 1954 but no money changed hands. The founder of Adidas, Adi Dassler, was just doing what he could to help his team to victory out of national pride, though it did also make excellent marketing and promotional sense. By 1966 there were complaints about sponsorship from the television companies, who were irritated at the trackside boards. They felt that the advertisers were getting free publicity, as they had made no payments to the television companies. By 1970, World Cup organisers were getting a little more excited about advertising sponsorship. That final, based in Mexico, brought in around $1.5 million, which was not a bad sum for the time. Some companies got their advertising free because signs that were already standing before the tournament were left up. This is in stark contrast to now, when any unauthorised – or non-paying – signage is taken down well in advance of games and tournaments.

Commerciability continued to rise and improve in a financial sense in the 1974 World Cup, where Germany applied all the lessons learned so far. There was more perimeter advertising, but it was hard to make out due to the distance between the cameras, the pitch and the boards. Nonetheless, the event was a success from a sponsorship point of view, with 20 million deutschmarks being raised.

It was the arrival of Joao Havelange as FIFA president in the same year that people now identify as one of the first moves towards bringing in more money, especially with his brash comment that:

'I have come to sell a product named football.'

Argentina in 1978 saw more money come in and Coca-Cola making its sponsorship entrance. By 1982, marketing and advertising men knew football had great possibilities. Coca-Cola, Gillette, Canon, Fuji Film and JVC all signed up; many of them are still involved today. However, some companies were becoming unwelcome. The 1986 tournament was the last FIFA event to have tobacco sponsorship, after it banned tobacco publicity and advertising. A hasty exceptional ruling, allowing it for the duration of that World Cup, was put through but it was the last time tobacco played a part. It would not be the last time rules were changed because of sponsors, however. After 1986 FIFA and its marketing partner, ISL, started negotiating deals for tournament sponsorship rights in longer steps, two and three tournaments at a time, claiming that this gave FIFA longer-term financial security, though some wondered if FIFA could ever go out of business.

The new longer deals also gave ISL a more coherent marketing programme on FIFA's behalf. Sponsorship started to change around this time, with billboards becoming only one way for a company to get noticed. More subliminal and subtle forms began to appear, with corporate boxes being sponsored and logos being put on equipment or shown during the credits of football shows.

The next big leap for football and sponsorship money came in 1994 when the tournament was held in the USA. After seeing how profitable the football market had been for Adidas, training shoe company Nike threw itself into sponsorship. It spent more than £30 million on sponsorship and advertising and would later spend £100 million on a training centre in Brazil. American sponsorship showed European companies just how effective the marketing dollar could be, and it cemented sponsorship's position as being as integral a part of the game to those in power as the 11 men in each team. Even the FIFA Web site states:

'For FIFA, the future means above all continuing to maintain the delicate balance between satisfying the demands of its corporate partners and preserving the dignity and the true character of the sport – a character which was largely responsible for attracting the corporate interest in the first place, many years ago.'

This is corporate romanticism. The only reason corporations got involved was to promote their own interests, and that means selling products. France '98 saw corporate interests and national laws clash again, with legal definitions being bent so that certain stadiums were not technically in France. The reason for this? So Budweiser could be advertised – alcohol advertising is not allowed in connection with sports events in France.

Until the 1998 World Cup, most people would have dismissed the idea that sponsorship could influence what happened on the pitch. One event at France '98 changed that for ever. One of Brazil's top players, Ronaldo, was left as a substitute on the early version of the team sheet produced just hours before the final against France was to begin. He had suspected ankle and knee injuries, and was not part of the starting 11. But just before kick-off a new version of the sheet appeared, with Ronaldo in the starting line-up. Brazil lost the game, and it was later revealed that Ronaldo had suffered convulsions for 30 seconds on the day of the final.

According to the player:

'I woke up with pains all over my body. It was something real bad that I had never before felt in my whole life. I really felt bad. I had a headache, my stomach hurt.'

He was taken to hospital and subjected to a barrage of tests, including neurological and cardiac, by the team doctor, Lidio Toledo. By this point confusion had already started to appear, as FIFA spokesmen had said that Ronaldo had gone to hospital for X-rays on his left ankle, which had been denied by Toledo, who later said the hype was affecting the player and making him ill. Ronaldo eventually declared himself fit to play and took part, though he looked a far cry from world class. His club Inter Milan were not happy, saying the Brazilian federation had behaved in an absurd manner because it was a serious mistake for him to play in that condition. FIFA and the Brazil camp were both widely criticised for letting him play so soon after his fit, but it was then rumoured that Nike had had a part in it all. Nike has deals with both the Brazilian team and Inter Milan, with a value of more than £250 million. Ronaldo had played a large part in the company's World Cup advertising. Nike put out a statement from its Italian branch following comments from its corporate headquarters in the United States, saying:

'Nike wants to emphasise that the report of such involvement is absolutely false.

'What is true is that last night's game was the most important moment of Ronaldo's career. To play the final of a World Cup is the dream of any player, Ronaldo included.

'In all of this, Nike did not interfere in any way. And besides, why should it have?'

To be fair to Nike, there is no evidence of their influence, but many feel the fact that Nike were put on the spot shows that one day a company could insist that a star player turns out for a game, even if he is not 100 per cent fit and to this day there are still those in Brazil who mutter about the company's involvement. A congressional inquiry into Nike's involvement is currently underway in Brazil (see Chapter 10).

As noted above, sponsorship has changed from being just about billboards, and Manchester United has shown that kit sponsorship is likely to change as well. Their most recent kit sponsorship deal was with mobile phone company Vodafone, for £30 million over four years. This ended an 18-year arrangement with Japanese company Sharp. However, the Vodafone deal was not just for a logo on a shirt. The deal also sees them being able to provide wireless Internet services to the club's 12 million supporters worldwide. Vodafone has said that it will be about four years before fans can watch a game live on their mobiles, but having beaten the likes of Microsoft to sponsor Manchester United, the company knows that being involved with the most famous club in the world gives them a huge head start over their competition. This is especially the case if it gets to a point where fans need a Vodafone to get the best mobile set-up, including the best picture quality, results update or club information.

Governments have not been blind to the power of sponsorship money in football. In England politicians are aware of the money being brought into the game and have tried to get it used for more than just lining the pockets of players, chairmen or shareholders. In 1998 MP Gillian Merron called for Parliament to take a lead and tackle the ever-growing financial divide between super-rich clubs and the others. She was of the opinion that if more funding was not reinvested then dozens of smaller clubs could collapse, dragging down with them the prosperity, well-being and spirit of some of the local communities that they represent. She called for a Football Sponsorship Levy, which would see the establishment of an independent representative board to distribute television money more fairly. She said:

'If politics is to re-empower the disempowered, replacing disillusion with faith and commitment, football is as good a place to start as any. Football is awash with money. In the past few years, hundreds of millions of pounds have come into the game through lucrative sponsorship deals, stock market flotations, merchandising and, above all, television deals.

'As time passes, we see also the greed of people who have a passion for making vast amounts of money, rather than for football. That is a source of aggravation and despair for fans of Premiership clubs, who want football to flourish and to be given back to the fans. This problem runs the length and breadth of Britain.

'The smaller clubs are being clobbered in many ways. The knock-on effect of the rich clubs being made richer by television wealth is the upward spiralling of wages and transfer fees.

'Why should we be bothered about smaller league clubs – the Lincoln Citys, the Burnleys and the Bournemouths? There will be plenty of others to support, and hours of football on the television to enjoy. Smaller clubs make a unique contribution to the economic and community life of their towns and cities across the land.'

Her last point hits the nail on the head, but also shows the problem with football being a business. The small clubs are important in an economic and social sense. On match day a stadium can be worth at least tens of thousands of pounds a year to the little shops and pubs nearby, and provide a focal point for the local people. But business does not care about that. In the world of the shareholder, all that matters is receiving the maximum profit from whatever you own shares in, and normally the best way to do that is by being the leader in your field, by being unique and having no competitors.

Football business analyst Dave Jones has pointed out that football is in a strange situation:

'In most businesses, the whole point is to be the best, to be number one and whether companies admit it, they all want to be the only company in their field. They don't want competition that limits what they can charge or that could put them out of business. Everyone wants to be Microsoft, who many feel was punished for being too successful.

'However, football is different. All the clubs need each other for survival and each level of club needs teams that are adequately matched so that there is some uncertainty. Now any sensible fan will tell you that they would go and watch their team every week, even if they knew they were going to win, and they would, but the uncertainty is what makes it exciting and helps make it such a marketable commodity like any other sport, so football needs competition while at the same time every top club is trying – for lack of a better phrase – to be Microsoft, to be the clear dominant winner.

'But just as Microsoft would have to acknowledge that it had help from elsewhere – the easy-to-use look of Windows is certainly inspired by what Apple had in its Macintosh software and both

companies were inspired by what companies like Xerox were doing
– football clubs at the top have to acknowledge that they get a lot
from below them and not just players.

'It's all very nice having clubs like Manchester United and Celtic
going to play fundraising games for Derry City, but they don't seem
to be doing that for clubs in their own lower leagues and even then,
that is just a token gesture. What should be happening is a regular
percentage – and a decent percentage, not a paltry 5 or 10 per cent
– should be trickling down to all the other clubs.

'Also in recognition of that, clubs in lower divisions should also
put some money into the lower leagues. Everyone should help
everybody else out and not just have the clubs at the top helping out.
Everyone should pitch in as it is in everyone's interests to keep the
game and the small clubs alive.

'It also wouldn't hurt for some big companies to sponsor small
clubs. Not only would that help, it would also appeal to the romantic
in many football fans with headlines like "Big firm backs small club"
and the firm could offer tickets to workers and so on. It won't happen
because the big firms only want to be associated with the big, high-
profile clubs that compete for and can win the big trophies, but it
would be a nice gesture.'

Marketing analyst Peter D'arbont feels a time may come when
sponsors will wonder if they are getting value for money:

'All it is is a more subtle, in some cases almost subliminal, form of
advertising. Companies will always want to promote their goods but
they may start to get the feeling that they do not get a return for their
investment. But let's be honest here. That money is getting put in for
a reason and that reason is to promote the company and the
company's goods.

'Just as fans want a say for their money, is it so unreasonable that
sponsors should want a say for their money? Shareholders get a say
in things after they put in cash, so why shouldn't this group?

'I don't think there's been much heavy influence yet, but what you
will see in years to come is sponsors advising clubs that they should
play certain friendly games or advise that it would be good to have
ethnic players – or even women players in some games where it is
permissible.

'However, if it starts to turn sour for the companies involved in terms of financial returns, you will see one of two things happen. They will either sponsor smaller clubs, which would be good in some ways, or they will pull out altogether, which benefits no one.'

Shares

As noted above, shareholders are the other group that want something from the game – and very often it is profit. Three types of people buy shares in a football club: fans, media companies and business investors. Fans buy either to give their club some extra money or to say that they own a part of the club. Media companies buy for a number of reasons, but the main one at the moment is the revenue that comes from the game. Business investors are there for only one reason, and that is to make money, just as they would from any other company. According to a survey by sports marketing company UFA Sport, about 40 million fans want to invest in the game. Interest is at its most healthy in countries where clubs are already listed on the stock market, although Germany is an anomaly. The UFA Sport survey found that in the UK more than 11 million fans held – or intended to buy – shares in a club that they liked. Second behind the UK was Germany, with about 7 million potential football shareholders, which was rather surprising because at the time of the survey (2000) not a single German club was listed on the stock market (Borussia Dortmund became the country's first listed club in October 2000).

Chairman of the Executive Board of UFA Sport, Bernd Hoffmann, believes the numbers will continue to rise and rise:

'The survey showed us that plenty of people in Europe are interested in buying football shares.

'From experience, we know that the relevant share prices depend too much on the sporting performance of a club, and less on its success from a business angle.

'For this reason, we consider football shares to be more of a fan article than anything else at the present time. However, the subject of shareholding in football will grow in importance as the sport itself becomes more and more professional and international.'

Just as with television rights, the UK has already stolen a march on the rest of the world in this respect. According to Dave Jones, some shareholding institutions are already starting to take a closer look at their footballing options:

'Up until now a lot of investments have been on a smaller level, but we are now at the stage where foreign banks and many large traders from outside countries where football is the dominant sport are putting money in or looking to put money in and these people have no emotion about the game. A lot of people think that there cannot be a further corporate change in the game, but most analysts think that so far has only been the tip of the iceberg.

'Say what you will about the broadcasting companies getting involved but at least to some extent they still understand the game and will let big name signings be made, wage increases go ahead and so on because it is in their best interests to allow the game to flourish. Investors with no interest in the game or the promotion of the game through the mass media aren't that interested. To them it's about a dividend, a return on their investment, profit or loss and that's it.

'As more of these people get involved you are going to see more tough questioning of boards. A good example could be if a player is bought and then gets injured or turns out to be a dud, for example when Manchester United went for Ruud Van Nistelrooy for a transfer fee of around £18 million. If the club had been stuck with him after the injury then there would have been some serious questions getting asked by the non-football shareholders. All they would see there is an incredible amount of money being paid for one employee who was not able to do his job. Any club that is a publicly listed company will have to worry about their shareholders when making an investment like that.

'Put it this way, the fact that any major football decision that can affect a publicly quoted company has to be announced to the stock market before the fans can be told shows you where things are going and where the power lies.'

But fans are wary. They may buy the shares, but that does not mean they are happy with the changing nature of their clubs. Again, there is rarely a questionnaire outside a ground asking fans if they think flotation is a good idea. A report, 'Ticket Pricing, Football Business and Excluded Football Fans', by the Sir Norman Chester Centre for Football Research showed that 75 per cent of those questioned felt flotations could produce serious conflict, as shareholders' and fans' interests are not the same. More than half were worried about investors with no interest in football buying into the club and 49 per cent felt it made it harder for the fans to get involved. There are also situations where fans buy shares in their club, but the club board may not have much business sense so the shares lose their value. Who bears the brunt of that? The very same fan who bought the shares, though other shareholders are also affected. In a submission to the Football Task Force, Richard Chorley of the Southampton Independent Supporters' Association made this point clear. He said:

'Having adopted public company status, Southampton have not progressed at all as a football club and are now resorting to severe price rises in order to balance the company's books and merely remain in operational profit.

'Investors purchased shares at a high price. Subsequently thousands of fans have lost money in the face of their [Southampton's] poor performance. It now appears that supporters are picking up the tab for the business decisions of... the... Southampton directors.

'In a bizarre twist the large percentage of supporters who purchased shares in the PLC now find themselves facing enormous season ticket rises in order to ensure a profit for the parent company and the accompanying payment of their own minimal share dividend.'

Conclusion

Sponsorship is very much the lesser of the two evils. While it may become insidious in the future, at the moment the worst it can do to fans is encourage them to eat and drink lots of fizzy drinks, beer, fast food and chocolate while wearing the latest training clothing. However, shares – and the overall pursuit of money – have led to fans buying into their clubs, fragmenting the ownership and allowing sometimes incompetent people to run the clubs poorly, while the fans are still expected to turn up and cheer on the team. The other scenario is that the club is a success, someone comes in to buy it, the fans' shares are still fragmented, and this stops them from mounting opposition to that takeover bid. Then when the new owner gets 90 per cent of the shares, the other 10 per cent have to be handed in, due to the rules involving a hostile takeover. Such was the scenario that faced Manchester United fans when BSkyB attempted a takeover, which is discussed in Chapter 19.

Nine

Europe

'It was the best of times, it was the worst of times.' The quotation from Dickens's classic *A Tale of Two Cities* sums up the current situation of football in Europe. There are some great teams playing, and there is a lot of money available, but there are those who are still not happy, who want more, and they could change the game for better or for worse.

Football is a global game, but the current economic powerhouse lies within Europe. As noted earlier, European club teams are the ones that get the most attention. Brazil may be the most renowned international team, but the most famous club teams are European – Manchester United, Liverpool, Barcelona and Inter Milan. For this reason, Europe wields an incredible amount of power within the game. Until recently the European game has been run fairly steadily – through UEFA – but that looks set to change over the next few years as clubs try to exert more influence.

UEFA was founded in 1954 to foster and develop unity and solidarity amongst the European football community. It is now one of the six continental confederations of world football's governing body FIFA, but it is not the same UEFA that started nearly 50 years ago. Even the organisation's Web site points this out, highlighting the new, business-like nature of the game:

'[UEFA] is a vibrant hive of activity with its own corporate identity and image, fully in keeping with the demands of the modern business world.

'As football has become more of a business, UEFA has given vital emphasis to reinvesting the vast sums of money generated by its activities back into the game at all levels. The football visionaries of the 1950s might hardly recognise UEFA now.'

Indeed they might not, but neither would they recognise the Machiavellian nature of the clubs who are not looking out for European football, but rather for themselves.

Until a short while ago there was another group meeting in secret – the G14. The name is derived from the G8 'supercountries', who determine the world's economy. It is not just hype or ego on the part of the clubs; they do have the clout to get what they want. The G14 clubs were officially institutionalised in mid-2000, when a firm was set up in Brussels to look after their interests. By that time, the fact that these clubs were meeting was also one of the worst-kept secrets in football, so it made sense for the clubs to come out and admit it.

The G14 group is unique in world football, as the teams have come together for no other reason than self-promotion. At the meeting in mid-2000, those present gave official titles to various members. The then Real Madrid president Lorenzo Sanz was named as the president of the organisation, with three vice-presidents under him: Ajax chairman Frank Kales, Bayern Munich vice-president Karl-Heinz Rummenigge and AC Milan vice-president Adriano Galliani-Sanz. Sanz, who is said to be very friendly with FIFA president Sepp Blatter, called it 'an important day for European football as the new organisation will allow us to defend our interests'.

Note the phrasing – 'our' interests, not the fans or the game as a whole, just the clubs. It could be argued that he meant European football, but UEFA already represents everyone in Europe. The G14 also released a statement saying that they wanted to help solve football's problems, which many football commentators thought showed either a hidden talent for comedy, or an unjustified belief that they may be part of the solution and not the problem.

The G14 clubs are from across Europe. From Italy, there is AC Milan, Internazionale and Juventus. In Spain Real Madrid and Barcelona are members. Manchester United and Liverpool are the

English contingent; Paris St-Germain and Marseille represent France; Bayern Munich and Borussia Dortmund are the German teams involved, while Holland's PSV Eindhoven and Ajax and Portugal's FC Porto round off the group. UEFA chief executive Gerhard Aigner has made no secret of what he thinks of the G14:

'Money is their only motive. This is motivated by selfishness. They are only defending their own interests and are not taking account of the interests of football in general. They are a self-proclaimed pressure group.'

The consortium showed it meant business when it appointed one of UEFA's top men to head up the organisation at its new base in Brussels. Thomas Kurth was head of UEFA's club competitions department and was the man responsible for the operational running and logistics of the Champions League. While UEFA has always known that these clubs are deadly serious, it was only after Kurth's appointment that the higher echelons started to see that the future might be turbulent. This was especially evident when the vice-president of Real Madrid, Juan Onieva, claimed that:

'Sooner or later the institutions of UEFA and FIFA will clash with our power. Our influence is increasing.'

There have been rumours of other clubs with large international support bases, such as Lazio, Roma, Chelsea, Arsenal, Valencia, Rangers or Celtic, joining the G14. The issue of allowing in a credible Russian team has also been raised, to try to tap that market. This would create a G22. Not all of the clubs suggested for the G22 have huge international appeal, but all have large fan bases and proven moneymaking abilities. By bringing in the best – or the perceived best – from so many countries the new league will appeal to expats across the globe as well as the die-hard football fans. The more countries involved, the greater the revenue possibilities, which is what this is all about.

Any eventual league would guarantee the death of one thing that football thrives on, even though fans hate it – uncertainty. Fans of the bigger clubs are normally confident of their team winning, but it is rarely guaranteed. The minnows can still occasionally pull off big surprises, especially in the cups. Clubs like AC Milan, Celtic and Rangers have found themselves knocked out in early European stages, which makes a considerable dent in terms of the money they expected to come in. By having a European league where there is no relegation, there is no worry about losing cash in this way, as most of the revenue will be from TV rights and sponsorship. These sorts of deals will always be negotiated years ahead with ticket sales low down on the agenda, which is just as well because only a few teams in the G14 are capable of winning any league they all take part in as, despite their financial clout and reputations, they are not all equally talented. Fans may or may not get bored with seeing their teams play the so-called cream of Europe, but there is a chance they will get fed up with being constantly 14th in a league when they can remember days of trebles and nine-in-a-row league victories. However, the business side of the clubs will be happy as long as the money keeps coming in and it would take a few years for any serious abandoning by the fans to be noticed by the bean counters. Of course the average fan doesn't matter here. There were no questionnaires carried out at Old Trafford or any of the other grounds. The fan will just have to take what is dictated to them and dictating is something that the current G14 group is very good at.

At the start of 2000 – before they were even an official organisation – Real Madrid, backed by others in the G14, demanded that they receive 50 per cent of any revenue received by national federations for international games. This alone would have brought in extra millions for the clubs, as they would be receiving money for games that may not involve many, or any, of their players or their facilities, making it money for nothing. This attempt at moneygrabbing was slammed by a number of footballing countries including Ireland, where the president of the football association, Pat Quigley, said:

'The small associations would go out of existence. We depend on our internationals to run our association.

'It's been said that the money would go towards the development of young players but in our case the money would be going outside Ireland to English clubs, so it does not benefit us.'

The G14 clubs then went on to demand that national games be played only in mid-May, June and the second half of October. And that was not all. They also wanted the release of players for national teams to be reduced to three days and players being allowed to transfer between clubs during UEFA competitions without being barred from playing for their new team (at the moment they cannot play in the European games if they sign for a new club after a certain date). They have also asked that Champions League and UEFA Cup matches should be suspended during future Olympic Games so that teams are not missing vital players. And to top that, they have also demanded new qualification criteria for the Champions League, in which sides would automatically be eligible to play in the competition if they had qualified three times in the previous five years. The scale of these audacious demands was further proof of how the clubs are seeking to run football, and their plan met with immediate anger from the domestic football associations. English FA spokesman Steve Double said it seemed as if the clubs are always working to their own agendas without concern for the greater needs of football fans across the board, while the German FA accused the G14 of having no concern for the general welfare of the game.

Even before that, however, the G14 were getting their way. In 1998, the threat of a breakaway European Super League involving the teams and sports marketing company Media Partners led to UEFA doubling the Champions League from 16 to 32 clubs and substantially increasing the money clubs receive from progressing through the tournament and the subsequent TV rights income. The UEFA Cup was also expanded to offer third-place Champions League clubs a place, giving them the chance to receive some of the money they would have made had they had a prosperous run in the Champions League. It was suggested at the time that this was the start of the slippery slope towards money-making, unofficial super leagues that are a future threat, not just to football, but to all sports.

One person involved with a G14 club who asked to remain anonymous told me:

'The clubs are frustrated at being held back. Some of them are looking at other European countries and are envious of what they have, so they have pooled resources to help look out for themselves. A lot of time and money has been put into this and I doubt it's just to have a lobbying group.'

Indeed, it has already been suggested that the ultimate outcome of the G14 will be a Europe-wide league that will run alongside other competitions before 2010. Early reports suggest that each club could receive up to £40 million in a new super league as well as millions for winning games, titles and so forth. Any new league would be funded by broadcasters such as Telefonica, the Kirch Group, Canal Plus, ntl and BSkyB, all of whom would pay handsomely to be involved in such a set-up and broadcast the games on a number of platforms including cable, digital and satellite television.

But the G14 might be beaten to it by their northern neighbours or they may even be giving them tacit encouragement to see if a pan-European league can work.

Since 1998 there have been rumours of an Atlantic League development, which would consist of Scotland, Holland, Portugal, Belgium, Sweden, Norway and Denmark, so clubs like Celtic, Rangers, Ajax, Feyenoord, PSV, Benfica, Porto, Anderlecht, Bruges, IFK Gothenberg, Rosenborg, Brondby and Copenhagen would be playing each other on a regular basis. The first moves towards this were proposed by Ajax – who is also involved in the G14 (it could be accused of covering every eventuality by having its fingers in every possible pie or perhaps of being a bridge between the G14 and the Atlantic League).

The main motivation for this is the generation of sufficient television revenue to ensure big clubs from smaller countries and leagues can still remain competitive in the top European football set-ups. For example, clubs like Celtic and Rangers receive only £2.5 million from TV deals, compared to the English Premier League where clubs can expect upwards of £25 million from the new deals with BSkyB and ntl. Ajax managing director Frank Kales admitted money from TV was a factor when he said:

'Television is a real issue. If Barcelona earns £50 million and Milan £33 million, then we have to have at least £17 million. But we only get £1 million. We have a big problem trying to make up that shortfall.

'Champions League qualifiers play three games at home, three away and that's the end of it if you don't progress.

'We must move beyond country borders. I hope, with discussion, to get there and if the authorities still say no then the only other option is to go into conflict mode. But that is the last thing we want to do.'

Therefore by its own admission – being set up to ensure that clubs can compete with the best in Europe – this is nothing more than the first step towards a European Super League.

The main catch for the Atlantic League clubs is that they would have to give up their domestic leagues. However, a compromise has been suggested that would see the clubs leave their leagues but still participate in national cup tournaments. The ruling authorities have hinted that this will be allowed as long as the clubs leaving the leagues compensate the smaller clubs for the revenue they will miss out on by not having league games against the larger teams.

The proposed composition of the league is four places to Portugal, four to Holland, three each to Scotland, Norway, Sweden and Denmark and two to Belgium. Qualification to the league would occur via a system of merit, whereby the top clubs in each of the domestic leagues of the nations involved would be invited to gain entry, with play-offs taking place to see who gets in. Plans are for the matches to be played at 1 pm on Saturdays, which would allow the clubs to compete in European and domestic cup competition midweek, and maximise television audiences.

The league makes sense from one angle. European football is dominated by the leagues of five countries – England, France, Germany, Italy and Spain – all of which have excellent TV rights, fan bases and a large number of teams. The other leagues do not. They have one or two big fish and lots of minnows. But if they combine, they could join the top five countries and play against them on a fairer basis, as they would have more money to compete equally. The winners of this league – and perhaps the second- and third-placed teams – would go into the Champions League. For the domestic leagues, the departure of the big clubs would open up competition again and make them more exciting, instead of having teams competing for third and fourth place year after year. It would also allow players in the lower teams to gain more prominence at home.

The proponents of the new league have also suggested that if the format is successful then other countries could start to reform their leagues to form four 'feeder' European leagues. This would give Europe 10 leagues: English, French, German, Italian, Spanish, the Atlantic League and then the smaller leagues – created on a regional basis – with the best all playing in the European Champions League. Another intriguing idea put forward is that of promotion between the leagues, which shows that if the Atlantic League went ahead, the changes to the structure of European football would not stop there. It does not take a stretch of the imagination to see regional leagues being set up: a Scandinavian League, a Southern Europe League, a UK League and so on. Alternatively, the clubs may – if the Atlantic League looked like being a success – cut to the chase and go for a set-up along the lines of the G14, with a First Division under that.

As noted above, the first attempts at breakaways failed for several reasons, including the fact that UEFA let it be known that it would fight tooth and nail to ensure that national league structures are kept in place. This is understandable because very few organisations willingly give away the jewels in their crown. The Atlantic League backers understood this and from early days had some big guns lined up to help suggest to UEFA that they wanted to work with them. Among these was Allan Macdonald, former managing director of British Aerospace in Asia and Africa.

Ajax spokesman Erik van Leeuwen said:

'We would like this to happen and you can reach this conclusion. We are interested because it is going to be very difficult for the likes of us to compete if we're not playing in a new league.

'In England, if Ipswich Town get promoted to the Premier League they are full with money but we are very poor compared to that country. But with good money from television then of course we would hope to compete.

'When you look at a game like Ajax vs Vitesse, it is only interesting to Dutch people. But Ajax vs Celtic or Rangers is interesting in Scotland and Holland and perhaps other European countries.

'Put simply, it means bigger money from TV, bigger stars for the club and it helps us to keep our home-grown stars. At Ajax, we are not happy that our younger players can leave here at 17 and go to Juventus.

'UEFA is now also wanting to talk about this, which is a good sign. They have to realise how hard it is to get involved in direct competition with England, Spain and Italy for us now.

'Although we haven't done as well in recent years, we still have the feeling we can cope with these countries. However, the gap is getting bigger fast and something has to be done.'

While the Atlantic League group, just like the G14 group, are making peaceful moves to the powers that be, this does not guarantee success. FIFA vice-president David Wills has spoken cautiously about the plans, reminding the clubs that they could lose out on a lot:

'Nobody can stop them going on their own and forming a league but they must realise they will be in another realm of football and not part of FIFA or UEFA.

'I am not saying there will not be an Atlantic League, but it must be done through the proper channels. UEFA must be approached first, and then FIFA.'

While Gerhard Aigner has appeared to be dismissive of the new possibilities offered by the Atlantic League, he has realised the far-reaching implications of the league being set up:

'We would have to be against it if we felt it was to the detriment of the general European football movement because we have a statutory mandate to look after the welfare of the whole of European football. Such a new project, which can have repercussions in other areas of the continent, which could also trigger off something in the five big markets, has to be carefully analysed.'

Aigner appears to be only too aware that if this is a success then the G14 would not be slow in pushing for more reform and attempting to get their own way if there is more money in it for them. To his credit, Aigner seems to realise that while the clubs are chasing more money, it is the fans that are losing money. But yet again, while the clubs talk of spending large amounts of money in order to keep up with the best teams who are winning the trophies, there has been no dialogue with the fans to see if they want to pay for more trips abroad – or even if they can afford to.

In February 2001 UEFA stated that anyone from the new Atlantic League would not take part in its competitions. This did not have the desired effect of frightening the clubs into submission. Instead they have taken the case to the European Commission, claiming that UEFA is acting as a monopoly by not allowing clubs to form their own competition, breaching European trust laws. At the time of going to press no solution had been reached but UEFA may be about to learn the meaning of the saying about the dog, its tail and who wags whom.

Arsenal and Rangers fan Mark Davidson is one of many who think both European League ideas may not be as wonderful as everyone suggests. He said:

'At first it all sounds really tempting, but so does a chicken curry every day for the rest of your life.

'You would end up getting fed up – fed up with all the travelling, fed up with a lot of games that didn't interest you but that you'd still be paying for.

'For example, say the rights to this are only available through digital or satellite television and it costs around £50 a season to watch the league. If Arsenal are in the top half of the league, the lower table stuff isn't going to interest me at all. Also, if it ends up more or less being the same teams year in year out then it's going to get boring.

'Also, knowing what would be happening every year would make things dull. At the moment you can be anywhere in Europe every year and you can have some cracking trips abroad and it feels special. You get all excited for it. With this a lot of the fun would disappear. The clubs should also look at providing cheap transport to the away games. In fact it wouldn't surprise me if some of them announce deals for people who join certain fan clubs.

'For example, join the Arsenal Euro Club and be allowed to fly on the reduced-rate fan plane. £20 a year membership to the club guarantees you first option for a seat on the plane at a reduced rate. BA or whoever puts on a plane at cheaper than normal prices in return for a guaranteed full flight.

'It might sound stupid, but clubs are trying to get into everything else, so why not this?'

But according to John Williams, Senior Researcher at the Sir Norman Chester Centre for Football Research, all this revolutionary talk may be a bit presumptuous. 'I've heard executives at Manchester United and Liverpool saying they believe the European league is some way off and that some of the radical proposals being suggested are not supported by too many. It could be more of an evolution than a revolution. Granted, the Atlantic League has a real possibility of going ahead and that may be a precursor to a new kind of arrangement between the top European clubs.

'I don't think the top clubs will ever desert the domestic game because I think they realise that they need domestic competition too, but I think they see their interests as lying with the larger European and world clubs and I think we're going to see more challenges to UEFA and FIFA.'

The famous line at the end of Dickens's *A Tale of Two Cities* reads: 'It is a far, far better thing that I do, than I have ever done.' Whether or not the clubs can see past their own interests to do what is better for their fans and football remains to be seen.

Ten

Corruption

There's no avoiding the fact, so it's as well to come up with it at the start: football is often a corrupt game. Many of the major footballing countries have been accused of corruption in some form.

Over the last few years there have been more and more cases of alleged or proven corruption.

Portugal

In Portugal, a referee and the former club president of Leca were sent to jail for fixing a match in 1993.

The chairman of Porto, Jorge Nuno Pinto da Costa, has come under fire for his possible role in a string of alleged European and domestic match fixing, including a 1984 Cup Winners Cup semi-final versus Aberdeen. Fernando Barata, who was president of another Portuguese club, Farense, claims to have acted as a middleman for da Costa in bribing Romanian referee, Ion Igna. The situation has been made more complicated by the convenient fact that da Costa is also head of the Portuguese league. This, it has been rumoured, put da Costa in the position of not only influencing, but also directly choosing, which matches referees will work.

Spain

Spanish football has for years been rife with stories and rumours that some clubs offer to pay other club's bonuses if they beat certain opponents. The European Champions League 2000/01 was rocked when it was claimed that Barcelona offered AC Milan more than £1.5 million to beat Leeds (a claim that all the clubs involved denied). However, Atletico Madrid's Jesus Gil has said that this goes on all the time and there have been calls to make it legal as it is argued that no offence is being committed. It is not a bribe for a team to throw a game, merely a 'bonus incentive scheme'.

Romania

In Romania, footballing legend Gheorghe Hagi has vowed to stamp out corruption in the game there, as he feels it taints anything the international team achieve. During recent years Romanian soccer has been frequently shaken by corruption scandals involving both the first and the second league, as well as heads of the national federation. Hagi has often criticised illegal deals between teams and has also pointed out the potential problems arising from Romanian soccer rules, which allow club presidents to sit on the board of the Romanian Soccer Federation.

Russia

In Russia a former coach has spoken of how bribery and corruption affect his country's leagues. Oleg Tereshonkov was manager of first division club Smena Saturn St Petersburg in the early 1990s, and has claimed that he regularly bribed players, managers and referees. Tereshonkov, in an article for a Russian magazine, portrayed the first division as being completely corrupt, with goalkeepers showing strikers where to shoot and referees asking for more money in the middle of a game. He said that at least half of all games in the first division are fixed and that clubs have whole teams of people in charge of bribes – for both referees and other teams – which could run into tens of thousands of dollars. He also claimed that in 1995 his club was so broke that it couldn't afford to travel to some away games and so accepted a bribe from a promotion-seeking team. Russian soccer officials concede that bribery is widespread:

'We admit there is a problem,' said Vladimir Rodionov, general secretary of the Russian Football Association. 'We know it is difficult to fight against. All these things happen behind closed doors.'

France

France has had some of the most humiliating accusations of corruption thrown at it, peaking with Olympique de Marseille forfeiting the European Cup in 1993 following evidence of bribes being given to Valenciennes players to go easy in a league match against Marseille.

Belgium

A survey in Belgium, for the magazine *Foot*, has shown that a large number of Belgium's first division soccer players believe the game is tainted by corruption, with one-fifth claiming they have been approached to rig matches. Sixty-four players said corruption exists in the Belgian professional game, while 12 said they had personally been offered bribes to throw games and 33 said they knew of other players approached to negatively influence the result of a match. Belgian soccer was rocked in 1997 by a match-rigging scandal when the former chairman of the country's most famous club, Anderlecht, confessed to paying a £20,000 so-called loan to the referee who oversaw the team's controversial 1984 UEFA Cup semi-final victory over Nottingham Forest. Anderlecht won the match 3-0, helped by a much-disputed penalty.

Ireland

In Ireland the football league is facing potential accusations of corruption after Lurgan Celtic football club launched judicial proceedings against it on the grounds of religious discrimination. The juniors have applied annually for the past five seasons to gain senior status, but have been consistently turned down, though no one at the club can work out why.

Germany

In Germany in 2000, in-fighting over the position of then national coach-in-waiting Christoph Daum was made worse when a convicted tax evasion criminal claimed that Daum owed him £1 million for real estate business.

England

In England there have been a number of incidents, and the clubs and FA have been very pro-active in trying to combat corruption, including setting up a Financial Compliance Unit, which consists of accountants making spot checks on clubs' accounts.

It was alleged by Brazil and Argentina in 1966 that England won the World Cup because then-FIFA President Sir Stanley Rous bribed referees and rigged the tournament so that Germany and England would meet in the final. The evidence put forward to support this was that a German referee was assigned to the England semi-final game, and an English referee to the Germany semi-final. It was claimed that they conspired to remove the South Americans from the tournament, by sending off South American players for no reason. The claims were never proved.

More recently, there have been two particularly prominent cases involving corruption in England. George Graham was sacked as Arsenal manager in 1995 for receiving £425,000 in connection with two transfer deals, which he claimed he believed were gifts from the agent involved.

The other, and most notorious, case concerned claims that former Aston Villa and Wimbledon striker John Fashanu, the former Wimbledon keeper Hans Segers, the former Liverpool and Southampton keeper Bruce Grobbelaar and Malaysian businessman Heng Suan Lim were part of a plot involving a Far Eastern betting syndicate to rig the results of Premier League games. It was alleged that Fashanu and Segers had been 'steeped in corruption' as their Wimbledon team reached its highest-ever place in the league, finishing in the top six in the 1993/94 season. Grobbelaar and Segers did admit in court that they tried to help the Asian syndicate forecast match results (which led to the FA handing them each a six-month ban and a £10,000 fine). But neither tried to predict the scores from their own teams' matches, they said. All parties were found not guilty and Grobbelaar later won a high-profile libel case against the *Sun* newspaper over the match-fixing allegations. Grobbelaar's lawyers described the *Sun*'s allegations as a 'classic scam', saying he had been wronged when he tried to expose corruption. The *Sun* launched an appeal against the libel decision and the verdict was announced in January 2001. As the paper itself might have said: it was the *Sun* what won it. The judges ruled that the jury's verdict was 'a miscarriage of justice' and that Grobbelaar's defence against the allegations printed in 1994 were not credible and could not be believed.

Brazil

Brazil is currently under the world's spotlight in terms of corruption in football. It has seen such scandals before, most notably when Mario Petraglia, the president of Atletico Paranaense and Alberto Duarib, president of Corinthians, were suspended pending investigation into claims that matches may have been fixed in the Copa Brasil. Ivens Mendes, who was the president of the Brazilian Football Confederation's refereeing department, resigned before he could be suspended after it was claimed that there was a tape in existence that showed him offering to have a referee give an advantage to Paranaense in their Copa Brasil match against Vasco de Gama. It was not disclosed how Mendes would get a referee to do this, though many felt it showed the man's influence – or that the whole department may need investigating.

However, it is the case launched by Brazil's Congress in October 2000 – a special investigative commission into corruption within organised soccer – that has all the footballing world's attention at the moment. The congressional commission has special legal powers to investigate, and was set up following the controversy surrounding the 1998 World Cup final, a poor performance at the Sydney Olympics and World Cup qualifying defeats against Paraguay and Chile. It is looking at allegations of failure of the clubs to make pension payments, tax evasion by coaches and claims that Nike has meddled in the selection of the national side to promote the players it sponsors. Nike denies this, and they have been backed up by former Brazil coach Mario Zagallo. He said, 'I picked the team myself; there was never any interference from Nike or the CBF [the Brazilian Football Confederation] and if there had been interference, I would have resigned as I have never accepted interference as coach of any club or national team.'

Another former Brazil coach, Wanderley Luxemburgo, is under investigation and a company called Traffic, which apparently brokered Nike's multimillion-dollar sponsorship of the national soccer team, has had its financial records seized.

Luxemburgo's former secretary Renata Alvez has alleged that he included players in the national side to raise their market value. She claimed the players would then be sold abroad and that he would receive a commission. It was also claimed that his tax dealings were improper. Luxemburgo, who has denied all allegations against him, has made the hearings almost as watchable as anything that takes place on the pitch, especially as he was quizzed about a fake birth certificate, why he had 30 bank accounts and how he had earned approximately £5 million over the previous five years. (Luxemburgo said he had received income from property and car sales, as well as inheriting a sum from his dead father.)

The hearing is also looking at the issue of fake passports being arranged for players. The passports – normally claiming that the holder is a resident of Portugal – often make it easier for Brazilian players to gain entry to the lucrative markets of Europe, doing away with much of the red tape that can hold things up. At least five Brazilian players have been caught in Europe with fake Portuguese documents in the last year, with the most high-profile case involving Corinthians midfielder Edu, whose transfer to Arsenal fell through when he was caught with a forged document at London's Heathrow airport and sent back to Brazil on the next plane.

While the commission is not expected to issue its findings until some time in 2001, not everyone is backing it. FIFA president Sepp Blatter has threatened to bar Brazil from the 2002 World Cup if the commission tries to meddle with international soccer rules during its investigations into soccer corruption. It seems to the observer that Blatter does not want people from outside the confines of FIFA looking into the game or interfering with it, though one would have thought he would have welcomed any investigation that would expose the corruption that taints football.

Blatter's threat came after the commission said it may call FIFA referees and members of FIFA's international soccer courts to testify at congressional hearings. Blatter was quoted in the weekly news magazine *Epoca* as saying:

'We won't tolerate investigations that put at risk the rules of soccer. It's not only the World Cup that's at stake. It's Brazilian soccer itself, a four-time world champion, that will be threatened.'

Blatter said that besides preventing Brazil's national soccer team from playing in qualifiers for a place in the 2002 Japan-Korea World Cup, a FIFA suspension also means that club teams would not be allowed to play in international tournaments. Players would not be able to transfer to teams outside Brazil, he said. Brazil's national under-17 and women's soccer teams would also be banned from international play. Blatter would do better to look at his own house, as we shall see later.

Referees

Players, managers and businesses are not the only ones accused of ruining the game through corruption. Referees do it too.

Ex-FIFA referee Kurt Rothlisberger was banned for life by FIFA after trying to arrange the outcome of a Champions League match between Grasshopper of Zurich and French side Auxerre, a game he was not even refereeing. Rothlisberger approached the coach of Grasshopper, Erich Vogel, and said that he was friendly with the game's referee. He told Vogel he could arrange with the referee, Zhuk, to have no unfavourable decisions made against Grasshopper for a sum of around 100,000 Swiss francs. While he was not involved in the game, the incident has clouded Rothlisberger's great career as a referee, and has created speculation about some of the more controversial games that he was involved in. One example was the 1993 Champions Cup final between AC Milan and Marseille. Rothlisberger's performance as referee drew no special attention at the time, but since then the match has taken on a rather sinister air. Marseille, the king of corruption in France throughout the late '80s and early '90s, was alleged not only to have bought off their French League match the week before the final, but also to have bribed two or three AC Milan players in the final itself. The first allegation was proved in a French court, and the second was expressed – though later taken back – in 1995 by former Marseille player Jean-Pierre Papin, who had played in the final for AC Milan.

There is also the matter of the European Championship qualifying tie between Switzerland and Turkey, where Rothlisberger claims that Swiss team sponsor Credit Suisse approached him about fixing the match with Romanian referee, Ion Craciunescu. However, Credit Suisse insisted that Rothlisberger approached them to do the same thing and asked for $64,000. Rothlisberger has denied all of the above, claiming that he did not understand any statements he signed admitting the charges, because they were not in his native language.

The issue of corruption goes beyond national boundaries. Investigative reporter David Yallop found himself being sued by Sepp Blatter after he wrote a book on corruption in the higher levels of football, looking at the matter historically from 1958 through to 1998.

However, FIFA has managed to avoid the sort of incident that engulfed the International Olympic Committee, which was hit by claims of a favours-for-votes scandal in 1998. FIFA have guidelines on gifts, which state that bidders for the World Cup should not give small souvenirs or presents worth more than approximately $100. FIFA has never had a large, internal, cash-taking scandal, but it does have closed back-room meetings, that, while not corrupt, do leave open the possibility of political machinations by members. For example, it has been claimed that in 1996 UEFA voted for South Korea to host the 2002 World Cup to spite supporters of the Japanese bid, forcing the situation that faces fans next year of two separate countries hosting games in the same tournament.

Football journalist Martin Harventon thinks the incidents of corruption are prominent but that football has nothing to worry about.

'Yes, there are incidents of corruption taking place but what you have to look at are a number of factors, including the countries where it takes place. If a country has a tradition of bribery and corruption in other industries then the odds are it will happen in football too, as the game operates within normal social parameters.

'UEFA and FIFA to their credit have reacted fairly quickly and ruthlessly when they have found proof of corruption in terms of bribes and backhanders and so on. What they also have to do though is work to eliminate any potential there is for corruption. That will mean radically overhauling internal structures, as much of football is discussed in back rooms and during closed meetings that the fan never has a say in.

'The thing is, most countries will be accused of it at one point or another as most people watching the game are hardly objective. But FIFA has to show that it will work with governmental and international agencies on getting rid of any problems. If it does not it may find itself being overruled as could happen in the European transfer scenario.'

Corruption is another factor that further removes control from the fans and destroys the ideal of the beautiful game where everything is decided on the pitch. Many organisations are quick to react to any accusations of corruption within their ranks, but this is not enough. All footballing bodies must work to eliminate any suspicion in the game, but the odds are this will not happen, as the people who benefit the most from backroom wheeling and dealing are those in the upper echelons of the game.

Eleven

2002 – The World Cup, Asia and Football

At the start of the 21st century football is watched all around the globe, but in some parts of the world, most notably Asia, Africa and the Middle East, its popularity is only now beginning to take off. Many people forget how massive these areas are; China alone has one-fifth of the earth's population, and cities that contain more than 20 million people. Deloitte & Touche's Gerry Boon has suggested that, if football becomes as popular in China as it is in Europe, China might one day be the wealthiest football nation in the world.

There has been a football regional body for Asia since the mid-1950s. Known as the Asian Football Confederation, it includes Vietnam, China, India, Pakistan, Burma (Myanmar), North Korea, Iran, Iraq, South Korea, Japan, Saudi Arabia, Kuwait and the United Arab Emirates. The spotlight has been trained on the area because of the upcoming 2002 World Cup, which will take place in South Korea and Japan.

While the 2002 bid was not as farcical as the 2006 bid (more of which in the next chapter), it had drama all of its own. The inspectors who went out to look at all of the countries bidding for the games were inundated with gifts, to the point where one person said that the only thing missing was a brown envelope full of cash. It reached the stage where gifts, including high-tech computers and cameras, were being returned as they were actually having a negative impact on the people that they were meant to be influencing. When it became obvious that it was a two-way race between Japan and South Korea, things started to get really interesting.

Japan has only recently started to develop an internal football league and structure, while South Korea has a longer history and international prestige. In matches between the two countries, South Korea has won 52 and lost 12, with 15 drawn. It is also, along with Thailand, one of Asia's dominant footballing powers, and has competed in a number of final stages of the World Cup. While the Japanese J League had done quite well in a short space of time, cynics have pointed out that this was due to a combination of importing European players and tapping into the amateur football scene, which had almost 100,000 registered players in the late 1990s. Critics of the World Cup taking place in the Far East point to the period around 1998 when the game plummeted – though it has started to recover since. Average attendances almost halved and merchandising money fell as the counterfeiters (of strips and other merchandise) moved in. However, proponents of the game point out that, at that period, Japan was going through an economic crisis, and also that televised games can attract audiences of more than 50 million.

The game in Japan is recovering but it could have recovered a lot quicker if the international and national bodies running the game had done more to attract fans from communities and grass roots, instead of appearing to be focusing on trying to maximise the amount of income they could generate. In the run up to the announcement of the winner of the 2002 bid, the Japanese seemed to have the edge, though some critics have said this was only due to the fact that Joao Havelange, then president of FIFA, favoured their bid. This was picked up by the South Koreans, who stated they were concerned about the fairness of Havelange, though they were not complaining about UEFA's Lennart Johansson, who seemed to support them. South Korea went crazy in its attempts to get the games, with President Kim Young Sam going jogging wearing a World Cup T-shirt, flags being flown with details of the bid and major publicity stunts, including the making of what was believed to be the world's largest football. The South Koreans also spoke of building a new airport at a cost of hundreds of millions of dollars, new stadiums, eliminating the 10 per cent VAT on hotel stays during 2001 and 2002 and creating high-speed rail links across the country. Football watchers were fascinated by the way the scenario was turning out, as politicians were dragged in and the whole situation started to look like a battle between UEFA and FIFA. FIFA had always backed the Japanese bid, and the Japanese felt that the backing of FIFA was enough to get the tournament. However, unofficial soundings showed that South Korea still had a chance, so the European contingent put forward a suggestion that the tournament be co-hosted in an effort to save the faces of those involved in the decision-making process. At the last moment it was agreed that there would be a co-hosted event, with South Korea hosting the opening match and Japan the final, making 2002 a historic occasion not only for football but also for the two countries.

But what will it be like? Few football fans know much about Asia and the way the game is played in that region. Is the game there actually any good? According to journalist Mike Simlett, who spent some months in China, Japan and Thailand, the answer is obvious: no.

He said, 'It's shite. Most of the expatriate players from the UK are has-beens or never-weres. There's also the odd Brazilian or African playing in China and Hong Kong and others dotted about Asia, and there are also a few East Europeans more recently, but they'd all be lucky to get a game in the [Scottish] Second Division.

'However, while the talent may not be up to much football is very popular, especially in Japan and Korea. FIFA are definitely trying to tap a new market but at least it's a market that is already there – unlike in the States – and when it [the World Cup] happens in 2002 then it'll be front-page news all over the Asian papers and not just the English language ones.'

Japanese and English teacher Grant Fraser has lived in Japan for more than a year and he thinks people are in for a real surprise in 2002:

'The J League standard is on a par with the Scottish Premier League for entertainment and what some players lack in skill they make up for in speed and the quality is constantly improving, though

I would say the game has a bit to go before it replaces baseball as the top game out here.

'But it's not just the teams coming here in 2002 that might be in for a surprise, fans will be too.

'The 1994 game was held in an English-speaking country, the '98 World Cup was held in Europe and many people know either the way to travel or the language and English is a pretty common second language. None of that applies over here. There will be language difficulties, travelling difficulties and a lot of other problems unless people really plan ahead.

'People coming here expecting it to be a normal World Cup are in for a big surprise. For example, there is very little in the way of English signposting so travelling can be problematic and not many Japanese know European languages, beer can cost £6, immigration is not equipped for large influxes of people and so on.

'A lot of fans might be thinking that to see a game in Korea it's just a case of jumping onto a ferry and then coming back, but it's not that easy as some of the journeys can take a long time and no one knows if the Japanese airports are able to take a lot more flights.

'The best thing FIFA could have done is split the tournament down the middle, with one part in one country and the other half in the other.

'Deciding to have a joint tournament was a good idea but it was done for all the wrong reasons. If the decision had been on the grounds of the history and politics between the two countries and this was an attempt to have them getting on better that would have been superb, but FIFA never realised it was a good idea for that.

'And while they are happy to be having the tournament I don't think they realise what's coming their way. As I say, immigration will be a problem, especially if people are constantly going back and forth between Japan and Korea.

'The police force is pretty lax and when it comes to dealing with any problems, I think there could be some surprises. I think they are actually hoping that not too many people come to the event – they are happy to have the prestige but the actual running of it might give them hassles.

'A lot of work is going to have to be carried out at the grounds.

At the moment most of them have one big stand, separate from the rest, and then the rest of the ground. For the rest of that ground there is no segregation at all and only one or two entrances and no electronic turnstiles, which I would imagine will be needed, so getting in can be a problem but once you are in you can walk around three-quarters of the ground.

'Getting to some of the games could also be problematic, as some of the games are taking place in rural areas, while some of the J League stadiums are not being used.'

What could hinder the transport situation is the weather. The air pollution and high temperatures in Japan will make playing uncomfortable, but even worse is the possibility of monsoons, if the World Cup is held in its traditional June slot. It has been suggested that the event is held at the end of August/beginning of September to avoid clashing with the Korean monsoon season, but this would conflict with the start of most domestic leagues.

So football itself in Japan may have some quick catching up to do, but in certain off-pitch matters associated with the game some parts of Asia are right up to speed with the rest of the world, including when it comes to hooliganism and corruption.

Hooliganism

In China, there have been reports of street battles involving hundreds of hooligans and police in areas like Xian. The riot there took place after a 1-1 game between Shaanxi Guoli and Chengdu Wuniu. A refereeing decision that denied Guoli a penalty resulted in fans gathering outside the stadium, attacking Chengdu supporters and then going on a rampage through the city, smashing cars, windows and causing general chaos. A penalty of 100,000 yuan was imposed and Guoli were also ordered to find another city in which to hold their home games. The authorities are also afraid that acts of hooliganism, normally started in response to refereeing decisions, could end up directed at the state. China's cabinet, the State Council, has called for stricter crowd control, saying that hooliganism must be eliminated to maintain overall social stability.

However, the riot in Xian was not an isolated event; there have been more than 50 crowd incidents in recent years as a result of refereeing decisions. And the problem is growing. The throwing of water bottles and firecrackers is regarded as a standard prelude to a fight and then a rampage through a nearby city centre. What can also lead to problems is the fact that many visiting fans believe that the police ignore violence from home fans and only target the away fans. This starts a cycle of violence, as the next time the visiting fans are in town they feel they have scores to settle with the police, as well as getting revenge on the other team's fans when it's their turn to attend away games. The police have not been slow to respond. Most games now have around 1,000 police and paramilitary on hand to deal with problems. Players on the pitch are not helping either. Three second-division footballers have been banned from the game for life after they attacked a referee and hospitalised him with serious injuries.

Chinese sociologists are having a field day with theories for the hooliganism. Some argue that the emotions of football run contrary to the restrained culture and state regulation of the country, and that when people – men especially – experience emotional outbursts these are much more severe and intense than they would be in citizens of other countries. Another theory is that football has become the new battleground for historical rivalries. Such clashes also allow the 'haves' to combat the 'have-nots', as fans from poor parts of the country clash with fans from better-off areas. While this is disturbing enough in itself, if this disenchantment with life spreads, the implications for China as a whole are not positive. Another idea being put forward is that corruption is seen as a part of many walks of life, which the average Chinese person can do little about. Not so with football, as a bad decision by a referee could result in a fan running onto the pitch to take issue with him. However, corruption in Chinese football is also on the rise.

Corruption

Corruption is a problem throughout Asia and the Far East. In an attempt to combat it, Singapore introduced legalised gambling, becoming the first region in Asia to do so, though the Singapore teams left the Malaysian league and started their own because of a gambling scandal. What was left of the Malaysian League could not gloat, though, because it had to start a new league after the old one carried out a corruption inquiry that showed 121 players and officials had played a part in fixing games. Indonesia's league also ran into difficulties after suspending 41 referees for taking bribes, leaving not enough referees to run games. Players from Singapore, Malaysia and Thailand have all been charged with corruption, as were 12 referees in Vietnam; allegations have also been made about results in South Korea, and for years Arab nations have been accused of fielding over-age players in youth internationals.

In 1998 China barred two coaches for match-rigging. Chen Yiming, coach of Chongqing Hongyan and Wang Hongli, manager of Liaoning Tianrun, had their licences revoked after their teams suffered humiliating losses at the hands of much weaker sides. According to a Chinese Football Association official the two clubs played passively and slackened off at a crucial point in the league. Both sides were each fined 50,000 yuan and Wang was sacked immediately after his suspension. Also in 1998 Hong Kong international Chan Tsz-kong was sentenced to 12 months' imprisonment for his role in fixing a 1996 World Cup qualifier against Thailand, as well as a series of Hong Kong championship matches.

One of the most embarrassing moments, though, occurred in 1998, when Indonesia scored an own goal to lose a Tiger Cup match against Thailand to avoid a semi-final match against the Vietnamese hosts. According to match reports, both teams played to avoid winning, with defenders tackling their own players and strikers running away from the ball. At one point the game became so bizarre that the referee booked both linesmen for not making proper decisions.

In August 2000 in Singapore Australian Mirko Jurilj was accused of accepting a $22,000 bribe, and German Lutz Pfannenstiel was said to have taken $12,000. Jurilj and Pfannenstiel, described in media reports as flatmates, were released on bail and ordered to forfeit their passports. Pfannenstiel had previously been questioned by the Corrupt Practices and Investigation Bureau, along with Billy Bone and Max Nicholson of England and Scot Brian Bothwell.

But match-fixing has a serious side, as players have been assaulted in connection with it. In Singapore, an attack on the Woodlands player Ivica Raguz on the eve of his team's match against Geylang on 21 July 2000 left him with a damaged knee, and raised further concerns over match-fixing. Woodlands team manager Vengadasalam was quoted as saying he believed the assault had been arranged by bookies.

The most recent foreigner to be exposed in Singapore was Australian Abbas Saad, who was fined in 1995 for match-fixing. A year earlier, Czech Michal Vana was arrested on similar allegations, but jumped bail and fled the country. The head of one Singapore-based syndicate was said to be earning tens of millions of pounds a year before he was arrested and jailed.

According to Mike Simlett:

'Overall the corruption thing is starting to be played to death though. Hong Kong is fairly safe, as is Japan and Korea. Malaysia is a bit dubious and you wonder about the Indonesian league. But the serious punters out in places like Hong Kong bet on the English Premiership, although it's technically illegal to do so, because the football is thought to be completely above board.

'Most leagues in Asia are relatively small scale in terms of revenue so any corruption would stand out a mile. Doesn't stop it happening though and you do wonder when you see some of the refereeing.'

Africa

As noted, the next World Cup will take place in Asia. If things had gone as most footballing pundits expected, South Africa would have been holding the 2006 World Cup, giving the developing parts of the football world two chances to show how they were doing in comparison with the established footballing areas. However, though Africa will now have to wait until 2010 to host the event – and it is more or less guaranteed that they will – it is still worthwhile having a brief look at the developing nations there.

African teams rose in skill and popularity during the 1990s, with countries like Nigeria, Morocco and Cameroon becoming more prominent on the world stage. Cameroon's entertaining style in the 1990 World Cup finals opened many people's eyes to the talent in the continent. However, while it may have some talent, it also has a lot of problems, a major one being money. Many countries do not have enough money for the basic necessities of life, never mind developing a football infrastructure. This means that it normally takes a lot of government intervention for the game to survive at the higher levels, though there is no doubting its popularity among the people.

Until the mid-nineties, African football was run on a more or less amateur basis, and certainly was amateur when compared to Europe, as there was little in the way of training facilities and the game's ruling bodies were full of bureaucrats and their egos. However, with the backing of FIFA things started to improve, as the powers that be realised the potential earnings to be made from the game through satellite television. In this way, the top African clubs have been influenced by the top European clubs, enviously eyeing the money they make and wanting a share for themselves. The 1990 World Cup also helped African players to move on, with the likes of George Weah, Abedi Pele, Finidi George and Tony Yeboah being able to show off their skills on a global stage, making them more marketable. The clubs themselves are slowly realising the possibilities opened by the influx of commercialisation, and in 1997 they created an African Champions League, to which, along with the African Nations Cup, the TV rights could be sold. The Champions League was the big success story, though, as it was the first time prize money was given to teams for appearances, each point gained and winning the tournament, helping many clubs survive.

Looking at football in the wider context of money-making, South Africa is the most advanced of the African nations, but it has not been easy. Allegations of corruption there reached a point where the Minister for Sport ordered a Supreme Court judge to look into the matter, and there were resignations as a result of what he found.

The African game is still hindered by two things. There is a lot of grassroots support for the game, but no actual development of those roots, and the political involvement is still too heavy-handed.

The lack of grassroots development is especially a problem when one considers that the top players are now jetting off to Europe to make more money, but there is no one of a similar calibre taking their place. This is leading to a drop in the number of people going to the matches, as they are not impressed with the entertainment on offer, which in turn reduces the money coming into the game. Unless some of the players who are going abroad just now come back home to coach when they retire from playing, the game may have difficulties maintaining its position.

The players who go abroad are also having to be more and more careful, as the first generation to move away found that while they were being paid good money by African standards, it was not as good as that of the European players and some felt exploited because of this. Come 2010, if African football does not start to look to the long term it is quite possible they will have national teams more or less comprised of players who do not actually play in their native country. The international game will be improving, but the local game will be floundering. And as always, it will be the fans who suffer because of this, having to watch poorer standards week in, week out, which could lead to the point where there are few local fans and people only get excited about the national game. (This would be an interesting contrast to the UK, where many fans dismiss national teams in favour of local ones.)

As mentioned above, South Africa should have been the hosts of the 2006 World Cup, but lost out at the last moment in scenes as dramatic as anything on the pitch. So what happened?

Twelve

2006 – Machiavellian Football

The drama surrounding the World Cup 2006 bid showed that anything football can do on pitch in terms of entertainment could be matched off the pitch. The bid to host the tournament saw moments of drama, farce and a last-minute winner – everything a 90-minute game can have.

Countries start their bids early to allow time for preparation. Bids for the 2006 tournament started in 1996, and the drama began in 1997 when Germany suddenly became vocal about a so-called gentleman's agreement that had allegedly been reached in the early nineties between themselves and England. At the start of the nineties England had announced plans to attempt to host the 1996 European Championships, which they were awarded, and the 1998 World Cup, which went to France. They had been looking at a double bill of the European Championships and the World Cup, providing a maximum return on the investment that was being used to upgrade the country's stadiums. The Germans claimed that the then FA chairman, Sir Bert Millichip and the then head of the German FA, Egidius Braun reached an agreement that Germany would back England's Euro '96 bid if England dropped any World Cup bid for 2006. The Germans say this was a gentleman's agreement and members of UEFA were present at the time to witness it. When England made a move for the 2006 event the Germans cried foul and this agreement was cited as the basis of their discontent. However, Millichip was no longer the FA chairman, which some claimed meant the FA could argue that as he was no longer in power any unofficial deals he had made would not be enforceable.

But the truth is there was no such agreement. Bert Millichip is not the villain that he has been perceived to be. What did happen was that in 1990 England announced plans for a double bid. Dropping the 1998 World Cup bid in favour of France was one reason they gained enough support for the Euro '96 bid, but FA bosses, including the then chief executive, Graham Kelly, said at the time that England would go back into the World Cup bidding if Euro '96 was deemed to be a financial and popular success. The only concession made was that England would pull out of the '98 bid; nothing more and nothing less. Sir Bert himself has always claimed that there was no deal with the Germans and that he did nothing against England's interests. In fact, an official FA meeting held in September 1996 shows how keen Sir Bert was for England to put in a bid. Others at the meeting included Graham Kelly, Euro '96 organiser Glenn Kirton, FA chairman Keith Wiseman and Football League chairman Gordon McKeag. At that meeting Sir Bert pointed out that England had put off the 1998 bid but that there was no reason not to bid for a later tournament, though it was not known who would back their bid. Germany was mentioned at the meeting and Sir Bert said nothing to those gathered that let them think there was a deal or anything that could cause embarrassment when the bid was announced. To further muddy the waters Kelly and Braun commented on their bids at a UEFA meeting in November that year, and the conversation between the men was said to be light-hearted. Indeed, at this point the Germans had not told anyone about the gentleman's agreement. They would not do so until 1997, months after England stated their intention to run for the tournament in 2006. However, the damage was done and UEFA backed the Germans ahead of the English.

For 2006 every country put in a spirited bid. Brazil was playing on being the home of 'sexy' football and having the most talented players in the world. What worked against it were worries over crime and poor infrastructure. In Europe, England and Germany were squaring off over bids, both having excellent infrastructures, and both saying they would have new national stadiums by 2006. England's bid cost £10.77 million, which came from the FA, the Premier League and Sport England's National Lottery World-Class Events fund, but it was seriously weakened by the German claims mentioned above. Even Manchester United did their bit, going to the World Club Challenge in Rio de Janeiro to boost England's chances, pulling out of the FA Cup in the process. They were under a lot of pressure to do so, having been told that not going would hamper the English bid.

And while there may not have been any underhand deals with the Germans, there were some involving the Scottish FIFA Vice-President David Wills. There were moves by the FA to have him replaced by the English Wiseman as the UK FIFA representative, which would give them some much-wanted clout at a high international level – something they did not have at that time. To do this they had to get two or three of the home countries to agree that they no longer wanted Wills in the job. The best way to do this was to promise development money in the millions. The Welsh went along with it, but the Irish said no and the Scots were considered above approaching for obvious reasons. The poor attempt at power-grabbing did the English no favours either when it came to the votes for the tournament. In an inquiry into the matter FIFA later cleared the Football Association of any incorrect or improper actions. Kelly and Wiseman were deemed by the FA to have acted without having consulted either the executive committee or the FA's full council, and the incident was dismissed as an error of judgement and nothing more.

Germany was operating a different style of wooing votes by being strategic in speaking to other confederations and countries to see what areas of mutual interest they had, instead of the more traditional method of visiting members, bringing them as guests to the country and so forth. Germany was also involved in scandal when it was claimed that they were blatantly trying to get the vote rigged (as compared to the more subtle ways others had done so in the past). It was claimed that the German bidding team was sending out letters offering cash and gifts to the FIFA delegates deciding which country would host the tournament. International members dismissed the letters due to their lack of authenticity and it was revealed after the vote that they had been sent by German satirical magazine *Titanic*. FIFA threatened to sue over the incident but did not pursue the matter.

In Africa, Morocco and South Africa were both battling for the tournament, though in a more civilised way than their European counterparts. Morocco's bid was severely weakened by poor infrastructure and facilities, while there were concerns about crime in South Africa. It was also pointed out at the time by those making bids for other countries that South Africa had never participated in the event.

A six-man FIFA inspection team travelled all over the world to examine the facilities. They were treated like royalty wherever they went, but despite their fine treatment in England – it cost £280,000 to take them around the country over a five-day period – they were not impressed, as their report into the country claimed England's facilities were worse than Germany's or South Africa's. The UK Government envoy for the bid, Tony Banks, called the report an insult to English football and he has never held back his opinion of who was to blame for it. He said, 'It was a studied insult to the whole of English football. We had problems on our hands because we've clearly got the UEFA machine working for Germany and the FIFA machine working for South Africa.

'It isn't FIFA, it's the FIFA machine. It's undoubtedly FIFA president Sepp Blatter and of course it's the FIFA inspection team. It's a blatant piece of political chicanery. If they really rated South Africa as being superior to England, then it wasn't an objective report.

'There are a lot of good political reasons, I can understand those as well, as to why South Africa should be favoured. I can understand that, but this is supposed to be a competition about who is best equipped to organise the World Cup in 2006 and that was England.'

As the date for the July announcement drew near, most people felt it was a race between Germany and South Africa. South Africa seemed to sew up the result before the official vote when Brazil pulled out of the bidding, leaving England, Germany, Morocco and South Africa. It was rumoured that Brazil was always on the verge of pulling out so that it could concentrate on a 2010 bid. If that was the case, it would have been looking for a quid pro quo agreement on voting. Brazil announced it would be pulling out and that the votes of Brazil, Argentina and Paraguay would be going to South Africa. It was suggested by football observers and those familiar with the politics surrounding World Cup bids that the vote for the 2010 tournament would see the favour returned as the Brazil, Argentina and Paraguay votes made South Africa the favourites for 2006. South African campaign leader Danny Jordaan admitted openly to the talks with Brazil and the South American delegates. He said:

'There are many examples in international sport when countries come together and discuss their mutual interest and see to what extent they can secure certain votes. We have gone down that route by talking to Brazil and many other confederations.'

England felt their chances were boosted after Brazil dropped out, as the Germans were worried that it would affect their bid. Franz Beckenbauer said:

'Not everybody is convinced that Germany is the ideal host for 2006 and what has happened between Brazil and South Africa is horse-trading, and now the vote will probably go against Germany.'

The first round saw Morocco eliminated. Germany had 10 votes, from Sweden, Italy, Belgium, Norway, Spain, Malta, Turkey, South Korea, Qatar and Thailand. South Africa had six, from FIFA president Sepp Blatter, Cameroon, Botswana, Brazil, Argentina and Paraguay. England had five, from Scotland, New Zealand, Costa Rica, the United States and Trinidad & Tobago, while Morocco's three came from Mali, Tunisia and Saudi Arabia. That result showed what the rest of UEFA thought of England, with the European bloc voting 7–1 against it in favour of Germany.

In round two England went out, as Saudi Arabia added its vote to the Germans, while Mali, Tunisia and all of England's backers, except Scotland and New Zealand, transferred their votes to South Africa.

With only two teams left, it was believed that South Africa had won, and that if there were a tie then Blatter would use his casting vote to give South Africa the tournament. Like many games of football, however, things did not go to plan. South Africa had the same 11 votes as Germany, Scotland transferred its vote to Germany and New Zealand abstained. All hell broke loose. The South Africans were distraught, while the Germans looked as if they thought it was a fake result. And it was all because of one man – Glasgow-born Charlie Dempsey, head of the Oceania confederation, which takes in Australia and New Zealand. The football world was shaken. Blatter – who had pinned everything on South Africa – was embarrassed and left politically weakened. To add to the intrigue, Dempsey left for home hours after the vote took place, explaining nothing. He then resigned his FIFA post and the Oceania presidency. He did eventually reveal what had happened and when he explained it, he showed how shadowy the whole process could be:

'The decision I made was for football and was not a political issue. The night before the FIFA meeting I received a number of anonymous calls which disturbed me. One of them was a threatening call.

'It had also been made clear to me by influential European interests that if I cast my vote in favour of South Africa there would be adverse effects for OFC in FIFA.

'My daughter obtained approval from six of the nine OFC members allowing me to abstain if I so chose and after careful consideration I decided to follow this course, acting on the knowledge that the majority of the executive committee had confirmed that I was now free to use my judgement to act in whatever I considered to be in the best interest of the OFC.

'I did not do it lightly. I do not make decisions like that lightly. I was under unsustainable pressure.'

As Dempsey was defending himself, there were accusations that FIFA had thrown away the opportunity to make football a truly global game. The African continent would now have to wait until 2010 if they were to stage the event, although they did consider going through the courts to see if the result could be overturned. After the result Danny Jordaan played on the emotions of all involved, saying:

'Africa is a member of the FIFA family and a family can't keep feeding one child and leaving the others to starve, which is what they have done. The World Cup would have made a major impact on our country, our continent and our lives.'

It was claimed by many in the African footballing scene that African football would suffer as there would not be enough money to keep top players, because clubs could not compete with the offers made by those in Europe. South African bid committee chairman Irvin Khoza hit out at Dempsey's claims that he was pressurised into abstention, saying Dempsey was not the type to be intimidated. Khoza and others also considered legal action against the result but Blatter told them that the result was perfectly legal and could not be challenged. He later told the press that the result was not the one he would have liked to have seen, iron-clad as it was. He said:

'It's the biggest disappointment of my career as an administrator. We had the chance to make history and we didn't take it. Europe had a great opportunity to make a grand gesture towards Africa. They didn't do it.'

The whole farce showed one thing if nothing else: that there had to be change. Unfortunately the country that will be worst hit by the proposed changes (that the World Cup should be awarded on a rotational basis to each of the six footballing confederations) is England, who may now have to wait a long time before it sees football coming home again. If the World Cup is rotated from now on, it will be more than 20 years before England has a chance of hosting it.

Blatter has also said that he will not be giving up power in 2002 and will stand for re-election so that he can oversee the next World Cup bidding. As he put it himself:

'I have conceded a goal, now it is up to me to equalise and score a winner.'

The bid process, spanning years and costing millions of pounds, has nothing to do with most fans, but again it is fans who will suffer, as they will have to traipse around the globe, going to countries that may care little for the game but are offering a lot of money to host it. While no one should criticise a democratic voting system, the whole procedure showed that perhaps there should be some wider form of discussion about the event that is meant to contain football's finest moments.

As an ironic footnote to the whole sorry saga, it is worth noting that Dempsey was replaced by Fiji's Sabu Khan, and Khan was voted through on a casting vote.

Thirteen

Football and Politics, Politics and Football

S port and politics are like potassium and water; when they meet there's nothing but trouble. In Europe it leads to that all-too-common phenomenon of people doing things behind the scenes, attempting to compromise to please everyone and ending up pleasing no one. Abroad – especially in African and Latin American countries – it has led to death, as social unrest has led to political statements against despots and governments being read out at sporting events, with riots ensuing as the authorities move in to quell those who go against the ruling powers.

This chapter will look at how politics has started to throw itself into the game like a burly tackler and how, as usual, the person who will lose out is the fan.

In most of the democratic world where football is played, there can be occasional chants of protest against governments at matches, normally if a politician is attending the game, but there is rarely more than that.

However, in continents such as Africa, large public gatherings like football matches are sometimes the only chance people have to speak out against less democratic regimes. One of the most tragic of these incidents took place in July 2000, when Zimbabwean police fired tear gas to control what they called 'unruly' fans watching a World Cup qualifying game between South Africa and Zimbabwe at the National Sports Stadium in Harare. In the resulting panic, 13 people died, including four children. It was revealed that the police had started firing after a few fans began chanting slogans backing the party in opposition to President Robert Mugabe.

Witnesses told reporters that many of the 50,000 crowd raised the opposition party's open-hand salute during the national anthem and continued to raise it throughout the match. The opposition Movement for Democratic Change's slogan 'chinja' – 'change' in the local Shona language – was also heard throughout the stadium.

Mugabe later said that a group of agitators had been planted at the stadium to shout slogans and display opposition party symbols before throwing bottles and other missiles onto the field, though witnesses said that the tear gas was fired all around the stadium and not just at the areas from where gestures were being made.

Football and politics also had a strange overlap when the Ivory Coast squad was detained – at gunpoint for a while, it is claimed – in 1999 at Zambarko camp, near Yamoussourko, after being put out of the African Nations Cup in the first round.

The Ivory Coast's exit from the tournament caused a massive public outcry and the army took the squad to the camp before stripping them of their passports and their mobile phones.

The official line is that it was a necessary exercise to ensure the players' safety, but many were not convinced of this and, while politicians criticised the detention, it took the intervention of FIFA president Sepp Blatter to get the players released.

In the UK and Europe political involvement involves more lawyers than bullets. Football has been used by politicians to 'show' that they are in touch with the working man, that they are normal people.

At the start of its elected term in 1997, New Labour supported populist subjects and considered no topic out of bounds. As some had expected, football came under its scrutiny, and within three months of coming to power it was announced that there would be a football task force headed by Conservative MP and football commentator David Mellor. The task force was instructed to look at several areas, including racism in football, wheelchair access to grounds, grassroots support for the game from top clubs and commercialism in sport. The resulting reports surprised no one, as they called for less racism, more access for disabled fans, and more grassroots work to be carried out to ensure the long-term future of the sport.

It was the final area of the task force's remit – commercialism in sport – that everyone knew would be controversial. David Mellor himself acknowledged that it was a contentious area, but no one guessed just how difficult it would be. Eventually two reports were published on the matter after it became obvious that there was a split between members of the task force as to how the game should treat commercialism.

However, there was some consensus, as both reports said that with the millions of pounds pouring into football, strict codes of practice over issues such as replica kit sales and ticket prices needed to be introduced. The main report recommended a radical programme of reform, most notably the establishment of a Football Audit Commission, which would be a permanent football regulator, and an ombudsman-type figure to report on individual complaints, while the second report called for a system with greater emphasis on self-regulation.

The first report (from here on known as the FAC report) also stressed the importance of keeping ticket prices low, demanding that all clubs stretch the range on offer, so fans paying the highest prices would effectively cross-subsidise those paying new, lower ones. Home and away fans should also be charged the same prices. The report said that offering 10 per cent of all tickets at half price for the under-16s and those in full-time education would help keep the young and poor interested in the game. It was also suggested that the lowest priced tickets should be increased annually by no more than the Retail Price Index and that the number of season tickets should be limited to encourage support from those who cannot afford to buy one.

The FAC report also recommended that all replica strips have a minimum lifespan of two full seasons, with the collar carrying a date showing when it would be replaced. Clubs were also to consult supporters on major decisions, such as ground relocation, stock market flotation and major share sales. All of this would be overseen by the Football Audit Commission, which would have a code of practice and set the minimum standards for how clubs would treat their fans. However, the other report, which was mainly by task force members representing football authorities, recommended that an independent scrutiny panel composed of independent members to enforce a code of conduct would be the best way forward. This panel would produce an annual report on the game, after working for a maximum of four weeks a year.

Sports Minister Kate Hoey was left to try and balance a way out of this. Her initial comments suggested that compromise would indeed be the way forward:

'One of the tasks of the government is to strike a balance between the necessary business interests of clubs and those of supporters, without whom clubs would not exist.'

At the time of going to press, it looks as though there will be some form of overseeing body created, but it will not be a statutory body. According to Dave Boyle at the Football Supporters' Association (FSA), current regulation will do for now as long as it is not just talk:

'The FSA have been working hard on the issue of regulation. We've campaigned for a statutory body but it seems we won't have that to begin with.

'Whatever it turns out to be, we'll be pressing it to get involved in issues such as ticket prices and distribution and to use its power and influence to peg back the game as a whole, to remind them [clubs] that their status as global businesses is secondary to their participation in a deep-rooted national game watched live by people from all incomes.

'We've also got the majority task force [report] and its 63 recommendations, which we will use as the benchmark to judge the regulator, whatever form it takes. The majority report is a good starting point, seeing as it was agreed by many different people coming from various perspectives, and represents a good "to-do list" to be getting on with.'

Indeed it is a good 'to-do list', but the danger is that like many wish lists, the things that the fans want the most may be the things they never get.

While the task force had the duty of trying to change the game of football for the better, another political body – with no specific loyalty to football – has been getting more and more involved, and not necessarily for the best reasons. That body is the European Commission. While the task force reports could have positive implications for football in Britain (if certain people genuinely work for change and stop looking after their own interests), politics at the European level are capable of totally transforming the game, to the point where hundreds of clubs across Europe could go out of business.

At this point people may wonder what politics has to do with court rulings. It is this: the original laws on employment came from politicians who did not have the foresight to see that areas like sport in general and football in particular may need some form of exemption. Just as many in the financial industry see football as just another business and try to treat it as such, there are those who argue that football is just another employment industry and it is in this arena that politics is transforming Europe.

Politicians have always been happy to wave a scarf to get votes, but when it comes to the heavier matters involving football, they shy away. There was no political pressure for convictions over the Hillsborough tragedy, nothing has ever been done about Scotland's sectarian problem and across the world there have been only knee-jerk attempts at dealing with hooliganism. Change can start with the fans, yes, but it takes political will for things to really improve as laws need to be made to really make a difference.

For years before Hillsborough, clubs could have upgraded facilities but did not, and afterwards it was a combination of the government-backed Taylor Report, political pressure and political announcements about funding that created change.

Politicians may set up laws with the best of intentions, but they have to look at how the real world – and different aspects of the real world – is affected. They also have to start taking more responsibility when it comes to the game and making harder judgements, perhaps even setting up independent football regulators to safeguard the spirit of the game.

European court involvement in football first reached everyone's attention in 1996, when Jean-Marc Bosman took UEFA to the European courts to contest a ruling that said that despite having ended a contract with a team, a player could not move to another club in the EU without a transfer fee being paid. Bosman argued that this held players back, as a club could hold on to them out of self-interest, despite the fact that the term of employment was up. By arguing in very general terms, which made football sound like working for any employer, and using the laws that the European Commission politicians had devised regarding labour movement, he won the case and UEFA rules changed to allow a huge movement of players on free transfers around Europe. Wages went up as a result, as clubs fought to keep their top players, but ironically Bosman himself faded into obscurity.

It was felt that the game could survive this, but in 2000 the European Commission and football met again when Italian side Perugia complained to the EC that paying a transfer fee for a player who was still under contract was illegal under the Treaty of Rome, because it infringed an individual's right to freedom of movement. The effect of this on the game, where players and managers would only have to announce they were leaving and perhaps work a period of notice, was immediately realised and football authorities mounted what is regarded as one of the largest efforts ever to preserve the status quo. There were a number of worries around this. First, clubs spend millions on developing new talent every year, signing up players from an early age in the hope of that player either turning out to be a superstar for them or someone who brings in transfer fees when moving on, recouping some of the outlay made on him. However, if players could just hand in their notice then clubs will be a lot more reluctant to spend large sums on developing new talent and may just find it more convenient and cheaper to let other, smaller clubs do all the hard work of training players, grooming them and so on and then come in and get the player they want. It also means that any player who wants to leave a club can, knowing that another club has, or is about to, make him an offer, hand in his resignation and go, without owing the club anything for all the training and time they have given him. Of course, this goes both ways. Players could also find themselves being sacked for poor performance.

FIFA general secretary Michel Zen-Ruffinen claimed that football would die unless it was argued successfully that the Perugia case be turned down. In August 2000 it was turned down but just as football chiefs heaved a sigh of relief the EC announced that major changes would have to be made to the current transfer regulations because they were against employment law. This did not signal any change in domestic transfers as the EC could only look at international transfers (they do not have any authority over domestic matters). The saga then twisted when Sepp Blatter said that paying transfer fees for players over the age of 24 was 'a thing of the past'. However, UEFA chief executive Gerhard Aigner said the matter was not closed and they would fight to keep transfer fees.

By September FIFA had set up a transfer task force to enter into discussions with the EC to try and find a legal solution. The task force included UEFA vice-president Per Omdal, Gerhard Aigner, Michel Zen-Ruffinen, Spanish League general secretary Pedro Tomas, German FA vice-president Gerhard Mayer-Vorfelder and chairman of European players' union FIFPro and chief executive of the Professional Footballers' Association, Gordon Taylor. National states also started to get involved at this point, with Tony Blair and German prime minister Gerhard Schroeder calling for the Commission not to do away with the system. All 51 members of UEFA united and issued a statement saying that if need be they would take this battle through the courts. A number of Europe's top coaches, including Sir Alex Ferguson, Arsène Wenger, Carlo Ancelotti, Fabio Capello, Hector Cuper, Sven-Goran Eriksson and Lorenzo Serra Ferrer, put out a statement asking for sense. It read:

'For the team-building process, the cornerstone of sport, it is essential that team managers can count on their players for a period of three to four years.'

By October the optimism had gone as Gordon Taylor threatened to quit the task force because he did not believe that the concerns of his members – players – were being looked at. He then did quit after the proposals of FIFPro were not discussed, and he became involved in a blazing row with Sepp Blatter. The task force also conceded that the diverse nature of individual European employment laws meant that a unified transfer system would be impossible to achieve. Taylor was then accused of turning traitor and backing the new proposals to change the system. The accusations of a U-turn started with an article he wrote for *The Observer* newspaper, in which he argued that players, clubs and fans benefited from the existing stability of players' contracts and that the change would be disastrous for the game. The problem came when this was contrasted with FIFPro's policy, which wants the EC to introduce a new transfer system. However, the accusations levelled at Taylor were harsh: if, as is claimed, FIFPro's proposals were not being looked at, what other options did he have to make his point? He had to look after his members and he has done that. What he has to do in his job may not be his own personal, private opinion but he is being paid to look after players' interests and he should be applauded for being principled, something a few politicians – especially in the European Commission context – should learn from, considering the scandals there have been over corruption in the European political system.

Also, as was pointed out at the time, what may be best for the players may not necessarily be best for football, but the players may just be thinking of themselves, as most workers do when considering their options.

For players the proposed new system would have pros and cons. It would be good for young or talented players wanting to move around a lot, and would drive up wages, but older players would be worried by the potential lack of security. Players could be sacked and only paid for their length of notice. The chief benefit to players would be that managers could no longer artificially raise their transfer fees to prevent them from leaving, as sometimes happens now. If a manager did so, the player could simply hand in his notice. Some feel that the system could lead to the end of youngsters coming into the game, as managers could just sign existing players, but there is little evidence to support this, as clubs need young players to try to boost their future prospects. In that sense, doing away with fees would see the return of more players wanting to play 'for the jersey', the team they grew up with. It would also bring agents into the game more, as they would try to negotiate more deals more often for players they represent. However, this could be offset by clubs attempting to get players to sign long-term or 'exclusive working rights' contracts, which would be the equivalent of today's contracts.

The Manufacturing, Science and Finance union (MSF), a union for skilled and professional people, even got involved in the UK. A statement from them read:

'Ending the right of clubs to charge fees for players over the age of 24 would mean a disaster for smaller British clubs in the lower divisions.

'In the long term it would mean the second and third divisions would be unsustainable. Thousands of jobs depend on the operation of football clubs around the country, as does the social cohesion of many towns in Britain.

'MSF, representing the 92 English and Welsh club managers through the League Managers' Association (LMA), fears the system of youth development, crucial to the survival of smaller clubs, will be decimated by the EC's plan. All 92 clubs operate Youth Academies or Centres of Excellence to bring on the stars of tomorrow.

'It costs in excess of £3 million a year to run a Youth Academy. Ten full-time coaching staff plus an education officer and top-class training facilities are required to keep standards high. If smaller clubs are unable to see a return on this investment through the transfer system youth development in football will wither and die.

'Without the development system British football will suffer, our national sides will find it hard to compete on the world stage and many of our smaller clubs will go to the wall.'

Agent Jon Smith, who represents players like Nwankwo Kanu, Steve Howey and Les Ferdinand, thinks the current system will come down sooner rather than later, as a single court case arguing that footballers are the last of the bonded employees would result in players handing in their notice and leaving after serving a suitable period of time. Bayern Munich vice-president Karl-Heinz Rummenigge said that abolishing transfer fees would have a devastating effect on European football:

'If the European Union succeeds and transfer fees are suddenly cut down, the salaries will go up and it will lead to the worst débâcle football has ever experienced.'

In the run-up to a deal a number of compromises were suggested, including using the Spanish system, where clubs signing a player specify the fee that must be paid for him to move on. Other suggestions included bans on international transfers for players under 18, unless their families emigrate, and a compensation package for players who move from their first professional club between the ages of 18 and 23. Problems with these proposals included the fact that the German Supreme Court had already ruled such compensation schemes to be illegal, so it would not – indeed could not – have worked in Germany.

However, the system could have been saved if UEFA and FIFA had argued that most transfers are based on national labour laws and national collective bargaining arrangements, which are areas where the EC cannot interfere, so it would have been powerless.

Then FIFA said it wanted players to be given the right to terminate contracts with a club over 'just sporting cause' like a disagreement over coaching tactics. FIFA's proposals would also have meant players giving just three months' notice when they wanted to leave a club. UEFA favoured five-year contracts, with players tied to clubs for an initial three-year period. To make matters worse, FIFA then started bypassing UEFA and dealing directly with the European Commission.

However, as *Football Inc.* went to press, a solution of sorts was found. It was announced that the European Commission had agreed a new system with FIFA and UEFA in principal that could be up and running for the 2001/02 season.

The system would allow players who had been at a club for longer than three years to terminate their contract by giving three months' notice. The player would be able to break the contract before that but that would lead to the possibility of suspension for up to one year and also a fine.

For players under 23 rates are to be established for each national association. Clubs would be compensated depending upon which division and league they are in and also how long the young player was with them.

A system of compensation for smaller clubs across Europe was also being proposed for when their players move on to greater things, though specifics had not been ironed out at the time of going to press. Compensation amounts and other related issues would be dealt with by the Dispute Resolution Chamber and the Football Arbitration Panel, both of wich will have members proposed by players and the clubs.

However, FIFPro refused to accept the agreement and hinted that it may launch a legal challenge. But top players may actually like the arrangement as clubs could be facing the prospect of having to renegotiate with them every year, as without pay rises the players could leave the club.

What was also unclear was whether the three-month notice period would apply only during the football season. For example, a player could say he was intending to stay at a club, then change his mind and serve his notice out during the summer break, which would mean that the club he was leaving would be paying him three months' wages without getting any benefit. However, if he handed in his notice in January, the club would still have him for three months of the season.

In this author's opinion the whole arrangement smacks of consensus by committee and will open up cans of worms for years to come and probably lead to more reform within a matter of years.

And who suffers most here? The fans, who will have to pay out for the wage increases, and the lower clubs, which are not only the lifeblood of the game, but in many cases are also staffed and run by fans.

The old system of transfers may not have been perfect but as time goes on, it appears that it may have been the best system. One thing that is becoming clear though is that the legal system is anything but the best for the game.

John Williams of the Sir Norman Chester Centre for Football Research thinks that the whole issue of intervention can be a tricky area:

'Broadly speaking supporter campaigners seem to say free market involvement is a bad thing and broadly speaking I agree with them that more regulation is probably required, and that if you allow the free market to rush in then what you get is a very distorted and imbalanced game.

'The problem then becomes at what point do you intervene in the ordinary operations of the free market? You might say that when Manchester United signed Dwight Yorke from Aston Villa a couple of seasons back that was the unacceptable face of the free market because he was on contract, was happy at Villa and then suddenly Manchester United come in and he wants a way to move. United were able to buy him because they were richer and stronger than Aston Villa.

'Now I don't think Manchester United fans would object to the operation of the free market in that respect. Without signing Dwight Yorke they wouldn't have won the European Cup in 1999 and that raises a very important empirical and practical question: at what point do you regulate and in what ways do you regulate?

'That becomes difficult when you've got UK clubs competing in Europe and it seems to me that any regulation would have to be Europe-wide. If that is done then I think there are some prospects for success but I think we're a long way off from regulation on that scale.

'It's interesting seeing the fans worry about the free market and the corporatisation of the sport but then when the EU – the public body – wants to intervene they say "football's a business, it's different from other types of business, leave it alone".

'The economics of this don't make any sense. Those who claim it is transfer fees that are keeping the smaller clubs alive clearly haven't looked in any great detail at the economics of how much transfer money on average smaller clubs take.

'In fact it would be much more efficient if we got rid of the transfer system and the larger clubs gave a percentage of every TV deal to the smaller clubs – a trickle down. That would make a lot more sense if we were really interested in the survival of the smaller clubs and it would be much more efficient rather than relying on a transfer system which can provide very small and patchy amounts of income for the smaller clubs.

'Losing the transfer system might have some positive effects – it would limit the activities of agents for one thing, limit the corruption that goes on around transfer deals and it would also offer the opportunity – though whether clubs take this up is another thing – to invest their money in different ways, to spend what used to be transfer money in different ways.

'I don't think losing the transfer system is the end of the world. I don't think anyone has really looked at what the effects of losing it might be.'

November 2000 saw another landmark decision involving the movement of players from Eastern Europe, when it was decreed by the European Court that players from countries with associate accords with the European Union (EU) had the same rights as any player in the EU.

The case involved Russian midfielder and Celta Vigo player Valery Karpin, who pointed out that football rules stated that clubs could only have so many non-EU players. This, he claimed, was something that discriminates against employees on the grounds of nationality – which is not allowed under the associate accords – so he should have the same rights as any EU player.

The decision could see Romanian, Croatian, Turkish and Slovenian players move a lot more freely as these countries also have associate accords with the EU.

While there is no doubting the good intentions of the Bosman ruling all those years ago, if football is forced to work in the same way as any other employer we will see – as in every other area of employment – a few doing well and the others being paid an average wage. In decades to come, and if football funding slows down or even reverses, then we may see all football players being paid average wages. However, where will this money come from? From television rights, which at the end of the day are underwritten by fans; from sponsorship, again eventually paid for by fans; and from generally increased costs, again coming out of the pocket of the fan.

The EC might think that it is doing some good in looking at the game and how the game treats the workforce, but perhaps it should be a bit more forward-looking and see how the game treats the consumers, who, after all, pay the EC members' wages.

Part Three

The Ugly Game –
How fans lost their game

Fourteen

Hooliganism

Big business, corrupt players, television rescheduling games away from 3 pm on a Saturday, poor refereeing. All of these things are said to be bad for the game, but if there is anything that has tarnished the game more, it is hatred – hatred for others because of their religion or their skin colour or even just because of the team they support. Hooligans will hate for the smallest reason and at times they have been the most destructive element in the game.

A football fan is passionate about his team, but it is a good passion; a hooligan is a distortion of a fan, his passion is to hate.

Contrary to popular belief, England was not the birthplace of hooliganism. The first incident occurred in 1908 when Manchester United players were attacked on the pitch during a game in Hungary. The following year there was a riot involving 6,000 spectators at Hampden Park in Glasgow, and there are records of incidents in the thirties, forties and fifties in France, Germany, Italy and Sweden. At the end of the fifties there were attacks and running riots in Turkey after games. In one game between Kayseri and Sivas 42 people were killed, over half of them stabbed to death. More than 600 people were injured in the battles following the game and it took the police days to restore order.

What is now dubbed hooliganism did not start to materialise in England until the 1960s. By then, there was already major violence in countries like Yugoslavia, where there were a range of attacks in the mid-fifties, when fans attacked each other with, among other things, hammers, pieces of wood and metal bars. As violence in England started to rocket, English clubs found themselves becoming dominant on the international and world stage; England won the World Cup in 1966 and Manchester United the European Cup in 1968.

During the seventies, English teams continued to do well in Europe. Nationalism was also rife, heightened by the success of the national and domestic teams. Some sociologists argued that as the game was increasingly televised – which meant that the hooligans' actions were televised – others were inspired to act in the same way. Violence begat violence.

And while English hooligans caused trouble abroad, it was nothing compared to the trouble at home. The reason for this was a simple economic fact. Holidays abroad – especially just for a few days – were not as commonplace or affordable as they would become and Britain's rail network at the time made getting about easy.

One can only speculate as to what sort of trouble there may have been abroad if the English could have afforded to travel there, but what is known is that on Saturdays in England during the seventies, train travel was risky if you weren't with a bunch of friends going to the football. Hooligans would pick on fans travelling if they were alone or in a smaller group than they were, and the situation cost British Rail thousands in carriage repairs and redecoration.

The fact that whenever hooligans were caught the punishments amounted to little more than slaps on the wrist did not help. The courts seemed unwilling to deal with a problem they felt was down to the football authorities to sort out, while the football authorities felt it was a social problem. The courts' and the football authorities' unwillingness to deal with the problem allowed it to flourish, and by the 1980s it was getting out of hand.

Just as the eighties began with hooliganism becoming a major problem, it was also the start of what would be known as the Thatcher era, and Margaret Thatcher caused problems for football, both directly and indirectly.

First, her party, the Conservatives, had never been associated with the working-class man, who at that time was still the main football fan. Second, as her anti-union attitude would show, she had a loathing of anything that gave the working class strength and unity of purpose. Third, her party worked on the assumption that money was all that mattered.

The conditions that were created at football grounds in the early eighties – high fences and pen-like areas – as part of their response to hooliganism seemed to be of no real concern to the Government. Their attitude was that if people wanted to act like animals, then they would be treated like animals. Unfortunately no thought was given to what would happen in an emergency and this would play a part in one of British football's most tragic moments, in 1987, in a stadium called Hillsborough.

As the eighties progressed, it became evident that a new type of hooligan was emerging, one who looked quite normal and not like the stereotypical skinhead psychopath. The 'casual' was born. He was given his name because he (very few, if any, hooligans have ever been female) wore the best clothing at the time, such as jumpers that had previously only been associated with golfers. Many of them had good jobs that a lot of working-class people aspired to. Often casuals were working-class people who had managed to benefit from Thatcher's reign. They had been to college or had some good school qualifications, had managed to get into a decent job, perhaps had even bought a house from the council. Casuals never wore club colours. They became known by reputation – most groups of casuals hung about in small numbers, which made it easier for someone to become a big fish in a small pond. Football authorities could see the reasons for the casuals' rise. At one point the secretary of the Football League, Alan Hardaker, told Thatcher to 'get your hooligans out of my game'; Kenneth Clark has admitted that the Iron Lady looked on football supporters as the enemy. In Britain this situation continued throughout the 1980s. The hooligans were treated with contempt, but little effort was made to understand the problem, although academic works on the subject began to be published. Casuals were also beginning to write books, glorifying themselves and regaling the reader with tales of violence, although a few did actually provide psychological insights into what created a hooligan.

In the attempt to eradicate hooliganism no one defended the fans, and they were treated terribly in stadiums as well as before and after matches. Relationships between fans and the police were very much on an 'us and them' level. The average fan was suffering because of the violent minority.

In the early eighties the mainstream opinion in Britain was that hooliganism was confined to Britain; this perception changed on 29 May 1985 when 39 fans died and more than 200 were injured in the Heysel Stadium, Brussels.

On that day, the European Cup final between Liverpool and Juventus had an uneventful build-up, with 60,000 fans making their way into the stadium. Many had spent the day drinking, as was the norm for football fans. But an hour before kick-off things went from being boisterous and slightly troublesome to disastrous, culminating in an incident that would never be forgotten, both on Merseyside and across the world.

At around 7 pm local time, a wall separating Liverpool followers from Juventus supporters in sector Z of the stadium collapsed. The full truth of what happened that evening will probably never be known, as no major inquiry was ever held to determine the facts. What is known is this: the fans were provoking each other, each side giving as good as it got, and bottles were thrown. Some people tried to get more involved in the trouble that was brewing. However, many people were trying to get away from the trouble. Their escape was blocked by a brick wall, which some of them scaled. This wall gave way under the pressure and collapsed.

Blame for the event has been cast everywhere. Some Liverpool fans claimed that Juventus supporters were hurling stones and other missiles, while the Belgian authorities were criticised for poor organisation, lack of policing and lack of crowd control. Juventus fans claimed Liverpool fans had been drunk and started to pick fights and throw objects. They claim the crush that started the barriers and walls collapsing was caused by people trying to escape rioting Liverpool fans. UEFA felt that blame lay with the Liverpool fans and banned all English clubs indefinitely from participating in any of the three European competitions. This ban was lifted five years later.

Heysel forced people to confront what was happening in towns across Britain every week. They were no longer able to dismiss the violence as testosterone-driven high jinks. It was no longer something the Thatcher-voting middle class could ignore.

Although some tried to dismiss it as the underclass showing their natural thuggery and yob mentality, the problem had become so bad that something had to be done. In true 1980s style there was a knee-jerk reaction: stadiums were made into pens and alcohol was blamed for a lot of the trouble. It was made an offence to carry alcohol on trains and buses being used to take passengers to or from a designated event, including football matches. It was also made an offence to possess intoxicating liquids, glass/metal containers and fireworks in a ground during a designated event. Unfortunately nothing positive was done, mainly because the Government did not care for the followers of football or their traditional backgrounds. Fans were treated even more like animals and this had terrible repercussions less than two years later in Hillsborough. What happened there is made all the more tragic by the fact that a Home Office report in 1986 laid a good part of the blame for hooliganism on the condition of football stadiums.

As the 1980s drew to a close domestic hooliganism seemed to be decreasing, but trouble caused by English fans abroad seemed to be on the increase. The Football Spectators Act 1989 allowed courts to impose restriction orders on people convicted of football-related offences in order to prevent them travelling to international matches. Failure to report to a police station at roughly the time the match was taking place was an offence. Football-related offences took in a diverse number of crimes including ticket touting and violence and public disorder, including racist chanting, committed within the 24 hours on either side of a domestic match, or longer for overseas matches.

As European football continued without the English, watchers of the game started to note that hooliganism was not an English-only problem. Many countries had a hardcore element that enjoyed the trouble it could cause.

In France, hooliganism took off in the early 1980s, but French police were always determined to clamp down on it. The French gangs are named 'kops' and 'ultras'. Ultras did not take off nationwide until after 1985, with fighting and vandalism in areas like Paris, Marseille and Bordeaux becoming more regular. A lot of French hooliganism has been linked to fascism and racism. Amongst the fans with the worst reputations are those following Paris St-Germain and Olympique de Marseille. Hooligans associated with Bordeaux, Metz, Nantes and St Etienne also have a reputation for violence.

In Belgium, after the Heysel disaster the authorities started looking at the problem a lot more seriously. It was discovered that a lot of the trouble was coming from the followers of only a few teams – Anderlecht, Antwerp, Beerschot, Charleroi, Clubb Brugge, RWDM and Standard Liege.

The Belgian authorities were determined to make sure that a tragedy like Heysel could never happen again, which explains their heavy-handed approach to football fans, which continues to this day (though it has relaxed a little since 1987, when 600 police guarded 300 Scottish fans during an international game).

In Spain, fights between supporters of different clubs are tied up with politics. For example, Atletico Bilbao gets a lot of support from Basques and anti-fascists living in other parts of Spain, who fight the supporters of clubs from other regions of the country and those that are seen as fascistic. As such much of the trouble that breaks out at matches is not described as football related. However, when there has been trouble on an international scale, FIFA has not been slow to react. For example, a 1987 match in Madrid between Real Madrid and Naples was played in a completely empty stadium as a result of disciplinary measures taken by FIFA in response to what they called 'the hooligan excesses' of Madrid supporters.

Europe has also had trouble throughout the nineties, though there has been an overall fall since the start of that decade.

In the Italian Serie A figures fell from the frighteningly high number of incidents that marked the start of the decade, when police detained more than 2,000 people in one season. However, the violence has not vanished, but has spread from the fans of Serie A to lower leagues and Southern Italy. Even in Serie A, however, there have been a number of events that remind the authorities they cannot be complacent, such as the 1995 stabbing to death of a 24-year-old Genoa fan by an AC Milan supporter.

In the Netherlands around 10 per cent of games in the top league now attract some form of trouble, though things have calmed down from the violent heyday of the late 1980s and early 1990s. Most of the violence involves fans of the high-profile teams like Ajax and PSV Eindhoven. The worst troublemakers in the Netherlands are known as Side or Siders, with each team having their own. For example, at Ajax they are the F-Side, while PSV's fans are called the L-Side and Feyenoord's troublemakers are known as the Vak-S and Vak-R. In December 2000, rioting in the Dutch city of Den Bosch saw a football hooligan shot dead by police as he approached an officer while carrying a large knife.

Some of Germany's problems are fuelled by neo-Nazism and problems caused by the reunification of the country. The main German teams all have gangs of hooligans attached to them. Bayern Munich has the Munich Service Crew, Düsseldorf has the First Class, Hertha Berlin has Wannsee Front, Schalke 04 has Gelsen Szene, to name just a few. Germany has had higher numbers of hooligans – or at least more high profile – than many other European countries, and the authorities have never had any hesitation in clamping down on them. However, there is still an element of trouble and German authorities have voiced their concerns that the troublemakers may wish to emulate the English model of following the national team, rather than just having domestic fights. For example, over the last few years German and Dutch hooligans have had running battles with each other.

There is little football violence in the Scandinavian countries. Likewise in Switzerland there is very little trouble, and when it takes place it is mainly between rival domestic clubs like Servette FC and FC Sion.

In the Czech Republic Sparta Prague has been the club most associated with hooliganism. However, it has diminished since the authorities brought in a number of measures including separate sections for away fans, giving police the right to search spectators, the banning of club flags and scarves and serving a weaker variety of beer at football grounds.

Hooliganism is not just a European disease – we have already seen the problems that Asia has. In South America, the Argentinian players' union Futbolistas Argentinos Agremiados went on strike in 2000 in protest at a brutal assault on players by rival fans. It took place at the end of the Excursionistas v Comunicaciones match, in the Metropolitan C Division, when local fans broke onto the field of play and attacked the visiting players. Many of them were beaten or kicked, and one, Adrian Barrionuevo, suffered head injuries, was hospitalised and later said he planned to quit the game because of it.

In 2000, first division Argentinian club Los Andes was forced to abandon a practice game when a gang of armed hooligans took to the pitch. The club coach Miguel Angel Russo threatened to resign if the club was not given safer facilities to train in, which it was.

Hooligans, known in Argentina as *barrabravas* (fierce gangs) are a feared group. The death toll involving the *barrabravas* makes chilling reading: eight deaths in the 1970s, 16 in the 1980s and 41 in the 1990s. What makes the situation even worse is the claim by some South Americans that some *barrabravas* work for their clubs and have a mutually beneficial relationship, with the hooligans sticking up for a manager or player – and not just by cheering for them on the terraces. Argentinian player and manager Daniel Passarella once said that the authorities did nothing until there were deaths, though little seems to change even then. Very few of the *barrabravas* go to jail or are even arrested for any incidents, as these people operate like the mafia. It is not all pitch invasions and terrace battles; they also work behind the scenes and, more importantly, when no witnesses are about. The rising drug problem in Argentina makes the situation even worse and football commentators who watch the area wonder how bad the situation will become in coming years.

Back in Britain, as the nineties wore on football administrators hoped that the scourge of hooliganism was behind them. One organisation that helped stop the trouble was the National Hooligan Hotline (0800 515 495). The creation of a Football Section in the National Criminal Intelligence Service (NCIS) was another improvement.

The Football Section acts as a permanent central co-ordinating point for intelligence coming into the NCIS from Football Intelligence Officers attached to league teams around the country. These officers are drawn from local police forces that have built links with their local football clubs. The Football Section also has a database that contains details of people involved, or suspected of being involved, in football-related violence or disorder. According to the NCIS, close co-operation between police and football clubs, the impact of all-seater stadiums, CCTV surveillance, better stewarding and an intelligence-led response to violence all played a part in reducing hooliganism in the UK.

And while some European countries are now emulating the working methods of the Football Section, hoping to repeat its success, Belgium has carried out one of the most major attempts to eradicate trouble – by introducing the fancard. It is now obligatory to display a fancard – which is applied for through the Belgian football authorities, who check for convictions – when buying a ticket, which means a supporter's background can be checked. Hooligans don't receive a fancard, so they're unable to enter football grounds. All fans have their own smartcard and PIN. Cardholders are legally responsible for their smartcards, which cannot be lent or given to anyone else. Each smartcard entitles its owner to one ticket per match. Troublemakers will have their smartcards refused or disabled.

When English clubs were let back into Europe the fans were well behaved, with only a small number getting involved with the police, and then normally for non-violent reasons like being excessively drunk, language misunderstandings and so on. While at home and abroad the authorities were congratulating themselves for the drop in hooliganism, there may have been a different reason that had nothing to do with the police and their initiatives – the mainstream use of drugs. This phenomenon has been studied by a number of people, including Stirling University's Rowdy Yates. He has noted the links between drugs and football over the last 15–20 years:

'Supply lines of drugs involving football have been quite interesting. For instance, you could see connections between Aberdeen casuals and a group working out of Liverpool and the Trafford end of Manchester United and they were purchasing large quantities of ecstasy, most of which was then going out of Dyce airport in Aberdeen and most of it eventually finding its way into Ibiza. Part of the thinking was that people coming out of Dyce were less likely to be implicated in the drug scene as compared to other airports like Glasgow, Edinburgh and so on.'

According to Yates, there were two significant developments in the early-to-mid-eighties that affected football's relationship with drugs and hooliganism.

'One was the whole business of middle-class interest in football, with the game becoming "sexy" and the other thing was the development of the dance and drug culture, and the two things brought football together.

'It brought clubbers onto the terraces and that was a fairly significant development, so by about the mid-eighties there was the beginning of a bizarre culture where you had things like Leeds supporters wearing T-shirts saying "LSD and 2 Es", Man City fans floating inflatable bananas at matches, and ridiculous symbols like that were picked up by other fans afterwards.'

The two events appear to have coincided. According to Yates:

'When the clubs got back into Europe, Man Utd fans were spending a lot on cannabis on away legs like games in Amsterdam and they were coming back as if they had been to Goa.'

Yates feels that while drugs played a part in the reduction of hooliganism, it is an over-simplification to say that they were all that was involved:

'Some people argue that the decline in hooliganism over many years was because of the widespread introduction of cannabis and there's something to be said for that, but the links are always more complex than that. Certainly there is clear evidence of those on the terraces becoming more and more aware of cannabis in particular at the same time as there is a pretty marked decline in football hooliganism. The middle-class impact on the game is still to be measured. I certainly think it was responsible for the removal of standing terraces. Without a significant middle-class audience you would have retained standing terraces. It's pretty clear that a lot of those middle-class drugs are being used in football as cannabis has become pretty much ubiquitous among young people.'

By the mid-nineties the game had calmed down. Reported violent incidents were down and the fact that the game was becoming more and more middle class – no doubt combined with the bans on alcohol and the increased use of other drugs – was making things more peaceful. However, with football coming 'home' to England in 1996 there were fears that it would be more than just the game that would be back.

Concern about widespread hooliganism with all the different nationalities at Euro '96 turned out to be unfounded. There were some incidents, but the overall impression was that hooliganism was still on the wane.

It took two years for that opinion to change. During the World Cup in France in 1998 there were running battles in a number of cities, with the English fighting anyone who would take them on. The French police waded in with a determination and severity that told everyone there would be no softly-softly approach. After the tournament, the usual soundbites were made about how to combat the problem, but little was done. In the UK, trouble started to rise. At the end of the 1990s, the number of arrests, 3,341, was the highest in years, though the 1999/2000 season showed a slight drop to 3,138. However, that season saw the number of incidents reported to the NCIS by Football Intelligence Officers and the number of post-match investigations rise significantly.

But do the figures tell the whole story? Apparently not, according to Bryan Drew, the Head of Strategic and Specialist Intelligence at the NCIS:

'Statistics for football-related offences have, in themselves, become an unreliable indicator in providing a true assessment of football hooliganism. There are many occasions when a major incident of disorder – quite often well away from a football ground – will lead to comparatively few or even no arrests.

'Conversely, a police commander might well decide to take action, in order to prevent disorder, that might result in a large number of arrests.

'The reports from the Football Intelligence Officers show the opportunistic and violent problem that we still face. Hooliganism is not just a football problem. The activities of drunken young Englishmen can be seen on continental beaches and outside English city and country pubs during the summer months. But football, with its inherent tribalism, passions and loyalties, has always been a beacon for such boorish behaviour.

'The numbers of people involved in individual incidents do, on the whole, remain comparatively small but we've seen an increasing number with larger groups getting involved.'

Scotland also has problems. The issue of the Old Firm will be dealt with in Chapter 16, but other clubs are also known for fighting. For example, during the 1999/2000 season, a running battle involving 150 people in the centre of Aberdeen caused a number of people to be hospitalised. According to Grampian police, it was organised hooliganism, with Chelsea groups being involved with Rangers hooligans and teaming up against Aberdeen fighters. There is a long-standing animosity between the two Scottish sides, and both had feared teams of fighters during the heyday of casuals in the 1980s. During that same season Leeds fans travelled up two weeks in a row for running battles around Glasgow, particularly in the East End, to fight with anyone who would take them on.

Just prior to Euro 2000, a report obtained by MP Jim Murphy reminded the UK that it could not be complacent over hooliganism. It showed Leeds to have the largest number of fans banned from attending games or who have restriction orders placed on them by the courts. From a total of 402 supporters who had been banned, 59 were associated with the West Yorkshire side, which had been working hard to eradicate its reputation for supporter hooliganism. Leeds chairman Peter Ridsdale said the fact that they were top showed that the club was doing all it could to stamp out trouble. He said:

'We believe the fact that Leeds United are top of this particular table is confirmation that we are proactive in working with the police and local magistrates to ensure that we do not allow such hooligans into our games and that restraining orders are in place when these hooligans are found guilty.'

According to the report, other clubs with a high number of barred fans include Stoke City (43), Manchester City (23), Chelsea (22), Millwall (20) and Sunderland (18).

Across Europe a number of measures were brought in before Euro 2000 to prevent trouble. In the UK, courts were given the power to demand that convicted hooligans surrender their passports. Germany brought in a new law, which it hoped would stop its most violent hooligans from travelling to the tournament. The proposal, which was aimed at approximately 3,000 of Germany's most violent hooligans, allowed known troublemakers to have their passports stamped to stop them leaving the country. If anyone with a stamped passport attempted to travel to the finals and was caught, they would have been liable for criminal prosecution.

French police started investigating what plans hooligans, especially fans of Paris St-Germain, had for the tournament, but they also started questioning supporters of a radical Algerian Islamic group who were suspected of planning to disrupt the championship.

In Holland and Belgium, a new beer brewed especially for the event had a low alcohol level of 2.5 per cent, and Amsterdam's coffee houses also stayed open in the hope that the legal cannabis would calm fans.

Internationally, the police were doing their bit too, setting up FIMES, the Football Intelligence Message Exchange System, which was the most complicated computer system ever undertaken for a football tournament. Up to 80 officers, including some from the 16 countries taking part, worked on it 24 hours a day once the tournament started. All 16 countries also sent a 15-strong police delegation to maintain co-operation with Dutch and Belgian authorities. The system required three years of planning and allowed every police station in Holland and Belgium to access the names of known troublemakers, to run checks on fans and to obtain a detailed profile of large groups of fans and where they would be staying. The central computer system allowed police resources to be diverted to areas where there was likely to be serious trouble. The 35,000 police officers on duty in Holland and 25,000 in Belgium were able to feed new information and names into the computer, as were foreign police forces. All supporters who travelled to Euro 2000 were categorised according to their willingness to take part in violence. Fans who avoid violence were categorised as A, those who take part in violence, category B, while those who start and organise it were categorised as C. The system also compiled a risk assessment of all fans who had pre-booked their accommodation. It was used a number of times to successfully block entry into the countries, but trouble still broke out.

Things started promisingly, with England playing Portugal. England lost the game, but there was little trouble and the Dutch police were praised for taking a 'softly-softly' approach. It was hoped that similar cool heads would be shown on all sides for the rest of the tournament. However, it was no surprise to anyone where the trouble really started: England v. Germany. While managers and players talk of dream draws, this draw is a nightmare for the authorities, due to long-term rivalries between the two teams. There was a lot of trouble after the game, with part of Brussels city centre being laid to waste, with both sides as bad as the other.

There were pleas for calm before the match, even from the then England manager Kevin Keegan, who said:

'We want the support behind the team, but we don't want the stupidity. What we desperately don't want is the wrong sort of people going for the wrong sort of reasons to do the wrong sort of things.'

The Belgian police warned that they would adopt zero tolerance tactics when it came to hooliganism, and that they would go for anyone within areas of trouble. They delivered on their promise when one group of English fans arriving peacefully in Charleroi were baton-charged getting off the train. The Belgians were accused of being far too heavy-handed, arresting people for public drinking or just wearing a football strip, but when you consider the behaviour of some English fans during the game you can almost understand why they acted this way. Thousands of them could easily be heard singing anti-IRA and war-related songs, adding to the tension. As the whistle blew, ending the on-pitch activities, many were wondering when the off-pitch activities would begin. It did not take long. Fans herded into areas of Brussels city centre fought back, some retaliating against what they saw as heavy-handed treatment by the police. There were also running battles with Germans and fans of other nationalities. Water cannons, dogs and riot equipment were all put to use, and the final tally was more than 900 arrests in the 24-hour period before and after the game.

There were immediate fears for England's hopes of hosting the 2006 World Cup, which were not boosted by a statement from UEFA, which read:

'The UEFA Executive Committee has called on the UK

government and the FA in London to take the necessary steps to stop English hooligans from travelling abroad. Following the violence in Brussels and Charleroi, the UEFA Executive Committee stated that these English hooligans are a disgrace to their country and a blight on the national team. The actions over the last 48 hours have left a scar on the tournament and left us wondering why more was not done to prevent them from travelling.

'Euro 2000 is a celebration of European football, not an excuse for a small minority of English fans to cause havoc. The UK government owes it to everyone concerned to take steps, similar to those taken in other parts of the European Union, to stop these so-called fans from travelling abroad. We cannot allow more people to spoil international tournaments for genuine fans. Other governments have shown that it can be done and we call on the UK government to take the necessary steps as a matter of urgency.

'UEFA will have to determine whether the presence of the English national team at this tournament may be maintained should there be a repetition of similar incidents.'

After the violence following the Germany game, there were worries and implied threats that the England squad would be thrown out of the tournament. After England had been knocked out, however, UEFA chief executive Gerhard Aigner backed down from threats of banning the English, saying:

'I think rather we must work in depth with the FA and the English government. It will be long, hard work but we must give ourselves the means of eradicating hooliganism.

'We must not exclude English clubs or England international teams because when there is an international competition held in England there is never the slightest problem. It's curious, isn't it?

'But we can't just continue like that, just making idle threats.'

What Aigner would have said if the team had got through to later rounds is, of course, unknowable.

There was other trouble at the tournament, in particular involving Turks, though Aigner dismissed this as having nothing to do with football, which caused outrage in the UK. He pointed out that the incident in question was not necessarily about football and concerned the resident Turkish community in Belgium. However, many felt that he was trying to paint the English as the black sheep of the football community. He said:

'If you do not provoke the resident Turks, then they are not necessarily violent... It was a joyful party that turned into a confrontation... But it wasn't an incident that could be characterised by unruliness of the masses, it was a party that turned into a confrontation and could be controlled fairly easily.'

The British Government was accused of being reactionary instead of proactionary and criticised for not doing more before the tournament. Political opponents claimed proof of this was the bringing in of new police powers after Euro 2000. Just after the tournament ended, a member of Greater Manchester Police Football Intelligence Unit told the author that police powers were limited, and though they did what they could, their powers could be increased. More condemnation followed when it was discovered that Germany and other countries had been proactive instead of reactive. Germany, for example, stopped more than 2,000 people on its own border. This is in sharp contrast to the British, who warned anyone with a domestic ban that the Dutch and Belgian police had their details, and that they were advised not to travel. Dutch and Belgian police were also given the names of another 500 people who had been convicted of football-related offences but not banned. This smacked to many of passing the home problem onto the foreign police forces.

When Germany was announced as the winner of the contest to host the 2006 World Cup tournament, the hooligans were blamed for England's loss. England's campaign director Alec McGivan said that he felt Europe might have turned its back on the bid after the scenes at Euro 2000:

'I think our hopes of getting one or two European votes died the day the hooligans took to the streets of Charleroi and if I'm honest I think that was an impossible position to recover from within the context of European opinion.

'We could have progressed if we'd got one or two votes and only one or two votes would have done the job for us from Europe. Right throughout this campaign we hoped that we could pick away at the German votes in Europe and achieve one or two for ourselves.

'If we could have built on five or six votes from either the South Americans or one or two Europeans this result today could have been very, very different.'

As noted, hooliganism is not a problem for just one country, so what can be done to save the game from off-pitch thugs? And what can be done to change this image of trouble abroad? Will it take tougher sentencing or more intensive social work? Home Secretary Jack Straw has said:

'Part of what happens when the English team goes abroad is undoubtedly the expression of a certain sort of national identity. That has been a relatively fixed feature of the behaviour of supporters of England for some time.'

But knowing that does not make it easier to identify or eradicate.

Politicians are reluctant to look at long-term issues such as social background, preferring a more rapid response. The Belgian fancard scheme may be the way forward, but this takes the game away from the fan who likes to just turn up and see their team. It may be an idea though to bring this in for those who support the larger clubs in the larger leagues and for anyone who wants a ticket for an England game. John Williams from the Sir Norman Chester Centre for Football Research feels it will take a lot of work to solve the problem:

'Hooliganism is an international problem, but that doesn't mean the problem is the same in every country or is as serious in every country or the manifestations are the same in every country.

'The way I see hooliganism is that it is right to point to the international manifestations of hooliganism but it is wrong to say that because lots of places have hooliganism then the problems causing it are the same in every place and all countries are blighted. Then there's no point in looking for particular cultural sources for hooliganism and that's what the problem is. I think there's all kinds of reasons. For example, drink has all kinds of different meanings in different cultures, masculinity is different in various cultures. Spanish, Italian, English and Scottish definitions are all different, for example.'

Different causes of hooliganism are easy to spot across Europe. In England, they include social class and regional inequalities; in Scotland and Northern Ireland, religious sectarianism; in Spain, the linguistic and political differences of the Catalan, Castilian, Galician and Basque regions; in Italy, the political and economic divisions between North and South and in Germany, the relations between East and West and political groups of the left and right. Williams believes that this is an area that should be looked at further because while there are international dimensions to hooliganism, 'there are also particularities that tell us more about themselves'. Unfortunately many people do not want to know what they tell them because they may not like what they hear, and as long as politicians go for the short-term answer the average fan is going to suffer – in more ways than one.

Fifteen

Racism

'You black bastard, you black bastard!' is a cry that decent people hoped had faded with the rampant hooliganism of the late eighties and nineties. But it never went away and it is on the rise, just like hooliganism.

In the UK, many think the problem was at its worst in the seventies and eighties but for years before that there was a more subtle form of institutionalised racism against players. It was not until the late 1970s that the number of black players within the ranks of professional British football gradually began to increase to significant numbers, though there have been black players dating back to the beginning of the 20th century. Now up to a quarter of the players in English football are black, but that is not reflected on the terraces. What is reflected from the terraces is hate and ignorance. Many fans think racism is no longer a problem, but lots of those fans now only see games in pubs where the noise drowns out any coming from the television, or at home after the crowd noise has been altered by the broadcaster. It is even quite possible to be at a game and not think there is a problem, only to discover that fans in another part of the ground have been screaming racist taunts at a player – usually one on the opposing team.

Racism is especially harmful to football as it shows that while it may be the global game, its reputation can still be tarnished by those who hate people who look different or who are from other countries. Across the UK and the rest of Europe, many clubs still have fans who chant racist songs during games or promote racist literature before and after a game. Newcastle United supporters still taunt Coventry City fans with comments like 'you're a town full of Pakis'.

'Racism is still a problem in the game today and the problems come in many different ways. There aren't quite the issues in overt ways where thousands of people would get involved in racist chanting but there are still problems,' says Piara Power of Kick Racism Out of Football, an organisation that was set up in 1993 by the Professional Footballers' Association and the Commission for Racial Equality. According to Power one of the main problems for ethnic minorities, especially in England, is that of exclusion:

'For example, the average percentage of season ticket holders who are non-white across the country is 0.9 per cent and when one looks at the places where those clubs have their stadiums and where they are located that is a damning statistic. Virtually every club in the country bar Sunderland and Ipswich is located in areas where there are high ethnic minority populations and only to attract 0.9 per cent tells you a little about the exclusion that is evident.

'But it's not just exclusion of the fans – it also happens to players. In England we know of the high levels of passion for the game amongst Asian youngsters yet we do not have a single homegrown [Asian] professional footballer.

'There are some starting to come through academies but we think it's a problem of stereotyping of attitudes by scouts, coaches and managers, who traditionally – because there hasn't been that record of achievement amongst Asian youngsters – haven't seen them as being talented enough to make it at the top level. This was the same sort of attitude that used to be about in the seventies and eighties about black players – comments about the sort of style they preferred, they don't like the cold, are not very fast and so on. We're seeing the same thing now but with reference to Asian culture.

'There are also comments like Asians not being interested in sporting achievements or that their parents are more interested in the children becoming doctors and lawyers and so on, which when you look at things like cricket, shows that lie for what it is.

'When that is taken together with a lack of a role model, football's not perceived as something Asians do, but the game is beginning to realise now that the talent is there and hopefully the players will start to come through.'

It is not just Asians who are suffering. Black players still face abuse. A survey carried out during the 1998/99 season in the UK showed that in all the large clubs, racial abuse was still a problem. Fans at games involving all four divisions of the English football league plus Rangers and Celtic in Scotland were surveyed and more than 33,000 results were analysed. Games involving Everton, Rangers and Celtic had the largest number of racist comments heard, the survey found. Fans were asked the question, 'Have you witnessed racism aimed at players this season?' The percentages of fans who heard racist abuse at Everton were 38 per cent, at Rangers 36 per cent, at Celtic 33 per cent, at West Ham 32 per cent and Newcastle 31 per cent, making them the top teams in a league of shame. The clubs where the least racist abuse was heard were Wimbledon on 11 per cent, Charlton on 12 per cent, Derby on 14 per cent and Southampton and Arsenal on 16 per cent. The work also found that racism at football matches seemed to be changing, as overt abuse, like throwing bananas on to the pitch and chanting abuse, was in decline and it was now individual bigots who were more of a problem. However, there appears to be a flaw in the study. It was not made clear where the abuse was coming from – home or away crowds – and at whom it was directed. For example, there is a difference between a Leeds United fan going to a game and hearing racist chanting coming from the opposition and hearing it from their own side.

There are other factors as well: a racist fan is unlikely to answer that he's heard racist abuse and also clubs with a higher score may simply have more enlightened fans, not more racist ones, that recognise and disapprove of racist behaviour.

Many right-wing groups have been accused of being involved with the racism in football. Freelance writer Nick Ryan spent a year and a half investigating the neo-Nazi group Combat 18, discovering the racist links from behind the scenes. He noted that it was more than just right-wing thinkers getting together for a drink and some singing of racist chants:

'It was a collection of guys who came predominantly from the football hooligan scene and many also had connections to the extreme Right. Many of these guys were basically brawlers and drinkers in their 20s and 30s – not skinheads – who had been involved with the National Front, British Movement and other extremist groups on marches or in a capacity in the past.

'At most I would say it had no more than a few hundred members. This could swell rapidly, though, with an influx of football hooliganism firms. Several of England's most dangerous hooligans have at times been involved within C18's ranks. So, for example, C18 was able to field over 600 hooligans to attack a march of Irish Republicans once.'

And while Ryan fears that incidents are getting more violent when they occur, he also thinks there is some hope:

'The UK far right is far more fragmented and fringe-based than many of our contemporaries. Also, many areas like the inner cities of London are just too racially mixed now, and most people in the under-30 generation simply accept living side-by-side with members of other religions and ethnic groups.'

British politician David Mellor has been heavily involved in trying to get racism out of the game in the UK. He believes that racism is a major stumbling block for ethnic minorities trying to get into football.

'Tackling racism is the key to encouraging more black and Asian children to play football. The threat of racism is a powerful deterrent to black and Asian people – and particularly young people – playing organised football. It can have a detrimental effect on a player's performance and persuade some to give up the game altogether.

'The emergence of an Asian player in top-flight football would do more than any other development to encourage wider participation in the game amongst the Asian community. And, as the number of black and Asian players increases, behaviour of racist character will be increasingly marginalised.'

He also wants to see the players do more about the matter.

'Not only do we need to get the anti-racist groups working together to combat the problem, but the footballers also need to be involved.

'Money breeds indifference and it is important that footballers know how lucky they are and they have to be involved in the community initiatives. Unity is strength in this matter and we should use this conference [the Council of Europe conference on "Harnessing the Potential", Strasbourg, 22–23 November 1999] to develop links.'

Players now travel across Europe to play their game and in travelling take not only their skills but also their attitudes. One of the worst recent incidents of a player being caught making a racist comment involved Rangers captain Lorenzo Amoruso during the 1999/2000 UEFA cup. Rangers were playing the second leg in Germany when Amoruso made physical contact with Borussia Dortmund's Nigerian striker Victor Ikpeba. Afterwards the Italian said he could not have said what he was accused of saying because he only swore in Italian, despite the fact that video footage showed him saying it. But there was a large public outcry and days later he repented, saying through a club statement that words were exchanged.

'However,' he added, 'in a highly charged football match it is not unusual for tempers to boil over and I do not remember making the remarks attributed to me.

'[This morning] I viewed the video recording of the game and, on this evidence, I cannot dispute the fact that I made the remarks. I would like to make an unreserved apology to Victor Ikpeba for these comments.

'I would like to make it clear that I am not a racist and deeply regret any upset I have unwittingly caused to the player or anyone else.'

Rangers never revealed if Amoruso was ever fined, though they did say that the club did not condone his comments and as a club they were opposed to racism. Some sections of the Scottish media leapt to Amoruso's defence, with television commentator Richard Gordon saying that it was all blown out of proportion and it was all down to the heat of the moment. Rangers' lack of public action was surprising as the club had not been slow in banning season ticket holders who chanted abuse at their first black signing, Mark Walters. Piara Power has his own thoughts on the incident:

'He denied it and then came forward, there were no sanctions applied to him by the SFA or UEFA and that sends out the wrong message – that tells people it's OK to do it.

'I don't know Amoruso but my perspective is that when he was cornered with TV evidence it looked as if he decided to come clean so that he would not look like a liar.

'On the pitch, saying something is just part of the game or psychological warfare is just a get-out and that is just turning a blind eye. Doing that just sets a bad example in the eyes of young kids and so on. What we do find is that in the odd situation involving coloured players they are afraid to complain because they do not want to upset the apple cart, especially if it involves someone from their own team. They may not be confident as to how the complaint will be taken up or how it will be viewed and how others will look at them for making the complaint.'

While some wondered what the club could have done to set a sufficient example of punishment for one of its more faithful players, few thought he would be told to leave the club, and he was not. German footballer Thorsten Legat was not so lucky though. Legat was sacked by Bundesliga club Stuttgart, after it was discovered that he had insulted a colleague. During training a poster of Guinean midfielder Pablo Thiam, showing the player advertising a soft drink, was defaced, with the words 'negro juice' written across it.

All the players present denied having anything to do with it and the club took the highly unusual step of calling in a detective and a handwriting expert to find the culprit. After confronting Legat with the evidence, he admitted what he had done. Days later he was dismissed from the club by way of a brief statement released to the media, which said:

'The club and Legat have severed their relationship with immediate effect.'

Stuttgart suggested the incident had more to do with player disharmony than racism, as Legat did have a bad reputation, especially after beating up a neighbour, but to most followers of the game in Germany it was fairly obvious why he had been made to leave.

While Amoruso's outburst was a despicable thing, he is not the only Italian to be accused of racism. Serie A club Lazio has a

notorious reputation, despite years of anti-racist initiatives. The club
has been fined thousands of pounds because of the fans making racist
comments. Fans have also been known to unravel banners and flags
praising murdered Serbian warlord Zeljko Raznatovic, Mussolini and
others. Some fans also use the club's full name, SS Lazio, as a way of
harassing AS Roma fans, many of whom are Jewish, by having
banners where the SS is written in the same style as the Nazi SS.
Despite the club's fines the fans do not appear to be taking any
notice, as was shown when Arsenal played Lazio in October 2000
(this match also showed the club's players in a bad light). The Arsenal
players were subjected to racist abuse by the fans, who pelted them
with debris at the end of the game. Arsenal midfielder Patrick Vieira
claimed Lazio's Yugoslavian defender Sinisa Mihajlovic made a
number of racist comments and gestures before, during and after the
match in Rome.

Vieira said, 'I've had abuse back in England, mainly because I'm
French, but this was all about my skin colour.'

The then Lazio coach Sven-Goran Eriksson suggested one
possible solution:

'Perhaps buying a star black player might help us get over these
problems of racism. I find it extremely sad that racism in football can
still be such a serious problem in 2000.'

Meanwhile Lazio president and owner Sergio Cragnotti has a few
plans too. He has threatened to order his team to play behind closed
doors if the abuse directed at ethnic players does not stop.

He said: 'I am ashamed at fans like these, who make racism their
banner. I don't want them at the stadium, as it's something I cannot
stand.

'The stupidity of these people is beginning to exceed all
reasonable bounds. All racist or political manipulation of soccer
should be totally eliminated from grounds.

'I'm preparing a series of measures because Lazio want to be
leaders even when it comes to our fans' behaviour, otherwise we'll
do without them and we'll just play our games without any fans at
all.'

However, some people deny there is a problem in the first place.
Italian national coach and 1982 World Cup winner Dino Zoff has

said, 'I don't know whether you could really call this racism. I think it could just be a question of people making fun of someone.'

What Zoff has never explained is why it only seems to be black players who have fun made of them.

It is not just in Italian and British football that racism occurs, however. Like hooliganism, racism is a Europe-wide problem. Red Star Belgrade was fined £15,000 for its supporters' unruly behaviour during the UEFA Cup defeat of Leicester City in Vienna in late 2000. Players Ade Akinbiyi and Andy Impey were subjected to racist chanting by fans of the Yugoslav club during the match.

At Paris St-Germain, those in charge of the club have in the past refused ethnic minority supporters entry to a part of the stadium known for its racist members. The thinking behind this was that they would be protecting the former, but they were criticised for appearing to give the racist chanters a place of their own from which to shout.

It is well known that football racists, especially in the Czech Republic and Poland, are using the Internet to spread their message of hate. There has also been concern that the Celtic cross is being used by some instead of the swastika as a racist symbol and sign of racial purity, upsetting those who see the cross as a religious icon.

The problem of racism in football has been discussed at the highest levels, and in 1999, Football Against Racism in Europe (FARE), the first European anti-racist football network, was founded. FARE is made up of over 40 organisations including anti-racist projects, fan clubs, football associations and players' unions from 14 European countries. It aims to engage in proactive networking among anti-racist football initiatives in Europe, through co-ordination and enlargement of the FARE network and public relations activities. It has its work cut out for it, says Piara Power:

'Clubs are doing more than they used to when it comes to racism in the terraces, but in our view they are still not doing enough.

'They are relying on economics to sort it out to an extent, with some people who may cry racist chants no longer being able to afford tickets, while a few smaller clubs have tried more and we've seen that it impacts on them in a lot of ways in terms of their club as a brand, their image, in the eyes of clubs and fans.

'For some clubs, there is a fear of alienating a part of their crowd if they start to pick on the racist chanters but for others it's a lack of inventiveness, a lack of understanding about some issues because in other areas clubs have not been shy of alienating their audience through things like ticket pricing, merchandise pricing and so on. Certainly at the top that doesn't seem to be an issue.

'However, fear of losing part of your crowd is not a good reason, it's absolute nonsense. In our experience if you take a positive stance and make examples of a few people, you are more likely to attract others who stayed away because of racism.

'You also have to remember that it's not just blacks and Asians who have problems, there are many white supporters who are turned off by it as they find it disgusting.

'Ways to go forward include marketing campaigns against racism as a positive process by forging links with the local community and also marketing anti-racist measures as a way of enhancing the so-called club "brand".

'In terms of the European position concerning racism in football, each country has its own specific problems because of the differences between their ethnic communities. We need better intervention by UEFA as they have the resources and the power to bring pressure at the local level.'

But there is some way to go. Just before this book was completed I attended a game between two English premiership sides where one section of the fans was taking great delight in abusing the black players on the opposing side, while praising their own. When asked if they didn't think there was an obvious contradiction one replied to me:

'Nah mate, our guys are on our side, their guys are the enemy. Besides, it's only words and they get paid enough to be able to take a bit of stick like this.'

Racism in football is not as bad as it used to be but the fact that it still exists at all is deplorable in a so-called civilised age. Fans of the game should do their utmost to change the attitudes not only of their fellow fans but also the clubs themselves, applying pressure for racist players to be punished as and when appropriate.

Sixteen

Sectarianism

Glasgow. Derby Day. The Old Firm, Celtic playing Rangers. Somewhere in the city, hours before kick-off, a mother may be about to say goodbye to her son for the last time because he'll be killed before he gets home from watching the football.

It would be nice if this were fiction – after all isn't football only a game? – but the recent statistics for Old Firm meetings show that at every match there will be a handful of attempted murders, scores of assaults and many casualties throughout the city, some of whom are people just unfortunate enough to get caught up in football's troubles. On occasion there will also be death. And why? Because of religion.

Religious bigotry between Christians is not a problem in English football. The fact that some faiths associate with one team rather than another is more to do with demographics than religion. However, in Scotland – and the west coast in particular, where both Celtic and Rangers hail from – religion takes on an importance not seen anywhere else in Western Europe, save Northern Ireland. There is nowhere else in the footballing world where two particular teams playing each other brings about so much hate because of religious differences.

While racism has never appeared to be as large a problem in Scotland as it has elsewhere, those who feel the need to hate someone still have a target – normally their fellow Scots – because in Scotland religious bigotry has always been the big issue.

To people from elsewhere – which in this case is anywhere outside a 100-mile radius around Glasgow – the Old Firm match is nothing more than another football derby, along the lines of Liverpool v. Everton or Manchester City v. Manchester United. People inside that radius, however, know it is a great deal more than that. It is a hatred that has cost the city considerable amounts of money. In 2000 it cost Glasgow around £5 million, when the director of the film *There's Only One Jimmy Grimble*, John Hay, said he needed a city with football rivalry but avoided filming in Glasgow because of sectarianism. He said:

'The problem with Rangers and Celtic is that you get a lot of politics, and you don't want to get into that. We ended up setting it in Manchester because the City and United rivalry is based purely on football.'

Trade union UNISON carried out an informal study in November 2000 after the Old Firm game at Ibrox, which Rangers won 5-1. The study looked at the number of assault victims needing hospital treatment compared to the weekends before and after the game. Across central Scotland, there was a dramatic increase – as much as nine times the normal number of assaults in some areas.

There is a Celtic song that calls for fans to 'know your history' and history is at the root of a lot of the troubles of Glasgow football.

Celtic was technically formed in November 1887, but formally established in 1888, by a Marist Brother named Walfrid. The club had two principal aims. First, to raise funds to provide food for the poor of the East End of Glasgow, an area of the city that was greatly impoverished and had a very high rate of infant mortality. Second, the club was to be a bridge in the East End between the large Irish community and the native Glaswegians, between whom social frictions were growing, especially as Scotland was traditionally a Protestant country and the Irish were Catholic. Brother Walfrid saw the need for social integration, and his vision was a football club that Scottish and Irish, Protestants and Catholics alike could support.

Rangers was formed when four men who wanted to form a team got together for a kickabout on Glasgow Green in 1872. The club, taking its name from an English rugby club, was officially formed in 1873, when it became businesslike, having its first annual meeting and electing a board. So, from the very start, there was a different ethos behind the two clubs.

From the beginning the two teams attracted different support. The East End and some of the north of the city rallied round Celtic, while the more affluent south and west sided with the Ibrox team, Rangers. Over the years the teams built up rivalry. It was soon obvious to all that mainly Catholics were supporting Celtic, and that few Catholics supported Rangers. To the people running the clubs, this was something that could be built on to generate support for their teams. As many families and shipbuilders from Northern Ireland came to Scotland, they adopted Rangers as their club. This helped to shape the division between the two teams, as many from Northern Ireland wanted nothing to do with anything that had connotations of southern Ireland. Those who came to Glasgow from the south of Ireland adopted Celtic as their club for similar reasons, and for the club's background.

At the start of the 1900s, a Glasgow cartoonist depicted the Celtic and Rangers treasurers greedily sharing out a huge bag of gate money. It was captioned 'The Old Firm' (which was then a popular term for well-established business partnerships) and the name stuck.

From the early days, the derby was a passionate and occasionally violent affair, with fights breaking out on a regular basis. The two clubs always measured themselves by the activities of the other, Celtic fans gloating when they became the first team in Britain to win the European Cup, Rangers fans revelling in Celtic fans' despair when Rangers equalled the East End club's nine-in-a-row league wins. As the years went on, after the world wars and into the sixties, it was an unwritten rule at Ibrox that only Protestants — or at least non-Catholics — could succeed at the top of the club. To be fair to Rangers they were not the only ones in Scotland with this policy; it was something that was reflected in everyday life (although it cost Rangers talent like Sir Alex Ferguson, because his wife is a Catholic). Celtic tried to convey the message that they were a non-denominational club and signed, amongst others, a Protestant manager, Jock Stein, and non-Catholic players. However, they were still tagged as the Catholic team of Scotland. This perception continued until the 1980s, both sides having boards that were firmly entrenched in their own beliefs and ways. Then Graeme Souness came to Rangers and dragged Scottish football into the latter half of the 20th century, spending millions of pounds under the eye of new chairman David Murray.

Souness held a firmly pragmatic view that religion meant nothing to him. He proved this in spectacular style when he signed Mo Johnston, an excellent striker who had previously played for Celtic, and had been on the verge of re-signing to them. Celtic fans were upset, but the reaction from the Rangers fans was one of disbelief. People burned scarves and season tickets, saying they would never go back to the club because Souness had destroyed its traditions, regardless of the fact that Johnston was one of Scotland's best strikers. To many fans, this was the ultimate betrayal. To their credit, Murray and Souness never backed down. Souness may not have cared about the religious aspects of the football, but Rangers supporters did, continuing to cry 'Fenian Bastard' (although the irony has not been lost on many that some of the original Irish Fenians were actually Protestant).

The myth of one side being Catholic and the other Protestant persists to this day. When Martin O'Neill signed as manager of Celtic, Leicester chairman John Elsom sparked anger by saying, 'In the end the pursuit of a personal dream related to his Roman Catholic heritage seems to have won the day.'

All of this would be history were it not for one thing – people are killed because of the derby. As noted, the game has always attracted trouble, partly fuelled by alcohol and emotion, but in recent years the problem has got out of hand, and it now endangers most people in Glasgow when it takes place.

Both teams have tried to improve the situation. Rangers has, until recently, been low-key in its efforts, but David Murray has been quoted on more than one occasion calling for fans to stop singing offensive songs at home and away games. However, few have followed his requests, as Rangers' opening game in the European Champions League 2000/01 showed. Newspapers commented on how the game was marred by thousands chanting, 'Are you watching,

Fenian scum?' Celtic took a public approach to the problem when chairman Fergus McCann, who said he was appalled by the bigotry he has rediscovered since his return to Scotland after a 30-year self-imposed exile in Canada, set up the 'Bhoys Against Bigotry' campaign, which organised a number of high-profile events to try and reduce the singing of sectarian songs and change people's attitudes towards sectarian groups. McCann was criticised by many for trying to change the club and outlawing certain songs. However, he was ruthless in his pursuit of these goals, having fans ejected for singing pro-IRA songs, many of which were mainstays of the fans' singing repertoire.

The first incidents that showed things had taken a turn for the worse took place in 1995, and they were in many ways the most tragic.

A young man was murdered in Dennistoun after he and his brother had watched the Celtic game live in a pub. They passed by the local hall of the Orange Lodge and were chased by a group of people hanging around outside. One of the brothers fell and was kicked and stabbed to death.

On the same night, 16-year-old Mark Scott was walking home with two friends after a game at Celtic Park. They were passing a pub in Bridgeton Cross when some Rangers fans started jeering at them. One of the group, Jason Campbell, a Rangers fan with Loyalist sympathies, pulled out a knife and slashed Mark's throat, leaving him to die a slow, agonising death on the pavement.

The west coast was shocked by the attack on Mark because he was from a well-to-do middle-class family; there was no hint of 'ruffian' in him that would have allowed people to dismiss the murder as thuggish violence. However, after a few condemnations the incident faded into the background. Mark's murderer was later considered for transfer to a jail in Northern Ireland to be nearer Loyalists, making the murder seem politically motivated. There was outrage both from the public and from Loyalists, who did not want to be associated with someone who had killed for something that, to any rational person, had nothing to do with their cause, so the transfer fell through at the last moment.

In November 1997 18-year-old Irish student Sean O'Connor was passing the same area, after being directed there by police and stewards, when he was attacked from behind and stabbed in the neck in an attack that bore similarities to Mark Scott's murder. His attacker ran off, and though a number of people chased him, he was driven away in a waiting car. This has led many to believe that this attack – and others – was premeditated. For Sean the day is one he will never forget. He said:

'I heard a move behind me and out of the corner of my eye I saw this guy come running up to me. I thought he had come to punch me and I just managed to get my arm up to block him. He ran off down an alleyway and the people with me said he was still shouting sectarian abuse as he went... It was only when I felt my shirt was soaking wet and saw the blood that I realised what had happened. Then I felt a huge hole in my neck. I was later told the wound was 6 inches.

'When I was in the ambulance the paramedic said to me, "You do realise that this is attempted murder, there's no doubt about that." But when the CID interviewed me in hospital they basically admitted that they are not really interested in investigating these kinds of sectarian attacks.

'The doctor who treated me told me that if the blade had gone 1 millimetre deeper it would have severed a major artery. She said that when that happens you lose consciousness in 40 seconds and will die within minutes.'

Police later admitted that in the two-year period between the attacks, 38 similar assaults had taken place in the area, all directed at Catholics or those wearing Celtic colours.

Despite this, the police do not feel there is a problem. In the second half of 1999, the author was told by Chief Inspector Kenny Scott, 'There is currently nothing to suggest that there is any risk to supporters travelling to and from matches at Celtic Park.' This comment was met with incredulity by the Celtic fans as Bridgeton and Duke Street – both within a mile of Celtic's ground – are seen as flashpoints for the worst of the violence. Fans find it hard to avoid these parts, as Bridgeton – an area with strong Protestant and Loyalist sympathies – is the nearest train station to the Celtic ground, and Duke Street is also a major transport route. It may be that the success of football club strip merchandising has contributed to the problem, as more people are wearing club strips now, so are easier to identify as a possible target, but it is a sad indictment of the situation in the city that a choice of clothing can mark you out for death.

May 1999 was the worst period. Rangers beat Celtic at Parkhead to win the league but the on-pitch activities were blurred by what happened off-pitch, with a number of incidents showing how bad the problem had become.

One Celtic fan, Carl McGroarty, was shot in the chest by a bolt fired from a crossbow as he left a pub. Another young fan, Liam Sweeney, was attacked after waiting for a meal in a Chinese takeaway. He was wearing no colours or Celtic merchandise, but his green jersey and the calling of his name to collect his food order may have been enough to identify him as a Catholic from an Irish background. He was followed from the restaurant by his attackers and stabbed several times. Liam lost more than four pints of blood and almost died as a result of this horrific attack. In Ayrshire two male Celtic fans and one female supporter were set upon by a large mob of Rangers fans. All three were hospitalised. One of the men had severe head injuries, and the other had a broken jaw.

However, the worst was to happen to another young Celtic fan, only 250 yards from where Liam had been attacked. Sixteen-year-old Thomas McFadden had watched the game live on TV in an Irish pub close to Hampden Park, where the Cup Final was played. On his way home from the pub Thomas was attacked by three Rangers fans, two men and a woman, and received fatal stab wounds to the chest. He died in the street where he lived. Tragically and ironically his mother had not allowed him to go to the actual match because of her fears of violence. While Thomas lay dying, in another part of the city Rangers vice-chairman Donald Findlay was caught on video singing sectarian songs about being up to his knees in Fenian blood, and other inflammatory songs like *The Sash*, *Follow Follow* and *The Billy Boys*, which is based around a 1930s Glaswegian anti-Semite who tried to set up a Scottish Ku Klux Klan. Findlay, one of the Scottish legal establishment's more colourful figures with his pork chop-shaped sideboards, flamboyant dress sense and strong, Conservative Party-backing views, has never made any secret of his loyalty to Rangers. He once said that he had never forgiven his mother for giving birth to him on St Patrick's day, and he always chose to celebrate his birthday on 12 July, which is the date of the Battle of the Boyne, a battle fought between the Protestant King William of England and the Catholic King James of Scotland over the future of Ireland. Findlay has also defended the murderer of Mark Scott and others involved in sectarian attacks, so he was familiar with how deep a problem it is in Scottish society. Also seen in the video are a few Rangers players, but the attention was on Findlay. There was outrage from all sides; not all in condemnation of Findlay. Some football fanzines published the names and addresses of the people believed to have handed the video over to the press and few believed it was so Rangers fans could congratulate the video-taker on exposing the incident.

Some newspapers said that the fact that Findlay had sung these songs did not mean that he hated Catholics, it just showed that he did not like Celtic football club – even though the club is not mentioned in the songs. Findlay resigned from the Rangers board, pleading that his behaviour had been 'an error of judgement', but he has been told by David Murray that he is still welcome at Ibrox.

Rangers fan Frank Forrester was stabbed to death in Ayrshire at the start of December, following a long-running feud with a Celtic supporter, though it has been suggested that there was more to this than sectarianism.

Composer James McMillan ignited Scotland with a damning speech about the situation later that year when he said that Findlay was not unique, saying what many, who had never spoken up, thought about the situation. Many people called him paranoid, while others applauded his bravery in speaking out about the matter. In his speech he said:

'Donald Findlay is not a one-off. To believe this is self-delusion. Because our professions, our workplaces, our academic circles, our media and our sporting bodies are jam-packed with people like Donald Findlay.

'There was a palpable anger with him anyway in some quarters for having given the game away. The sanctimonious Scottish myth that all bigots are uneducated, loutish morons from the lowest level in society was undermined at a stroke... there is a very real resentment against him for having so foolishly squandered the alibi.'

Scotland's largest-selling paper, the *Daily Record*, summed up the feelings of most of Scotland in an editorial:

'He has been caught, condemned out of his own foul mouth among his toadies, where, no doubt, he arrogantly assumed he was safe.

'Findlay with his courtroom skills, sharp intelligence and brilliant mind is not stupid. Except that that mind appears to be a closed mind, a narrow mind, pickled and distorted by his innate bigotry.

'He was knee-deep in it. He wallowed in it. He gloried in it. If he was simply stupid, it might just be understandable. But Findlay always knew exactly what he was doing. That is what makes everything so much worse.'

Findlay is not the only person to be caught out, however. One-time Rangers goalkeeper Andy Goram has never made any secret of his sympathies for the Ulster Protestant cause. He has made a number of trips to Belfast, even turning on the Christmas lights on the Shankhill Road in 1995. In 1998, he wore a black armband just days after the murder of notorious loyalist Billy Wright, who was also known as King Rat. Goram's excuse to the public was that it was a delayed expression of mourning for an aunt who had died in October 1997. Pictures of Goram with a UVF flag were eventually published, but not until after he had left Rangers and gone to another club.

It is not the game's fault that this problem exists, but the game is now the focal point for it, and the average rational fan has, for now, lost this game to something worse than big business – thuggery. To make it worse, Scotland tries to pretend there is no problem. When two Leeds United fans were murdered by Turkish supporters in 1999, there were pages upon pages covering the incident – what had happened, what the background was, was it hooliganism or something else – no stone was left unturned. In Scotland, after an Old Firm murder, the traditional reporting has been a day's coverage of the matter and over the next few days appeals for the murderer to be caught, alongside pictures of where the person was attacked. There is no examination of the wider causes; no attention is paid to the social background; no one asks why this is happening. The media –

print and non-print – have found themselves in a bind over the matter. As a senior journalist at one of Scotland's larger-selling papers told me:

'Sport journalists don't write about it as they are covering the game and they also don't like to get into the deeper dimensions of it, but some newspeople put it down as football-related so sport should cover it.'

But there is another problem. The majority of the attacks have been carried out by Rangers fans against Celtic fans. In Scotland, where there are more newspapers per person than anywhere else in the UK, and all are involved in tight circulation battles, to point this out could be seen as circulation suicide, as many people take offence at having their group linked with murderers.

Some people are trying to fight back and change things. Cara Henderson was a schoolfriend of Mark Scott. After Donald Findlay was caught on tape, she sent a letter to a newspaper and the response from that inspired her. While there was some negative feedback, which only confirmed to Cara that something had to be done, a lot of people agreed with her. She has set up a poster and education scheme called 'Nil by Mouth', with pictures showing harrowing images of people who have been attacked and scarred by the violence surrounding the Old Firm. Both clubs have helped with funding for the scheme, and it marks the first major public effort made by Rangers to stamp out the problem. Cara feels there are a number of matters that have to be addressed, but people have to accept there is a problem first:

'Ultimately we're trying to challenge people who say the word "huns" or sing "hello, hello we are the Billy Boys" because no one seems to have stopped and thought about it. It's like people who are not out there fighting are using these words and thinking that it's all right because everyone else is doing it, so it can't be wrong, but we're saying is that the case, is it all right?'

Cara went to Oxford to complete her education, getting a history degree, and she feels that it's when people move away from Glasgow that they see how ridiculous the situation is:

'Going out of Glasgow you encounter how others see it and many have a complete ignorance of the problem. To them it is not an issue in the slightest, whereas in Glasgow it totally consumes some people.

'Everyone here accepts the way things are, but that does not mean it's OK or that we should leave it this way. People who stay in the west coast in and around Glasgow and never go elsewhere don't see that it's not an issue elsewhere.'

Cara feels that pointing fingers at one group of people is not going to help achieve anything, as there are attitudes on both sides.

'We're not trying to label people as bigots, what we are trying to show is that we all share this mindset, there's no one to blame, but let's acknowledge there is a problem and let's try to deal with it together.

'The media have an important role because they set the tone for how people perceive things. Without a doubt the media play to the whole thing tacitly. The whole build-up. Football rivalry is a good thing, competition is a good thing, but this is a unique situation and the media know it is a unique situation.

'What frustrates me is their reporting after it. In the *Herald* this was in the same article as the match report. The media don't deem the attacks often to be newsworthy enough on their own.

'Ignoring the problem plays into it and if the facts are that more fans from one side than the other have been murdered then newspapers have to report that and distance themselves from the events. They cannot be concerned about how others will perceive this.

'However, the most depressing aspect is that there is a silent majority in the west of Scotland around Glasgow who do not speak out against the minority or criticise something sectarian when they see it. Some people won't change, but if the majority do not speak out then the kernel of sectarianism will always be at the heart of society.

'As far as I can tell, there is a genuine desire at both clubs for change; they are not benefiting from sectarianism now and really want to distance themselves from that element of it.'

Another group, Campaign Against Sectarian Attacks (CASA), has called for Celtic to provide a train station near the ground, so fans can avoid the flashpoints of Duke Street and Bridgeton. However, setting up a station is something that will take time and millions of pounds. The spokesman for CASA, Bernard O'Toole, said:

'The facts are that most of this so-called "Old Firm hatred and violence" is a one-sided affair. Sure, Celtic supporters have no particular love for their rivals from Rangers and over the years there have always been some hooligan clashes between the supporters. But the latest acts of violence are not the actions of organised groups of hooligans on both sides. They are or at least appear to be the random acts of a group of Rangers supporters whose hatred of all things to do with Celtic and Ireland knows no bounds.'

Dr Joseph Bradley is a lecturer in Sports Studies at Stirling University and has written widely on ethnic, cultural and religious identities in Scottish football as well as in Scottish and Irish societies generally. He believes that while what we hear and see in relation to football cannot be dismissed, fans should not simply be judged or categorised by their behaviour at or near a football ground:

'The things people often say, do and sing, in relation to football, shouldn't always be taken literally. Much of what we witness can constitute the unthinking and in a football context, simply joining in. However, that's not to say football fans shouldn't think about what they do and say.

'Football can be an exaggerated social environment but this should not minimise what happens. This understanding allows us to contextualise behaviour. That said, I believe that the songs sung repeatedly by fans over the course of time do reflect meaning in their lives, their identities as well as their perceptions of those they sing for and against.'

Dr Bradley also feels that the term 'sectarianism' is thrown about without any real understanding of its sources and nature in Scotland. He feels it is a widely abused term, especially in the media, and this can actually lead to sectarian attitudes and judgements.

'My research amongst not only fans but generally in Scottish society shows that there are varying perceptions of what constitutes bigotry and sectarianism within the "Celtic and Catholic" community and the "Rangers and Scottish Protestant" communities. There is also a recognisable difference of opinions and behaviours where religious identity is concerned. This is important in that formal and spiritual religious adherence often says something about the nature and depth of dislike or hate. I tend to believe that on the whole, those who are closer to the practices of their Christian faiths are less likely to be sectarian or bigoted.'

Until the bounds are curbed and everyone in Glasgow accepts there is a problem and deals with it, the most prominent colour in a town of green and white fans and red, white and blue fans, will be blood red. There may be hopes of peace in Ireland, but Glasgow has some way to go yet.

Seventeen

Hillsborough

If there is one word that brings a chill to anyone who knows anything about football, it is Hillsborough. 15 April 1989. An FA Cup semi-final between Liverpool and Nottingham Forest. Liverpool fans hoped it would be the prelude to an all-Merseyside final against Everton, but minutes after the start, none of that mattered. At 3.06 pm, six minutes after kick-off, the game was brought to a finish. Supporters were being crushed in one area of the ground where too many fans were being allowed in. Fans were suffocating after being pushed up against the fences at the front of the stand. Ninety-six people died.

It was later revealed that there had been a crush of fans at the turnstiles and the authorities were worried that someone could be injured or killed. So Exit Gate C was opened to relieve the pressure. But after the gate was opened, thousands of fans went through a tunnel, which led into the already crowded pens three and four on the terraces.

What happened next has been well recorded: the *Sun* newspaper blamed the fans. Liverpool manager Kenny Dalglish and the players attended the funerals. The families banded together to fight for justice. The Taylor Report; a public inquiry; an inquest; legal scrutiny and a High Court judicial review; Virgin's Richard Branson underwrote a benefit concert for £100,000 that raised more than £500,000; Home Secretary Jack Straw said there would be no fresh inquiries into the matter.

It is now accepted that the fans were not at fault. The incident was due to overcrowding, and not hooliganism as was suggested at the time. The Taylor Report itself said that South Yorkshire police's failings had played a part in what had happened. What never happened, however, was any conviction. If anyone was responsible for the death of 96 people one would think it only right and fair that they should be held accountable. But there was never a public prosecution. While the families never saw justice, a prosecution or compensation, a few police officers did receive compensation, which only added to the outrage felt by the families. Fourteen officers won settlements totalling more than £1.2 million for the post-traumatic stress of dealing with the tragedy. There are many other cases from that day involving police still to be heard.

For the vast majority of people, Hillsborough faded into the background, but the families never gave up, and in 2000 they had one last chance to get justice. They managed to bring a private prosecution against former chief superintendent David Duckenfield and former superintendent Bernard Murray, who were in charge of crowd control that fateful day, and who are both now retired from South Yorkshire police. Duckenfield was match commander while Murray was ground controller. They were charged with the manslaughter of John Alfred Anderson and James Gary Aspinall, and also of wilfully neglecting to carry out their public duty.

Before the trial at Leeds Crown Court the men's lawyers put forward the argument that they would not get a fair trial due to the amount of publicity there had been about Hillsborough, and the length of time since it had happened. However, the prosecution went ahead. The trial and jury deliberations lasted for six weeks. I attended parts of the trial, which was the most solemn event I have ever been to. Football is a game about passion and noise and life, but this was the opposite. More than 50 relatives could be found in the public gallery every day during the trial. There was passion, but it was not positive; it was a spent passion, an angry passion directed at the men in the dock and the system that allowed the families to go without justice. The atmosphere was always heavy. This was the antithesis of all that football should be, which in a way was appropriate, because this was football's darkest hour. Even during the trial, you occasionally had to remind yourself that this had happened because of a game. Just a game. The quote by Liverpool manager and football legend Bill Shankly about football being a matter more important than life and death seemed hollow in the circumstances.

The trial started with Alun Jones QC and the case for the prosecution. He told the court the tragedy could have been averted if the defendants had ordered officers to block or close off the tunnel leading to terrace pens three and four. It was his belief that the police had a duty of care to look after the fans in the ground and the pens, and they were as responsible for the fans' safety as an aeroplane pilot and his co-pilot are for their passengers. Jones claimed that not directing fans away from the tunnel to the busy pens amounted to criminal negligence, and was tantamount to manslaughter. According to Jones, Duckenfield – who had only taken up the post that made him responsible for policing at Hillsborough less than a month before the game – spoke to FA chief executive Graham Kelly minutes after the disaster, recognising very quickly the causes of the tragedy, and that he was responsible. Jones said:

'He realised that a man like Graham Kelly would be likely to talk within minutes to the media and he sought to deflect the blame from himself and place it on the people at the game.

'Duckenfield deceitfully and dishonestly concealed from those men that he had himself ordered the exit gates to be opened because the crush at the turnstiles had become so severe.'

Jones added that Duckenfield later gave two accounts of what he had said to Kelly. The first was that the gates had burst open themselves, and the second was that he feared crowd disorder if he admitted he had given the order to open the gates. Jones claimed that six weeks later Duckenfield changed his account under public questioning when he made a public apology for suggesting that Liverpool spectators caused the disaster. The court heard a statement that Duckenfield was supposed to have made during an earlier inquiry. It was claimed that he said he did not want to order the gate to be opened because it could have allowed in fans – drunk or sober

– without tickets, but he decided he had no option because of a message from outside the ground that there might be injuries and deaths if he did not.

Video footage of the disaster was shown to the jury. Members of the victims' families wept as the four-hour footage was played, and several people left the courtroom. The start of the video showed the stadium entrances at the Leppings Lane end where the tragedy happened. A commentary pointed out the blue-shuttered exit gate which, the jury was told, was opened on Duckenfield's orders to allow fans into pens three and four, where the victims died in the crush. It also showed the tunnel leading to the terraces, which, the jury was told, was not blocked off by police, allowing hundreds of fans to flood through. The film showed Gate C being opened at 2.52 pm, and thousands of fans pouring through towards the tunnel leading to pens three and four. Jones said a superintendent outside the ground had made about four requests over a seven-minute period for the gate to be opened to relieve the pressure at the turnstiles. Footage taken inside the ground showed that pens three and four were packed by 2.40 pm, but other pens still had plenty of space. Jones told the jury that neither defendant had done anything to stop the game until 3.06 pm, when another superintendent ran on to the pitch. He said that by then people in some distress had already been seen climbing out of the pens. The jury was also shown a mock-up of the police control room that was in use that day. They could not be taken to or shown the original because that had been destroyed, and a new one was then in operation.

Liverpool fan Colin Moneypenny described all too vividly the feeling inside the pen:

'I was literally carried off my feet for 30–40 feet – I had no control of my actions from there until I landed and at one point was within feet of the perimeter fence at the front of pen three and had no choice about staying in that position for the next 15 minutes. I was fighting for my life.'

High court judge Sir Maurice Kay recalled that the area in front of the turnstiles at the stadium was very busy and congested about half an hour before kick-off. He said:

'As time went by there seemed to be an emerging danger from the crowd, too many in too small a space.

'Within a couple of minutes one was caught up in movement of an involuntary kind and it took the form of being moved both forwards and sideways. There were so many people in such a small space it was very uncomfortable. One was aware then that something very serious had gone wrong.'

A GP, Colin Flenley, recalled the press trying to warn the police:

'Reporters were trying to get hold of officers in the police box, saying "Can't you see what's going on?" '

Graham Kelly took the stand at one point and told the court he had held a meeting with Duckenfield 15 minutes after the game was stopped. According to Kelly, Duckenfield told him that fans had pushed through a gate, causing a crush on the terraces. Duckenfield is also alleged to have said to Kelly that there had been some fatalities and the game would have to be abandoned. Kelly agreed with Duckenfield's QC, William Clegg, that the police were responsible for protecting spectators from attack. Clegg put it to Kelly that the police were not responsible for the safety of the spectators when they were in the ground, to which Kelly replied that that was the responsibility of the club as the holder of the safety certificate. Clegg also pointed out to the jury that:

'His [Duckenfield's] job was to protect people from danger, not expose them to it.'

Off-duty police officer James O'Keeffe said:

'I believed at that time the police were at fault... The central pen was grossly overcrowded. There was no movement in the crowd whatsoever. I knew I was looking at something that was extremely dangerous.

'Although I was shocked at what I saw, the injured and dead, in no way was I surprised at what I saw given that the terrace was so grossly overcrowded at 3 o'clock.'

Roger Houldsworth was monitoring crowd control on the day and he told the court that he heard a message saying: 'If we do not open a gate someone is going to die' and a reply coming back saying: 'If someone's going to die, open the gate, open the gate.'

But it was not specified which gate should be opened. Houldsworth said he saw on the monitors a large build-up outside the ground and the crowd surging through when Gate C was opened. On-duty police officer Adrian Brazener said he thought it was a pitch invasion at first but when he got to the penalty area he knew it was not a hooligan incident.

'I could see something was amiss. People were on the fencing pushing people back down to the pens. I could see officers pushing people off the fences, on the floor, onto people struggling to get back up.'

He told the court that someone at the game's morning briefing told officers working in the Leppings Lane End to take a meal break at 2.45 pm, which he thought was unusual as it was close to the kick-off time.

At one point Justice Hooper discharged the jury from giving a verdict on the charge of wilfully neglecting to carry out a public duty, saying:

'We have considered count three and we have decided it does not really add anything in this case and I am discharging you formally from considering it.'

One of the most emotional moments came when Murray took the stand. While many had thought of him as an evil man (some whispered 'bastard' when he took the stand) he came across as remorseful, claiming to be haunted by the thought that if he had closed a central tunnel to the Leppings Lane terrace lives might have been saved.

He said he thought the terraces were safe and his main concern had been to get people away from the crush at the turnstiles. He said:

'I am very much aware that there was a course of action which, if I had thought about it and realised I could have taken, it might have prevented people going down the tunnel. Its effectiveness I do not know, but it's something I might have done.

'I never considered there might be a problem with the terraces... I thought the terraces were safe. People seemed to be coming in really responsibly.

'I am a parent, I have a great deal of sympathy for the families and I know what they have lost, I know how they must feel and I know a lot of them blame me. I just hope they can be a little understanding because it does affect me.'

Murray also recalled a two-minute breakdown in police radio communications that occurred as the incident was becoming a tragedy:

'It disrupted my train of thought. If we had not had a radio fault or problems I do not know what my course of action would have been. It might have been I would have been thinking about delaying a kick-off.'

When Justice Hooper summed up, before letting the jury retire to come up with a verdict, he let them know what he thought while directing them. Chairman of the Hillsborough Family Support Group, Trevor Hicks, has claimed that the summing-up swung the verdict in favour of the police because it made it literally impossible for the jury to convict the men. One thing that people pointed to as an example was the wording of four questions that Justice Hooper gave the jury. The questions were the same for each defendant, apart from 'match commander' for Duckenfield being replaced by 'ground controller' for Murray. They read:

1. Are you sure that, having regard to all the circumstances, it was foreseeable by a reasonable match commander that allowing a large number of spectators to enter the stadium through exit gate 'C' without closing the tunnel would create an obvious and serious risk of death to the spectators in pens 3 and 4?

    If the answer is 'yes', then go to question 2. If not, your verdicts must be: 'Not guilty'.

2. Are you sure that having regard to all the circumstances, that there were effective steps which could have been taken by a reasonable match commander to close off the tunnel and which would have prevented the deaths through crushing of spectators in pens 3 and 4?

    If the answer is 'yes', go to question 3. If not, your verdicts must be: 'Not guilty'.

3. Are you sure that the failure to take these steps was negligent? The failure would be negligent if a reasonable match commander would, in all the circumstances, have taken those steps.

    If the answer is 'yes', go to question 4. If not, your verdicts must be: 'Not guilty'.

4. Are you sure that, having regard to the risk of death involved, the failure to take those steps was so bad in all the circumstances as to amount to a very serious criminal offence?

If the answer is 'yes', your verdicts must be 'guilty'. If not, your verdicts must be: 'Not guilty'.

Nonetheless, it took the jury of eight men and four women four days to come to a verdict. By the third day Justice Hooper told them he would accept majority verdicts on which at least 10 of them were agreed, instead of requiring a unanimous decision.

Anticipating the emotional outcry that could come with any verdict, the judge warned members of the victims' families who packed out the public gallery that they must not react when the verdict was announced, as it would be a serious contempt of court. Murray was the first to be cleared of the two counts of manslaughter. He held his head in his hands, and there were tears from some in the public gallery who had held on for so long to this last hope of justice. When asked by the judge if there was a realistic possibility that jurors would reach a majority verdict in the case of Duckenfield, the jury foreman said they might if they had some more time. However, on the following Monday time was up for the jurors and Justice Hooper discharged them.

Justice Hooper ordered – after some heated debate in which Jones accused him that his directions to the jury had been misleading in parts – that there would be no retrial on the matter. He also ordered that the majority of the cost of the case – believed to be more than £4 million – was to come from public funds.

Duckenfield, who was revealed to be suffering from post-traumatic stress disorder, never took the stand during the trial. His only comment was a statement put out by his solicitor, which read:

'As a husband and a father he has every sympathy with the victims' families for the loss of their loved ones. He respectfully asks that he and his family are now left alone to try and rebuild their own lives, away from the glare of publicity.'

Trevor Hicks said the families did not think they had been completely defeated:

'It is not quite the result we would have liked but it is a limited victory. We may have lost the war but we have certainly won a lot of battles on the way.

'We said we would be bound by the verdict and we will be. We've put our case in a court of law and we have nearly won. We have not lost... we were not looking for scapegoats... we think we are totally exonerated in what we have done.

'Our lives have had to continue for 11 years. This will be one part of our lives which will not continue.'

Nevertheless, a part of the families' hope died with this, the last ruling there can be on Hillsborough.

And the families are yet to know peace. The pre-Christmas 2000 release of the Hollywood movie *Gladiator* on DVD brought with it an unwelcome and inaccurate extra. A second disc contains a commentary featuring scenes from the Hillsborough disaster, linking it with violence. The feature looks at the background of gladiator games and the relationship between violence in public entertainment and sport. The Hillsborough footage is shown between players competing in a Rugby Union match and a boxing bout, while a voice-over states: 'The connection of violence in public entertainment and sport has continued to thrive and can still be found in modern sports today.'

But if the police have not been found guilty, who else is there to blame? At one point during the trial, Murray's counsel, Michael Harrison QC, argued it was the situation that led to football supporters being caged in pens, rather than the failures of the police, that caused the tragedy. If one accepts that argument, then surely it is wise to look at who was responsible for the pens. On one hand we can blame the hooliganism of the time, but we can also put blame on the people who decided to treat the fans the way they did. For that we can look to the then ruling party, the Conservatives, and their leader, Margaret Thatcher. Thatcher was never a football fan. The whole football environment – or working-class people banding together – was something her party hated. Treating the fans as animals and as hooligans regardless of what they were doing played a part in the tragedy. Blame can – and should – fall upon those running the country at the time. Tony Blair always claimed to be a football fan, supporting the team in his constituency. However, appeals to Blair's government for justice were ignored, and one got the feeling that the subject was too tricky, too emotional, too real for a government obsessed with media-friendly pop culture. Pop stars may be welcome at 10 Downing Street, and Blair may like to go to cup finals, but when his party had the chance to do something positive, it failed, making sure that 96 families will never know true justice in the Land of Hope and Glory. Cool Britannia indeed.

So then, who is to blame for Hillsborough? Certainly some of those mentioned above. However, there is one other group that deserves mention. It comprises every person who moaned about the treatment of the families but did nothing about it, who made no complaints to the press and directed no campaigns at politicians. They are the average person: you, me. We are all a little responsible for the lack of justice from 15 April 1989.

Eighteen

Newcastle

Fans at clubs across the world suffer for their teams: this is the truth of football. Fans put up with treatment from football clubs that they would not accept from anyone else they were giving money to. In Britain, Newcastle fans have suffered on numerous occasions, but no one ever thought the club would be so low as to battle its own fans in court – a case that was so unique in football, it gained attention across the world. It is a situation that every fan of any club in the world could find themselves in and as such has relevance for everyone.

The roots of the court case lay in 1994 when thousands of fans – some of whom were already season ticket holders, some of whom weren't – read literature from the club that said that if they paid £500 they would be allowed to keep the seat they had for 10 years. As well as enticing literature on the matter, it was also heavily promoted by the then manager Kevin Keegan. Fans were also told by the club that they could not guarantee any seats that were not bonded, so many bought out of fear. When existing season ticket holders bought the bond they were given the option of changing their seat to a better one if they wanted to. It was a successful sales pitch, with 7,232 fans taking up the offer, providing the club with an extra £3.6 million.

However, in 1999 the club told the bond holders that they would either have to move to seats in the new upper tier to make way for hospitality units or pay £1,350 or £995, depending on the seat, to stay in the area they were in. The club planned to build hospitality units as part of a £45 million redevelopment of the ground, which would bring in an extra 15,000 supporters, taking St James's capacity to over 50,000. The corporate hospitality unit would bring in around £3 million a year. The club claimed that the bond guaranteed the fans a seat but not necessarily the seat they were in and on that spot, and they were told they would get a seat. However, the fans felt it guaranteed them a specific seat, the one they picked in 1994 and that any attempt to move them was wrongful and unlawful, so six of them went to court claiming breach of contract and misrepresentation.

The fans – Tony Coutts, Jane Duffy, Geoff O'Brien, Brent Pitcher, Alison Waugh and Colin Whittle – were fighting on behalf of 2,140 of the fans who had bought the bond, on the principle that they had each paid £500 in 1994 for a bond that would allow them to keep the seat they had for 10 years. They had already shown they were serious when they appeared on consumers' rights show *Watchdog*. The battle lines had been drawn then, with Newcastle saying it had tried to keep the number of people affected to a minimum. The club also admitted that it had tried to find a solution that would not involve moving fans, but it was not possible.

On the first day of the case in February 2000, when Miss Duffy told the court the reasoning behind her actions, you could feel the other fans in the courtroom beaming with pride for her, almost as if she were a player in the team. It is doubtful that club chief executive Freddie Fletcher and chairman Freddy Shepherd, who were also in court to hear the evidence, felt the same. She told Justice Blackburne:

'I have a seat on the halfway line, which gives me one of the best views of the pitch and I'm here because I don't believe the club has the right to take that seat away from me.

'When the information came through about the bond I thought I had to buy it because it gave me a season ticket for 10 years and most importantly I suspected there was no chance of being moved out of my seat.

'I knew that what I was getting was my seat for 10 years and I could heave a sigh of relief. If I move it will be to a vastly inferior seat.'

The first day's excitement at the trial taking place was nothing compared to the buzz that was expected for the second day, as it was believed that Kevin Keegan would be giving evidence on behalf of the fans. Getting Keegan on board was a triumph for the fans on a legal basis, because he was someone who had been an employee of the club, who had been used to promote the bond, yet was willing to give evidence against the club. On a personal basis he was someone held in the highest regard by Newcastle fans and was regarded as an honest man by most people in football. As someone who was the current England manager, to be willing to give evidence in court on behalf of ordinary football fans spoke volumes for the man, as he had nothing to gain whatsoever. However, Keegan was only to appear if the club was going to contest his statement. They did not challenge it. If he had turned up in the flesh, the damage and embarrassment would have been immense. As it was, his statement was still pretty devastating and gave the Toon faithful another reason to love the man.

Keegan's statement was admitted to the court as evidence, with parts read out by Jonathan Crystal, barrister for the Save Our Seats campaign. The statement alone shows the love the Newcastle fans have for their club, but also how grounded that feeling is.

One part read:

'Several times during the early stages of the bond scheme I can recall numerous occasions on which I met groups of fans and individuals who were attending St James's Park for the specific purpose of picking their specific seats.

'On occasions people would spend two or three hours choosing their seats. I would often go and speak to these people and I could sense the importance they attached to choosing their own seats.

'There was no doubt from the overall promotion of the bond scheme and the way it was sold that the bond holders would retain their own personal seats for 10 years.

'It is my belief that the purchasers of United bonds are entitled to their own designated seats for the remaining life of the bond.'

After Keegan's statement the club got a chance to fight back. It said that the money from increasing corporate hospitality was needed to keep the club at the highest level and that the work would allow more people into the ground. Freddie Fletcher said:

'The reason for the level of corporatisation in this stadium is to raise the money to spend £45 million to develop the stadium to allow more of those people who cannot afford the corporate hospitality to get into the stadium.

'Around 10 per cent of the seats in the ground are reserved for corporate hospitality but that brings in about 40 per cent of the total revenue from the gate.'

Fletcher said he disagreed with Keegan, but couched it in soft enough terms so as not to draw further wrath from the fans, saying:

'I am sure Kevin thinks what he said was true. He's a strong-willed, honest and decent man.'

When pressed on the point that brought them to court Fletcher denied the claims that the club had broken the promise made in the bond that fans would have the same seats for 10 years and pointed out that the small print said they could be moved.

'We gave them terms and conditions that we wouldn't move them unless there were exceptional circumstances. The last thing any club wants to do is upset loyal fans, but what we were attempting to do was solve the capacity problem for Newcastle United because the demand was there from fans who couldn't get into the ground.'

The club also claimed that nearly all bond holders affected had already chosen new seats within the revamped stadium and had taken advantage of an offer to select a second seat for a friend or family member.

Jonathan Crystal summed up for the judge exactly why this was an important issue, when many people could not believe that a case about football seats had gone to court:

'For these fans this is their life. They want the seats where they are. For them it's everything and that's what they were promised.'

The ruling came on the fourth day, not long after noon – high noon, as more than one person quipped. It added to the sense of drama, although the Newcastle fans had their own feelings about who the cowboys were in this case and who was being scalped. Around 70 fans sat in silence in a packed public gallery at the High

Court in Newcastle as the judgment was read out. For just over an hour they heard that the small print did allow the club to move them and that they should have been aware of this. Justice Blackburne said:

'The claimants' challenge must fail and their claim must be dismissed... but having witnessed the keenness with which many supporters have followed the proceedings and sensed the intensity of feeling, I would have preferred to have come to a different conclusion.'

But the judge did give the supporters leave to appeal on the grounds that the club had misrepresented its original bond offer in 1994, and he also issued an injunction prohibiting the club from proceeding with the corporatisation of the affected area until the matter − if it went to appeal − was completely concluded.

Colin Whittle remembers how they felt afterwards:

'We were very disappointed to say the least − especially on the evidence before the court. The general view of everyone who had heard the evidence was that we had won convincingly.

'Neither of the club's witnesses came up to proof whereas the general view was that our witnesses had.'

After the hearing, the club blew the chance to start developing goodwill towards the fans when a very businesslike statement was put out, which read:

'Newcastle United naturally welcomes the decision of the court. It is advised that the court's judgment was correct in all respects and will be upheld in the event of an appeal.

'We are keen to ensure that any issues over costs are resolved as quickly as possible and we will be working towards an early resolution of them.'

However, less than a week after the case, the club looked as if it was learning. In what was seen as a positive step − the first in a long time − the club commissioned respected football researcher Dr Rogan Taylor to conduct an independent review of the club's handling of its fans. Dr Taylor's background is one of the finest in football academia. He was the inaugural chairman of the Football Supporters' Association, formed after the Heysel disaster in 1985, director of the Football Research Unit at Liverpool University and on the planning committee for Euro '96. At a press conference he revealed some of his plans, including a 300-strong forum of fans to air supporters' grievances. Dr Taylor said:

'We all know that relations have been strained for various reasons over the past few years and this is an opportunity to build a decent system for proper fan representation.

'I get the impression that there has been a recognition that the club has made a mess of a lot of things in the past.'

When asked about the High Court costs he suggested the club should meet the costs as a peacekeeping gesture:

'I hope that the board deals extremely sympathetically with this question of costs. It is an excellent opportunity for the club, and it should, without a doubt, take it. I think the fans had every right to bring the case and this is a great chance for the club to make a clean break.'

It took the six bond holders some time to decide whether or not they would appeal, as it was becoming apparent that money would be a problem, but like footballers they played into the legal equivalent of extra time and appealed. They decided to go for the appeal after their legal team advised them that the High Court judge had reached the wrong decision and in their view they would be successful on appeal. This was confirmed by their insurers' legal team after they had considered the papers and the judgment and before they agreed to provide them with cover for the appeal.

Just to make sure they thought they had a chance, they also asked an independent QC to look at the papers and he reached the same view. The appeal was heard in June 1999, but it was another defeat for the fans, leaving them to worry about an £80,000 shortfall. Lord Chief Justice, Lord Woolf, said the club did have the legal right to move the fans 'however sympathetic one may feel' towards them, but he also hinted that the club should not press for the charges that the fans were now eligible to pay. The club ignored this and put in a claim for £197,000, to which Ms Duffy said:

'The indications now are that they want to claim to the bitter end. I can't believe that the club can justify these costs. It seems to me that the club wants blood and that makes me very, very bitter and angry.'

Ms Duffy, who had not missed a home game since 1976, claimed the ruling and the appeal would have wide-ranging implications for every true football fan in Britain. For her this was the final straw.

'We are staggered by the costs reportedly incurred by the club. Is that to be taken as an indication of their regime of letting fans have their say?

'This ruling, if unchallenged, will change irrevocably the face of football, legitimising the replacement by corporate interest of genuine supporters.

'What this case has done has given out a message to fans not to take on their clubs because Newcastle have as good as proved that if you do, the club will beat you into submission.

'I have been a lifelong supporter of Newcastle, have not missed a game since 1976 and remain a fan of the team but I don't think I shall be going back to St James's Park. There are always away games to watch.'

Not all the fans agreed, feeling that their argument was with the club, not the team on the pitch, and some took up new season tickets elsewhere in the ground.

One solicitor at the firm representing the fans put the ball firmly in Newcastle's court when he said it was up to the club as to whether they wanted to make their fans bankrupt and put them at risk of losing their homes. As well as being an emotive comment, it also referred to people at the club saying that the last thing they wanted to do was take houses from individuals. But the club has never offered the six an olive branch, confirming Colin Whittle's suspicion that it, or certain people there, wants to teach them a lesson.

'I expect the club to pursue the issue of costs, which is an own goal of mammoth proportions. PR-wise, it would be sensible to write them off. As it stands, when the matter goes to taxation the costs will be reduced and the club will take another bashing in the press.'

Refusing to pay such a sum, the fans have taken the proceedings to taxation, which is where the court will assess the costs. The fans' argument is that the costs are unreasonable and over the top. The taxation hearing is set to take place at some point in 2001. If it rules in the club's favour then the six will have to pay any shortfall between their insurance cover and the final figure, which could see them all bankrupted. They are currently accepting donations from fans, and their situation has touched the hearts of many who realise who is important in the game. They have even received a £20 contribution from a Sunderland fan who lives in Australia, which was especially touching as Sunderland and Newcastle are strong rivals.

Since the appeal, things have improved in part. A shareholders' trust has been set up and the new chief executive, David Stonehouse, seems supportive of the fans. The new ground has opened to acclaim, but the memory of the court case still lingers like a hangover after drinking too much of Newcastle's famous ale. For the club on and off the pitch it is business as usual, but the business has improved. Newcastle's last accounts showed they made a profit of nearly £2 million. To the club's bankers and owners the £197,000 involved in this case might be a not inconsiderable sum, but in the eyes of football watchers it has cost them a lot more than that.

Part Four

Extra Time –
Fans getting the game back

Nineteen

Manchester United

In September 1998 English football was getting into the swing of another season. It was a season that would end with Manchester United winning the European Cup, but at the start of it they got everyone's attention when it was announced that BSkyB had put in a £623 million bid to buy Manchester United PLC and take control of the football club. No one had expected it and pundits immediately thought the club's days were numbered before becoming a part of BSkyB and the News International Corporation.

Part of this thinking was due to the friendly relationship between Murdoch and British governments. Up until the 1997 UK general election Murdoch's newspapers had been pro-Conservative and both sides benefited from the friendly relationship.

However, in 1997, Murdoch's papers started to back Tony Blair and the Labour Party instead of the Conservatives. Media watchers at the time noted that Murdoch is a businessman above all else and they wondered what benefit he would get from allying with Labour, who won the election.

Thus when the Manchester United bid was announced there were fears that due to the close links between party and papers, the Government might back off from intervening in the matter, allowing the club to be taken over, even if it was not for the good of the club or the game in general.

Instead, the bid to buy the club would remind the two men – who know of socialism and the idea of 'power to the masses' – exactly what the masses could do, and the attempted takeover helped spark the desire of fans wanting to get control of their game.

But on that second week in September no one knew this. All the shareholders did know was that for each Manchester United share, they were being offered 0.2537 of a new BSkyB share and £1.20 in cash, which when combined was an offer in excess of the share value. Shareholders were also offered a straight £2.40 per share deal. While the offers shocked most, there was one piece of news that was not a surprise to those familiar with the club's then-chief executive, Martin Edwards. Edwards had spearheaded the deal, and as part of the package he would be joining the board of BSkyB. It was not the first time Edwards had tried to sell the club. The first had been in late 1989 when he decided to sell it to businessman Michael Knighton for £10 million, which was at the time considered excessive. Edwards's fellow directors, including Sir Bobby Charlton, resisted the sale, and in the interim period Knighton's backers withdrew.

There was no mystery as to why BSkyB wanted Manchester United, aside from the profit that could be made from a global brand. As mentioned elsewhere, the television rights to football are an incredibly powerful thing to control, and owning a club would not only allow BSkyB a seat at the negotiating table to see all the offers being made, it would also place them in a better position to put forward the case for splitting up the negotiating rights, if they wanted to do so. Manchester United in many ways was, and still is, the perfect team. They are a global phenomenon, with supporters' clubs in nearly every country in the world, particularly in the growing markets of Asia and the Far East. Research from China shows that United has an almost 80 per cent unprompted name awareness, showing that many people in many parts of the world know something about Manchester United, even if they know little else about football. This level of rating is phenomenal in marketing terms and can only be beaten by multinationals like Nike, McDonalds, Adidas or symbols like Superman's 'S' or Batman's bat emblem.

To cash in on this awareness, the club has plans for retail stores in Singapore, Japan, Taiwan, Indonesia, Korea, Dubai, Cape Town and

Hong Kong. China, Korea and Japan will have a combination of retail space selling anything that can take the club's name or badge, screens to watch matches, food and drink areas and perhaps even Internet cafés and online betting. But for the club to be that famous, it has to be seen, and this was one of the reasons for Murdoch's interest in Manchester United. As well as BSkyB, Murdoch's News International Corporation owns Japan's JSkyB, Asia's StarTV and the Fox broadcast network in America.

In Manchester the fans were moving as quickly as Beckham through a defence. Roger Taylor, drummer with the band Queen, donated £10,000 to the Independent Manchester United Supporters' Association (IMUSA) to pay for a supporters' rally at Bridgewater Hall and to set up a headquarters. Taylor got involved because his son Rufus is a Manchester United supporter. Taylor also upped the ante for all the media trendies and luvvies − many of whom had taken the Murdoch penny − by calling for them to get involved. He said:

'As I was in a position to help I felt compelled to do so. I'm hoping that others will now come forward and want to do the same, to help those grassroots fans hold on to the club they love.'

Murdoch and BSkyB were painted as the bad guys in the affair, but according to football author and Manchester United fan Jonathan Michie, there were others at fault:

'To be fair it wasn't as much a takeover attempt by BSkyB, it was Martin Edwards wanting to sell the club, get £80 million for it and get a seat on the board of BSkyB. He came into the boardroom, announced he had sold it and that was the end of it.

'However, Edwards and the others were completely stunned by the backlash, especially the campaign by the fans and the way they were taken seriously. It was never thought that the fans would go to the lengths they did.'

At that first meeting in Manchester the fans served notice on Edwards that they would fight for their club, with more than 1,000 people attending. At that meeting IMUSA issued a list of 10 proposals for assurances to be met by any organisation seeking to take over Manchester United, including demands that the new parent company would not interfere with the team, that ticket prices would not be increased unreasonably, that the domestic football structure remain in place and that fans be consulted on any changes. The bid attracted worldwide attention; even American newspapers commented on the deal, which was worth more than $1 billion – a record even in the United States.

Former Manchester United manager Tommy Docherty was one of the first to put the boot in, saying:

'I doubt very much if he [Murdoch] even knows where Old Trafford is... Not being a football man, he will not understand the true feelings of football people.'

This was untrue. Murdoch knew exactly what the game meant to people, how important it was and how much they needed it, hence the generous share offer. Worried fans pointed to the fact that when he bought the Dodgers baseball team for $311 million he more or less instantly replaced key people in the team. The club countered these claims through the chairman of the United PLC board Sir Roland Smith, who claimed BSkyB would not interfere in team affairs and transfer policy if the deal went through. He said in a document sent to shareholders:

'Alex Ferguson will be in charge of team selection. Alex Ferguson and the board of Manchester United will be responsible for the acquisition of new players.'

He added that ticket prices for matches at United's Old Trafford home would not be affected by the bid and that the United management team of chief executive Martin Edwards, deputy Peter Kenyon and finance director David Gill would stay involved in the club's daily operations.

The supporters realised that merely putting on a campaign for fans, appealing to shareholders and buying shares where possible would not be enough to save their club. It would take a concerted effort aimed at those who had the final say on the bid. This meant taking on the Government, as the Office of Fair Trading would be advising the Department of Trade and Industry on whether or not the bid should be referred to the Competitions Commission, then known as the Monopolies and Mergers Commission (MMC).

But it was not just the fans who had objections. The stock market was not as cock-a-hoop as expected. Some were saying that the £623 million offer, which was more than the £400 million stock market value of the club, did not take into account other factors like individual television rights for the club, which could be worth the value of the offer themselves. The share price reflected this and it was possible to buy shares at prices well below the BSkyB offer. Television authorities were also putting forward their objections to the deal to the Independent Television Commission in order to block the bid. However, their claims were not helped by the fact that every TV company with enough money was circling around other football clubs that had potential on a similar scale to Manchester United.

Politicians were also letting it be known that they had concerns, with Chris Smith, Tony Banks and Gordon Brown all said to be worried about how the bid would affect the average football fan. Smith also voiced the inherent contradiction between football and big business:

'As soon as football clubs become PLCs, they find themselves subject to predatory takeovers. Yet they can't be treated like products in a marketplace as allegiances to them are based on cultural affinities.'

But because they are in the marketplace they have to be treated like commodities – that's the law.

At the end of October 1998, the bid was thankfully referred to the MMC. The MMC – for the first time ever, reflecting the level of public debate on the matter – revealed the issues it was considering. These included the wider public interest, whether or not the takeover would see fans losing out as games were rescheduled to suit the TV channels, whether or not it would give BSkyB an advantage over other broadcasters in its talks for screening rights to Premier League football and if it would speed up the introduction of pay-per-view games or a quicker increase in prices. Murdoch's papers were doing all they could to keep the deal alive, pointing out how good BSkyB had already been for the game, and how much better it would be in future if the deal was allowed.

As 1999 started it was felt that there would be a compromise, with BSkyB getting the club as long as there were concessions on the matter of television rights. 12 March 1999 was the deadline set for the MMC to report back to the Government. Then on 9 April, the

Department of Trade and Industry surprised almost everyone with the announcement that they had blocked the bid due to the conclusions of the MMC report. Analysis of the report shows that it did not hold back in stating its opinions:

> [The Commission was] unable to identify any public interest benefits from the proposed merger. We therefore conclude that the proposed merger between BSkyB and Manchester United may be expected to operate against the public interest. We think that the adverse effects are sufficiently serious that prohibiting the merger is both an appropriate and a proportionate remedy.

If the deal went through it would:

> enhance BSkyB's already strong position arising from its market power as a sports premium channel provider and from being the incumbent broadcaster of Premier League football. The effect would be to reduce competition for Premier League rights leading to less choice for the Premier League and less scope for innovation in the broadcasting of Premier League football.

The report also considered the implication that if one broadcaster was allowed to buy a club, others had to be allowed to do the same:

> If rights were sold on an individual basis and there were several mergers between broadcasters and Premier League clubs precipitated by the BSkyB/Manchester United merger, all of the feasible outcomes would be less competitive than the situation in which rights were individually sold and no broadcaster/Premier League club mergers had occurred.

And just to hammer the point home:

> We also think that the merger would adversely affect football in two ways. Firstly, it would reinforce the existing trend

towards greater inequality of wealth between clubs, thus weakening the smaller ones.

Second, it would give BSkyB additional influence over Premier League decisions relating to the organisation of football, leading to some decisions which did not reflect the long-term interests of football. On both counts the merger may be expected to have the adverse effect of damaging the quality of British football. This adverse effect would be more pronounced if the merger precipitated other mergers between broadcasters and Premier League clubs.

BSkyB took the decision as well as could be expected. A company statement read:

> BSkyB is disappointed that the acquisition has been prevented from proceeding. BSkyB remains convinced it did not raise any competition or wider public interest concerns and that, had the acquisition proceeded, it would have been good for fans, good for football and good for Manchester United.
>
> This ruling sets an unfortunate precedent for other British clubs and companies who may have wanted to work together to improve and invest in the future for the benefit of clubs, players and fans alike. This is a bad ruling for British football clubs who will have to compete in Europe against clubs who are backed by successful media companies.

Not everyone agrees with Sky's view, though. Jonathan Michie is of the opinion that the case was a landmark because it triggered the end of the free rein that media companies and businesses thought they had:

'It brought about a qualitative change in the determination of supporters and their efforts of reclaiming the game.

'It wasn't just that until then media companies thought that they could make their own decisions on how to use football – or not – in their battles with each other and do what they decided and that was the end of that, it was also that fans started looking at the whole issue of them accepting that football owners could do what they want –

the Ken Bates, the Martin Edwards – and that was brought under more scrutiny. That came to an end with the end of the BSkyB bid.

'Fans realised they could – and can – separate the money coming in and the influence and power that it buys. They showed they can separate it and take control themselves if they want – to a degree – and still have the money coming in on their terms.'

The Manchester United bid proved that fans could, if they worked together and attracted enough public opinion, be influential. However, it also showed the opposite to many, that fans could not have a large say, because at the end of the day, any club on the stock market has to play by stock market rules, which in many cases is simply a matter of the highest bidder wins, regardless of the institution at stake. Manchester United got away with it this time. Other clubs may not be so lucky.

Twenty

Northampton

Northampton. An English town with a population of 200,000. An ordinary place in an ordinary part of the country. Except for one thing. Years from now it may be remembered as the place where the fight to return football to the fans began.

Northampton Town is not a team known for winning European Cups or being top of the league every year, but when you walk about Northampton you see something that is very rare. There are fewer Manchester United, Liverpool or Chelsea strips here than anywhere else in the country. Here the strip to wear is the local one, and it is worn with pride. But less than 10 years ago it was not such a cheerful picture.

At the end of 1991 some of the fans were told that the club was in serious debt and that the players' wages were being paid by their union, the Professional Footballers' Association. At that time the club was not doing well. Their ground, County Ground, was one of the worst in the league. For example, there were no ladies toilets except under the stand. Unfortunately, for safety reasons the stand had been closed, meaning the toilets could not be used.

The state of things – on and off the pitch – became so bad that a group of fans got together and called a public meeting entitled 'Tell Us The Truth'. They asked the then chairman to attend, which he declined to do. He went on to rubbish the meeting in the local paper, saying that if there was a need for a public meeting, then the club would call it themselves. The meeting took place in January 1992 and about 600 people turned up, which was approximately one-third of the gate at the time. At that meeting it was disclosed that Northampton owed £1.6 million – about two years' income – and the fans decided to start raising money to save the club. However, they didn't want to hand it over to those in charge at the time, so a resolution was passed to start a trust that would raise money and keep it until the club was in good hands, when the trust would then hand it over. To all intents and purposes it was a statement of no confidence in the chairman, but also a statement of intent from fans.

Brian Lomax, a long-term fan who was heavily involved in trying to save the club, remembers the time well:

'People were not happy at all with the way things were going and they were not going to hand the money over and see it disappear into a bottomless pit. What they wanted was some form of proper say in the running of the football club in return for the money.'

Three months later the fans got their chance after the chairman put the club into administration. The administrators invited the trust to elect two members of the board in April 1992, which they did, those two fans becoming the first directors elected by fans to a British football club. The trust then handed over the £30,000 they had raised, for which they received a shareholding of around 8 per cent. At the same time as the fans were doing their bit, the local council was also getting involved. Amongst the proposals being pushed by councillors, including the present director of Northampton, Tony Clarke (who is now the MP for the area), was for the council to develop a new ground for the club. The proposals were fairly radical and European for their time. They were European in the sense that in countries like Spain, most – if not all – of the country's grounds are owned by the local government, who pay all the costs and charge the teams who play there a rent.

In the case of Northampton, in return for a new stadium the club would have to hand over 20 per cent of every week's gate. At the time, some criticised the council for spending £12 million on the site that would come to be known as Sixfields, though to date more than £6 million has been recouped from the development of the area, which now has a modern stadium, cinema and pubs. Part of the conditions attached to the stadium was that it was to be used regularly by the community and not just for football once or twice a week.

It is an excellent deal for the club. In return for that one-fifth of the gate money, which is in reality a rent fee, the council looks after the stadium and deals with ticketing, policing and stewarding. At the moment the council makes a loss of £250,000 a year. However, the council has maintained since the area's inception that first, there is more to it than profit, and second, some of the council's parks and leisure centres have running costs that are in excess of Sixfields', so in comparison it is quite good value. Since the move the club has improved in ways people would never have thought possible at the start of the nineties. The community has rallied round the team and on the two occasions that it has reached Wembley for play-offs there has been a healthy travelling support of around 40,000–45,000 fans.

There are now monthly meetings between the fans and directors, though players, managers and other club staff come along to explain what is happening in their part of the club, too. The meetings are open and no questions are avoided (though some issues like individual players' wages and contracts are not discussed as they are confidential matters). Fans who attend the meetings learn and see the constraints that the club operates under, and it allows them to be realistic, as they know what is going on. Brian Lomax remembers an occasion when ticket prices had to be negotiated:

'When we have to raise ticket prices, we talk to the fan base about what they think would be a decent and fair increase in prices. We don't just announce a rise and wait for the criticism.

'I think that without fan involvement in this sort of thing we would have just had criticism and fans saying we don't want any kind of ticket increase, but now they are saying they understand why there is an increase – wages are going up, money is needed for players – it's not just an order handed down from on high.'

This policy of openness gives the board and others at the club some breathing room because when there are a few bad results, the fans don't heckle the board and call for sackings, as they understand the situation. It is also extremely good customer relations, and other clubs have occasionally carried out similar meetings, though not on as regular a basis. As Tony Clarke says:

'The board are seen as true supporters and our fans are seen as educated supporters in that they know what is going on. My mail from fans shows that. It talks about issues on policing, wages and so on, it's not just about the on-pitch performance and results, they are looking at the other activities.'

The club has also commemorated its – and the community's – roots by erecting a monument to one of Britain's first black players, Walter Tull, who was also the first black commissioned officer and who died in the second battle of the Somme. The statue forms part of the area's garden of remembrance for those who died in the war, and many supporters have their ashes interred around the area and the monument.

Northampton showed how it could be done and this – along with similar institutions at a few other clubs – inspired Brian Lomax to help form Supporters Direct. The idea was to prevent things getting as bad as they had at Northampton, but also to give the fans more say and involvement in their club. The scheme offers legal and other forms of advice, plus free banking from the Co-operative Bank. Non-legal advice is provided by Birkbeck's Football Research Unit, which is directed by Dr Christine Oughton. Supporters' groups are also able to get advice from other fans who have first-hand experience of establishing their own trusts. Lomax sums it up fluently and passionately:

'We want the fans to have genuine ownership and control. A lot of fans don't realise the power they have.

'There was an element of doffing your cap in the 1960s and there was a belief that no one was profiteering from the game, but the old-style supporters' club was too easily impressed and too easily accepting of the club taking money and so on without getting anything really meaningful back.

'In a situation like we had in the early nineties, if things are being done wrong, and there's a supporter on the board, he can come back to the public and blow the whistle, which benefits all unless there's something untoward going on. No board has anything to fear from the fans or us if they are doing the job properly – nothing at all.'

Lomax's aims were backed by a report by the Football Task Force in January 1999, which recommended the formation of trusts that can acquire a shareholding as well as having direct election to the boards.

Supporters Direct was formally launched in mid-2000. It is chaired by Brian Lomax. Professor Jonathan Michie, who is Head of Birkbeck's School of Management, a football author and chair of Shareholders United (Manchester United's shareholder and supporter group) and Trevor Watkins, chair of AFC Bournemouth, are also actively involved.

Backed by Kevin Keegan and Sir Alex Ferguson, funded by £250,000 a year for three years from the pools' betting duty and agreed by the Government via the Football Foundation, it was an immediate success. Ferguson said:

'Supporters Direct will strengthen the bonds between supporters and their clubs. That can only be good for the game.'

Culture Secretary Chris Smith believes that Supporters Direct is what the game needs to recognise the effort put in by the fans:

'Supporters are the lifeblood of the game. Where clubs have been in crisis, more often than not they have been saved by their fans and emerged stronger for it.

'The more enlightened clubs know it is in their own commercial interest to value their supporters and involve them in the affairs of their club. That is the simple philosophy behind Supporters Direct: supporter involvement is good for clubs as well as fans.'

Within three months it had beaten its target for the year as fans swamped it with demands for information. More than 80 supporter groups across England and Scotland got in touch. By the end of its first six months 14 trusts had been established at a number of clubs including Walsall FC, Lincoln City, Bournemouth, Manchester United and Crystal Palace, where 4,000 Palace supporters paid £20 each to join the trust, plus raising £1 million in loans to help the club through a crisis period. At Luton Town, Supporters Direct helped Yvonne Fletcher become Britain's first democratically elected woman director. She said:

'Supporters Direct is the logical next step in a journey that began with fanzines and the Football Supporters' Association. Not only does it give supporter groups more credibility because it's backed by the Government but we'll feel more confident because we have all the relevant, up-to-date information on shareholding.'

One problem Supporters Direct does have is helping Scotland. Under the terms of its funding, it cannot get involved heavily or give financial backing because of devolution. According to Brian Lomax:

'We are informally helping Scottish fans and clubs but it is on a voluntary basis as we cannot use any of the money we received from Culture, Media and Sport. It cannot be used in Scotland and until we get extra funding from other sources we can't officially set up in Scotland.

'Now the Scottish supporters clearly want us to be involved. I attended a conference in Edinburgh in the early months of 2000 and there was a very high level of desire to have at least either a Scottish Supporters Direct or work through the existing Supporters Direct on Scottish cases.

'We've got files open and communication with fans and some other members of clubs on more than a dozen Scottish clubs. It's easier with some clubs than others. For example, it is easy to have dialogue with Partick Thistle because it's owned by the fans. Now we'd love to do the same in Scotland as we do down south, but that will take help from either the Scottish Executive or businesses to fund us to around £80,000 a year to ensure we could do up north what we are doing down south.

'It would be wonderful if the clubs and FA, SFA and so on would fund us up and down the country. I know the Scottish FA were present at the Edinburgh conference.

'Politicians were also present and it was interesting to see that the SNP and the Conservatives didn't think any funding should be coming from the public while Labour and the Liberals did.'

Nonetheless, the organisation helps where it can in Scotland, and as it helps more and more clubs in the UK it has been able to develop three basic models for the constitution of a supporters' group, which allows it to deal with the vast majority of situations that arise.

The first of these is the unincorporated trust that has weighty personal responsibilities for trustees and restrictions on the freedom of trustees to delegate responsibility. It is ideal in situations where shares have to be held on behalf of a group; it is in the interests of Supporters Direct and those who have donated money that the responsibilities of those who hold the shares are clearly defined and limited. The trust is the obvious vehicle for a pooled investment in a PLC – private limited company. For the same reasons a trust is less attractive where the group intends to spend money in other ways or to take on employees; the trust deed has to be broadly drafted but still leaves the trustees at risk of personal liability if they, or the people they employ, act outside their powers.

The legal structure of a trust does not lend itself to control by the membership in the way of a company or an industrial and provident society. The control in a trust is the trust deed and the actions of the trustees are judged against the wording of the document. Trustees are answerable for the way they carry out the instructions in the deed to the people who are supposed to benefit from the trust. Many supporters' groups that use a trust model will have some form of membership organisation linked to the trust through which supporters receive information and participate in debate.

Supporters Direct has stated that it prefers the more direct democratic model, where the trust deed will stipulate that the membership organisation nominates trustees and the rules of the membership organisation will provide for elections.

The second option is a Company Limited by Guarantee, a CLG.

The key features of a CLG include limited liability for members, defined responsibility for directors, freedom for directors to delegate responsibility, a constitutional requirement not to return profit to members and flexibility in aims and objectives. This makes the CLG an ideal choice for a supporters' group that intends to be active, entering into contracts or financial commitments or employing staff. A CLG can also hold shares in a club and can, in principle, have an active membership that elects its directors. Alternatively, its constitution may allow directors to be nominated or appointed by organisations or groups, or for new directors to be appointed by the existing directors. In that case, the membership of the CLG may be nominal and supporters may be offered a 'club'-type membership, where they pay a subscription, receive information and are invited to participate in debate.

The third type of scheme is that of an Industrial and Provident Society, or IPS.

Supporters Direct sees the advantages of an IPS as including limited liability for members, defined responsibility for directors, freedom for directors to delegate responsibility, potential for a two-tier structure, defining the role of elected directors and executives, freedom from investment regulation and a constitutional requirement to operate for the benefit of the community. An IPS is an ideal vehicle if significant money has to be raised by the public. It also allows the group to be active (which a CLG also delivers), but keeps the restrictions on basic principles which a trust has. Also, IPS is a legal definition. It is basically akin to a non-profit-making limited liability company. The main difference between an IPS and a trust is that the trustees of a trust carry unlimited liability, whereas the board of an IPS have no more liability than a company director. None of the models is as perfect as the Barcelona model, where the club is owned by its 120,000 members who elect the president and board, or 'Junta', every five years, but it is a start and an infinite improvement on what has happened in the past.

There is nothing like Supporters Direct elsewhere in the world. Just as many see English football as being the pinnacle of the game at the moment, it may be that the English fans are leading the fight to save the game – or it may just be that English fans have less say than their counterparts across the globe.

As mentioned above, in Spain fans hold elections to see who will take to the boards of football clubs, but this is very much the exception in the dictatorial football world, where fans are expected to take whatever is handed out to them, whether it be in Rio, Reading or Rome.

Supporters Direct is having an influence though and other countries – large and small – are now seeing what they can do to get more of a say in their clubs.

Even in tiny Nepal, which is a small country big on football, there have been recent attempts to make fans and clubs become closer. Nepal Football Fan Club has been running for over a year now. According to its president, Bikesh Shrestha, the club is non-profit, non-political and non-religious:

'The main objective of our club is to support our dear football players, [provide] information to our members, organise football competitions, pressure government for infrastructure building, players and fan meeting, participating in various meeting, seminar, publish football magazines and books to inform about football events around the world.

'Nepalese are very fond of football and our club hopes that football is [the] only way to develop Nepal's image in an international arena.

'In Nepal, youth have no jobs and no entertainment facilities so we would like to establish local football clubs, organise occasionally a football match between various ward, school and clubs.'

Trusts, then, may be the way forward on an international level for fans to get more say. However, John Williams of the Sir Norman Chester Centre for Football Research feels that trusts and Supporters Direct may take on a slightly different role to what they envisage. He said:

'I think the supporters' trusts are a good idea but I think substantially they are likely to intervene at the symbolic level rather than at the material and ownership and control level.

'They will voice the views of the fans, perhaps in the face of the worst excesses of corporate finance in the game, but largely to try and control important symbolic aspects of the game – what is the club called, what are we going to call the stand, those kind of issues are the type that fans will have control over.

'The symbolic issues are important for football and football supporters but actually intervening at a structural level is going to be much more difficult for fans and I don't see the fans as such wresting corporate control from corporate interests. I think they can act to limit the transformation – on cultural and symbolic levels – of football but it's hard to see how they can interrupt the control and ownership dimensions of the game. I think that's much more difficult.'

According to Williams, controlling or having an effect on the ownership of major football clubs is becoming increasingly difficult because the ownership of clubs is getting much more complex. He has a point. It is very hard to track who the owners of the very large clubs are, particularly the floated ones, because ownership is quite disparate – in real terms it is concentrated in the hands of a relatively small number of institutions or individuals, but they are not always easy to identify. Another of Williams's concerns is that people may assume that because they all support the same team, they will all agree on other matters.

'There is this assumption that because a large number of fans hold shares that fans will all feel the same way or think the same way or have a common interest or perspective on the way the clubs are run and I think that's a difficult, perhaps dangerous, assumption to make.

'You can have 50,000 fans of a club and all they have in common is the supporting of that club. Their politics may be different, their ideas for the club may be different. They may be able to agree broadly on one or two certain issues but once you get into the level of detail of how a club should be run and what its ambitions should be they may all have different ideas on it.

'I've no doubt that many types of supporter exist and it's not always possible to align democratisation and sense of involvement of supporters with wider global ambitions in clubs.

'My concern with what some people say is that they talk for supporters without really knowing what most ordinary supporters want or feel. I think there is a slight element of romanticism to it.'

If there is an element of romanticism to the idea of trusts and fans owning their clubs, it is hardly surprising, for football is a game of romantics and it is the fans' idealistic belief that things can get better, that they can win the league, win the cup, stop their star player going to a bigger team that fuels the game. With Supporters Direct the first rallying cries have been made at clubs across the UK that not only can things get better, but that the true fans will get involved to make things better. As I wrote at the start of this book: game on.

Twenty-one

The Future

Picture the scene. 2018. The World Cup has been played in Germany, South Africa and Australia, and is now gearing up for Brazil, which has spent millions preparing the country. Critics have argued that the money would have been better spent on social care and welfare for Brazil's poverty-stricken people, but that is all in the past and everyone is looking forward to a July kick-off in the National Pele Stadium.

Most fans will only see a few of the games, as only the semi-finals and final are available on non-pay-per-view television. In the UK fans will have to pay even for the final, because the only television signal in the country will be a paid-for digital one. For the dedicated fan, there will be packages of varying complexity and price allowing them to watch some games, some teams or the entire tournament. There is outrage in England when it is realised that not all of the country will be able to see the strongest national team in decades and a deal is soon reached with the dominant multimedia company, allowing England's games to be shown for free. Everyone is too busy being swept up in football fever to wonder what the deal – for an undisclosed sum – has cost, but no one is surprised months later when another deal goes through giving that company a virtual monopoly in a chosen area.

FIFA, now fully professional, having abandoned any pretence at amateurism, declares the games to be a great success, with billions of dollars flooding into its coffers, merchandising for the first time overtaking ticket sales and television rights.

No one bemoans the new rules. While everyone welcomes the abolition of offside, older football fans say the ban on any form of tackling has taken a large chunk out of the game. The increasing use of technology is seen as a mixed blessing: there are some reservations about the American football-type microphone used by the referee to explain his decisions. There are also health concerns about the infrared beams in the enlarged goalposts. The beams are there to ensure that the ball is fully over the line, confirming it is a goal.

Meanwhile, at a national level the game continues. Thanks to the new worldwide football calendar, all leagues – the Pan-European and domestic leagues – start at the same time. While the domestic leagues still exist, the elite European clubs play in a two-division set-up of 24 clubs, as envisioned by the G24 back in 2010. Promotion to this lucrative group is achieved through each country's domestic league winner going through a series of play-offs and meeting strict stadium and financial criteria. Two teams get in to the second of the two divisions and the bottom two teams always drop out, though this has caused some geographical anomalies for the league, as the southern teams perform better than the northern teams in the play-offs, following a trend in European football from the end of the 20th century. As well as the leagues, there are other tournaments. The Pan-European League teams still take part in domestic cup games, but using their B squads. There is a European tournament for all the domestic cup tournament winners. It has been suggested that the tournament involving all the winners of the major leagues – the Brazilian, US, Japanese, European and so on – should be widened to include more teams from other nations and continents. FIFA fears that this is the beginning of a worldwide league breakaway movement and long-term football pundits say it reminds them of the breakaway threats made by clubs in England and Europe in the 1990s and early 2000s...

The future of football or fanciful nonsense? The truth is that no one knows where the game at a local, national or international level is going. The terrifying thing is that there is no one looking to guide it at a local or national level anywhere in the world. FIFA exists, but that is what FIFA does best – making sure it keeps going, as there has been little real development in taking the game forward.

It seems very likely that whatever happens, the fans will increasingly suffer. In terms of economic advancement, players will continue to get more and more money as television companies put more and more money in. Advertising companies will feed into this orgy of flowing mass millions, but one group will not see a penny of it: the fans. In colloquial terms, if there is an orgy of companies involved in football, then it is the fans who are being screwed – and without much pleasure. The fans will no doubt face a continuing rise in prices – tickets, merchandising, TV packages, including pay per view, and computer games featuring their team. They will not be happy about it but there will be little they can do. They won't even get to see their team as much. All the big games – Manchester United against Arsenal, Celtic against Rangers, Merseyside derbies, AC Milan against Inter Milan – will be snapped up by the season ticket holders of the respective clubs, so fans will either only see their teams on TV or at the less important games. But this will only be a problem for the successful clubs. The clubs that languish mid-table in whatever league they play in will have average crowds, with all the spending on large stadiums wasted, as they will only be filled once or twice a year. As the team remains average year after year, some of the less dedicated fans will start supporting another team. If one nearby is more successful, then that team will get the support. It has been suggested that in the future everyone will support Manchester United, as they'll always be winning. While this may be the case for some, for others the opposite will happen.

Over time fans may become disenchanted with the overpaid prima donnas, the cheating where players dive just to gain advantage, the lack of sportsmanship, not being able to see a decent game and so forth. These fans might then go down to their neighbourhood pitches, if local authorities haven't been forced to sell them off, and watch a team of youngsters. They might stand on the touchline, surrounded by people screaming at their children or friends, who are trying their hardest, playing with spirit, pride and in some cases, skill. If they are old enough, they might remember that this is what it used to be about, swapping comments with a stranger beside them:

'D'ye see that?'

'What a shot!'

'Did you think that was a foul?'

These fans are enjoying a game of football, with some of the men or boys they just watched probably staying in the area, returning football and some of the fans – the real football fans – to the grass roots.

However, the large clubs may do something to get the fans back, something that harks back to the old days of football – reinstating standing terracing. While many people could not or would not stand for the two hours it takes for a full game of football, there are those who would. While it may seem that the days of standing terraces are gone, over time it is not inconceivable that stadiums will change to have three seated areas and one standing. Laws could be changed to enforce strictly controlled entry and safety conditions to prevent another Hillsborough. Just before Christmas 2000, the UK Sports Minister Kate Hoey announced she was to investigate whether it is possible to reintroduce standing areas that are safe and in January 2001, the UK tabloid the *Sunday Mirror* launched a survey that asked fans what they thought of the proposals to bring back small, secure standing areas at Premiership stadiums. Seventy-eight per cent of respondents were in favour.

Bringing back terracing would open up the game to fans who had deserted it, as well as perhaps bringing back some atmosphere to grounds. Clubs may even reintroduce terracing at a reduced price (but still enough to make a profit) to allow fans to get back into the game, opening up a market that had perhaps closed itself off for financial reasons or because of disillusionment.

Just as terracing or other initiatives will be brought in to maintain clubs' relationships with fans, the relationships professional clubs have with each other will have to change if they are all to survive. Clubs will grow closer as the football associations relax rules when they realise that if they do not allow the large clubs to adopt or take over the smaller ones, then clubs will go out of business. Otherwise many of the smaller clubs will run on little more than the kindness of a bank manager, nostalgia and a pittance. John Williams of the Sir

Norman Chester Centre for Football Research thinks that England will follow the European model in this regard:

'I think we'll also see closer ties developing – and being allowed to develop – between the smaller and larger clubs in England.

'There's a couple of informal relationships already existing, for example, with Southend and West Ham, Liverpool and Crewe Alexandra. Leeds wanted to set up youth academies at Oldham and elsewhere, using them as nursery clubs.

'Ninety-two football league clubs – if the larger clubs are unwilling to spread some of the television money – is a large number to sustain, and with some of the lower clubs only attracting 200–300 fans, the economics do not make sense, so I can see more formal relationships and nursery clubs developing like they do in Spain and Italy, but I think all of this will take time. I don't think there will be an immediate transformation.'

Supporters' organisations will try to keep the flame alive, but as share issues get more and more diluted, meaning there are more shares going around, the fans will only own tiny percentages of clubs.

For players, the years ahead could be revolutionary in many ways. Their wages will continue to go up and club loyalty will become even rarer than it is now, but players will face dangers, not only from their own rock and roll lifestyles, but from new drugs, which, while helping them play when not fully fit, may take a long-term toll on their health. It can also only be a matter of time before a celebrity footballer decides to become a politician, and while no one is holding their breath for Prime Minister Beckham, it may not be long before someone follows in Sebastian Coe's footsteps to Westminster or even the European Parliament. Managers will continue to face trying times as the clubs become more and more businesslike, with a few weeks' poor results being enough to trigger stock market panics and the manager's sacking.

TV rights, as mentioned above, will increase and continue to mutate to take advantage of new technologies. Just as fans get all of their favourite games on DVD, a new format will be announced and everyone will have to buy the same again, just as many people did when going from vinyl to CD. Games will become watchable on broadband cable television and computer thanks to broadband cable technologies like ADSL, and mobile signals may also offer a limited type of service. Clubs, liberated by gaining copyright of all their old games after lengthy court battles with the football associations, will release a stack of games and eventually fans will be able to watch these on a pay-per-view basis. Television companies will find their costs for the game decreasing. A new company will emerge, one that will deal with camera coverage at each ground, or perhaps each club will hire their own equipment and staff, and the TV studios will only have to provide commentary and analysis as well as a mass distribution system. Clubs may eventually bypass even this stage, and offer their services direct in an increasingly fragmented broadcasting market.

Technology will also help to develop a new bartering system for players. A secure Internet service will see more players' transfers taking place electronically, with clubs discussing and transferring players more quickly than before. The technology will have to be secure to prevent a repeat of farcical incidents like the one in 2000 when Aberdeen believed they were receiving a bid from Swedish side AIK Solna for midfielder Eoin Jess. The negotiations were carried out by e-mail, with a bid of nearly £600,000 put in for the player before the club said no. They then learned they had been tricked by a prankster who had no connection to Solna. An Internet-based system may not only lead to a decline in agents due to clubs carrying out all their transactions directly between each other, but also to an increase in scouts, though not scouts working for clubs. Just as today's Internet search engines have so-called 'intelligent' computer agents that look for data, companies could employ scouts to go out and write reports – to be placed on secure Internet sites – for managers to look at. For example, a manager is looking for an aggressive, young, Spanish left midfielder under the age of 25. He enters these details into a system and it comes back with profiles of everyone relevant stored on its database, along with club and contact details. This is not as far-fetched as it sounds – there is already an early version in development. Known as SoccerScout, the system – designed with the assistance of Leeds United and Tottenham Hotspur – has branched out to include information on players from Belgium, Denmark, England, France,

Germany, Holland, Italy, Norway, Portugal, Scotland, Spain, Sweden and Switzerland. The company behind it, Touch-Line Data Systems, are now working on a global model. Lynne Stewart, editor of SoccerScout, believes that the only way is up for their product and that it will grow as the game continues to expand:

'SoccerScout allows registered users to search its database for suitable players, while also providing an excellent document-management system. This allows clubs to extract maximum value from their own scouting and information gathering resources.

'But it's not just clubs we see as a market. Media and soccer game manufacturers are also interested in the data and information we have on the database, opening up further markets for us.'

One company that has looked at the future of the game is Deloitte & Touche. According to Gerry Boon, head of its football industry team:

'Looking at Europe and Asia, the growth of the game is dependent upon the markets – primarily, the demographics of the fan base and the depth of the corporate customer market – into which clubs and league competitions can tap.

'In the long run, the game will grow alongside penetration and value of pay-TV markets and ultimately broadband markets.

'Player wages will rise in line with club revenues. Football clubs have always spent all "spare" cash on player wages. There may be periods when wage growth outstrips revenue growth, but in the long term wages will increase in step with revenues. Accordingly, wages will only reach a ceiling if revenues do. Unfortunately, should it arise, the wage ceiling will probably be reached after the revenue ceiling. Players and their agents are usually one step ahead of club management.

'TV money will only dry up if there is a substitute threat to football – ie football loses its popularity or when penetration of football on television reaches its global limit. The only other proven driver of pay-TV is movies, and they're not as good as football.

'The TV money will move around, following the big clubs into the competitions where they participate and, of course, in the long run who's to say there won't be big clubs from other markets outside the big five, say from Eastern Europe.

'Clubs should be making provision for the stages after TV – broadband, mobile communications, etc. As long as football remains popular it will remain killer content for all technologies and as technologies develop to reach more fans, more quickly and more often, money to football will grow – but increasingly concentrated on a small group of elite "global brand" clubs, which have an international appeal.

'Clubs should recognise where and how value in football is created – not as a provision for if or when TV values decline, but to develop their businesses across a broader revenue base and lessen exposure to a worsening of any of its markets. At the end of the day it is the fan who drives value; directly through "the gate", in the shop and at the stadium, and indirectly by providing the fan base which underpins TV values and sponsorship rates.

'What this means, of course, is that as in any market, it is the customer – in football's case, the fan – who will dictate what the product will look like, what it will cost, how it will be presented and so on. It is those football clubs that successfully embrace this concept who will thrive in the long term.'

But regardless of all the money and technology, at some point over the next 20 or so years, football is going to get as big as it can. There will come a time when the market can no longer sustain high prices and football will settle back to a level where things are affordable. The game's calendar will eventually merge into one, bringing with it the problems of different climates and trying to fit games into a schedule that suits everyone. International friendlies and the Olympics will probably be the first to suffer here. According to John Williams:

'[There will be] more tensions arising between dominant powerful clubs – in Europe especially – and national teams. It will be asked, for example, why they have to play friendly matches and why do they need the players at particular times during the season. Some chairmen don't see the relevance of routine national team football.'

Football journalist and author David Conn is in no doubt as to where the game will go:

'It's depressing to admit, but it does look as if football will follow the course of every industry or profession which has been subjected to market forces without any form of regulation, which has to happen in my opinion. If there is no regulation then it is more than likely that every decision will be taken on the basis of whether it will make more money for the clubs, owners and corporations that will already be rich.'

Whatever happens in the future, one thing is painfully clear: if fans do not take more of an interest in their clubs than just reading the back page of a tabloid and going along to the occasional game, they will lose football.

It could be argued that the game has already been lost because big businesses are involved and governments have not intervened, but that is not the case.

Just now is football's extra time. If the fans rally enough, fight enough, campaign enough, they may be able to ensure a healthy future for the game. The people's game. Your game.

Bibliography and Further Reading

Most of what is listed below is easily available and is recommended for anyone wanting to find out more about the game off the pitch.

Books

Conn, D (1997) *The Football Business*, Mainstream, Edinburgh

Devine, T (ed) (2000) *Scotland's Shame*, Mainstream, Edinburgh

Hamil, S *et al* (eds) (2000) *Football in the Digital Age*, Mainstream, Edinburgh

Hamil, S *et al* (eds) (1999) *A Game of Two Halves*, Mainstream, Edinburgh

Sugden, J and Tomlinson, A (1999) *Great Balls of Fire*, Mainstream, Edinburgh

Szymanski, S and Kuypers, T (1999) *Winners and Losers*, Penguin, London

Articles and reports

The first nine reports are from the Sir Norman Chester Centre for Football Research and can be viewed by going to their Web site (address listed below).

Black Footballers in Britain

Fan Power and Democracy
Football After Taylor
Football and Football Hooliganism
A History of Female Football Fans
Racism and Football
Ticket Pricing, Football Business and Excluded Football Fans
Why Support Football?
Women and Football

Deloitte & Touche Sport (2000) *Deloitte & Touche Annual Review of Football Finance*, London, August

Deloitte & Touche *Sport* (2000) *England's Premier Clubs – A Review of 1998/99 Season*, London, April

English FA (1995) *1995 FA Carling Premier League Fan Survey*, London

Managing Injuries in Professional Football: The Roles of the Club Doctor and Physiotherapist. Report was based on research undertaken by Centre for Research into Sport & Society's director Ivan Waddington, Martin Roderick and Graham Parker, Leicester, 2000

Rt Hon. Lord Justice Taylor (1989, 1990) *The Taylor Reports* (interim and final), HMSO, London

Turner, A P and Coventry University colleagues (2000) Report on Osteoarthritis in Football Players, *British Journal of Sports Medicine*, October

Web sites

Centre for Research into Sport & Society:
    http://www.le.ac.uk/crss/
Deloitte & Touche Sport:
    http://www.footballfinance.co.uk
Football Governance Research Centre:
    http://www.football-research.org
Football Unites – Racism Divides:
    http://www.furd.org/
The Footy Business:

http://library.thinkquest.org/C005849/index2.html
Hansard and other government publications:
  http://www.parliament.the-stationery-office.co.uk/
Sir Norman Chester Centre for Football Research:
  http://www.le.ac.uk/snccfr/
Stonewall (lesbian and gay equality site):
  http://www.stonewall.org.uk/
Supporters Direct:
  http://www.supporters-direct.org
Topica (hosts a number of football e-mail lists):
  http://www.topica.com
University of Liverpool's Football Research Unit:
  http://fru.merseyside.org/

Newspapers

The *Daily Express*, the *Daily Mail, Evening Times*, the *Guardian*, the *Herald*, the *Independent*, the *Independent on Sunday*, the *Mirror*, the *Press and Journal, Scotland on Sunday*, the *Scotsman*, the *Sunday Herald*, the *Sunday Mail*, the *Sunday Mirror*.

Magazines

Attitude, Business 2.0, The Economist, FourFourTwo, Private Eye, Punch, When Saturday Comes.

Other media

Championship Manager 2000/01, FIFA 2001, *Gladiator* DVD, ISS Pro Evolution.

Index

About the Author

Born in Glasgow in 1973, Craig McGill is an experienced news, sports and features writer. His articles have appeared in many newspapers, magazines and Internet sites, including *TIME*, the *Guardian*, the *Sun*, the *Daily Express*, the *Mirror* and the *Scotsman*, with his work having been translated into Norwegian, French and Italian, amongst other languages.

He is currently a writer for the *Sunday Mirror* and is also editor-in-chief of the upcoming Web site Scomics.com.

Craig has been a football fan for more than 20 years.

Future work includes books on Munchausen Syndrome by Proxy, the murder of Asian Scot Surjit Chhokar and novels.

Currently based in Glasgow, Scotland he can be contacted at the following address: mcgillcraig@hotmail.com.